The Control Paradox

The Control Paradox

From AI to Populism

Ezio Di Nucci

ROWMAN & LITTLEFIELD
Lanham • Boulder • New York • London

Published by Rowman & Littlefield
An imprint of The Rowman & Littlefield Publishing Group, Inc.
4501 Forbes Boulevard, Suite 200, Lanham, Maryland 20706
www.rowman.com

6 Tinworth Street, London SE11 5AL, United Kingdom

British Library Cataloguing in Publication Information Available

Library of Congress Cataloging-in-Publication Data

Name: Di Nucci, Ezio, author.
Title: The control paradox : from AI to populism / Ezio Di Nucci.
Description: Lanham, Maryland : Rowman & Littlefield, [2021] | Includes bibliographical
    references and index. | Summary: "Through the notion of the control paradox, Di
    Nucci shows how the lack of direct control within representative democracies could
    be motivating populism and argues that a better understanding of delegation is a
    possible solution"—Provided by publisher.
Identifiers: LCCN 2020035960 (print) | LCCN 2020035961 (ebook) | ISBN
    9781786615787 (cloth ; alk. paper) | ISBN 9781786615794 (paperback ; alk. paper) |
    ISBN 9781786615800 (ebook)
Subjects: LCSH: Social control. | Social control—Political aspects. | Artificial intelli-
    gence—Social aspects. | Democracy.
Classification: LCC HM661 .D52 2021 (print) | LCC HM661 (ebook) | DDC 303.3/3—
    dc23
LC record available at https://lccn.loc.gov/2020035960
LC ebook record available at https://lccn.loc.gov/2020035961

a Cate Franz Lola Usa

Contents

Preface

This book introduces, analyzes, and then applies what I call the "control paradox," the idea that the very technologies and practices we develop in order to enhance our control end up undermining it. The main aim of the book is to use this new analytical tool to better understand and navigate technological innovation, avoiding (geeky and corporate) uncritical enthusiasm on the one hand but also techno-apocalyptic skepticism on the other.

In order to demonstrate how the control paradox works, I will spend quite some time unpacking the practice of delegating a task and describing how the concepts of control and delegation interact: basically, when you delegate successfully, you voluntarily give up direct control in order to enhance overall control. Delegation, properly understood, ends up being both the source of the control paradox and also its proposed solution—but that will depend on a lot of other conditions and different interpretations of the paradox, all of which taken together make up the theoretical core of this book (in parts I and II) and cannot be summarized in this short preface.

The rest of the book is dedicated to applying the control paradox and my understanding of the practice of delegation to a selection of new technologies and other complex practices, including, ultimately, political representation and power. Through these applied exercises (parts III and IV), you will get the benefit of further extrapolation of both the control paradox and the concept of delegation. But there is also novel analysis of some of the most successful and controversial technological innovations of our time, such as artificial intelligence (AI), drones, autonomous weapon systems, self-driving cars, video-assistant referees (VARs) in football, and, finally, the way populism has recently threatened the foundations of representative democracy.

The book is structured around four parts and divided into twelve chapters. In part I, the paradox is introduced and presented in all its different versions and possible interpretations. In part II, the book's two most crucial concepts—control and delegation—are analyzed and also applied to contemporary technological and social practices. Part III applies the control paradox to exemplary technological developments, and part IV applies the control paradox to exemplary political developments, also dealing with the question of responsibility.

A note on the introduction: think of it as a long abstract or short summary of the overall book—for those of you worried you might not make it to the end. If you are of the confident sort, you might even consider something daring: skipping the introduction and beginning with chapter 1.

On a personal note, I finished writing this book at the end of March 2020, during the COVID-19 lockdown, with my university, my wife's theater, and our children's school and kindergarten all closed. I had to resist the obvious temptation of applying my new toy—the control paradox—to the new coronavirus crisis; after all, we have all had to give up control of our lives in order to try to get the pandemic under control. But adding a chapter on COVID-19 felt like shamelessly jumping on the bandwagon of tragedy, so I decided against it. I guess I don't believe in philosophy *that* much, after all.

Acknowledgments

I hate the name-dropping typical of acknowledgments sections in books (particularly academic ones—and philosophy is one of the worst offenders). Still, some thanks are due, but I will keep it brief. I had the basic idea for this book while at a conference in Chemnitz, Germany, at the end of 2016—yes, it has taken me a while, I know. So many thanks to that conference's host, Minkyung Kim, for an inspiring environment. Thanks to another organizer of that same conference, Thomas Grote, who has followed this book's development from the beginning and has offered valuable comments. Thanks to some of my collaborators on tech and other issues relevant to this book, for example: Cory Robinson, Filippo Santoni, Aaro Tupasela, Rasmus Thybo Jensen, Jeanette Knox, and Isaac Wagner. Thanks to Iben Mundbjerg Gjødsbøl, Mette Nordahl Svendsen, Sven Nyholm, and Olsi Kosta for comments on early drafts of some chapters.

And speaking of my wonderful local colleagues in Copenhagen, apart from the ones mentioned above I must at least also thank Signild Vallgårda, Jan Friis, and Rikke Bentson—really everybody at the Centre for Medical Science and Technology Studies and the Section for Health Services Research, Department of Public Health, University of Copenhagen. Thanks to the many audiences to whom I presented ideas from this book: I believe my first talk on the control paradox was at the end of 2016 in Karlsruhe, Germany, and the last one was recently in Eindhoven, the Netherlands—thanks to those audiences and all the ones in between. Also thanks to those whom I will have inevitably forgotten.

Thanks to everybody at Rowman & Littlefield and especially Isobel Cowper-Coles, who encouraged me to make this book more political. And then there is obviously my family; they are way too important to be mentioned by name in an acknowledgment section I'm afraid.

Introduction

The Control Paradox for Dummies

Most people—even most academics—don't read books. And most who do don't read whole books; mostly they read just the first chapter. So this introduction is written for those of you who read only the first chapter of books. It superficially and quickly covers the argument of the entire book, like an abstract. If you read this introduction, you will know what the book is about—fulfilling the classic function of an introduction. But if you read only this introduction, you will know only what the book is about, not what it actually says: claims without arguments, in short. So do read the whole book, please. And if you are confident that you will make it to the end of the book, you could even skip this introduction. To turn to chapter 1 or continue reading below . . . that is the question.

* * *

Technological innovations are supposed to give us more and better control over ourselves and the environment; often, though, we also end up losing control as a result of these very innovations. This is the control paradox, which I present in this book by applying it to a series of recent technological developments, from self-driving cars to drones and autonomous weapons, from smart environments to passwords. In trying to enhance control, we end up losing (or at least increasing the risk of losing) the very thing we meant to improve. I show that the control paradox applies not only to complex technologies but also to simple artifacts such as bike locks. Furthermore, the paradox is not even restricted to technology, as a version might apply to both human behavior and political power. At the core of the control paradox is the practice of delegation, and better understanding what happens when we delegate can also provide a solution to the paradox.

Some might argue that being in control is a valuable asset and that—other things being equal—more control is better than less control, just as better control is preferable to worse control. And if you think that control is necessary to freedom, liberty, or autonomy, then most philosophical and political traditions should be committed to establishing control as one of life's most valuable components. So what's wrong with caring—even caring *a lot*—about control?

The problem with control is—or so I argue here—that often trying to gain more and better control simultaneously increases the risk of losing control. This is what I call the control paradox. It is not restricted to technology, but I will illustrate it with technological examples. We will begin with so-called autonomous (or self-driving) vehicles.

SELF-DRIVING CARS AND DRONES

What's the point of self-driving cars, apart from the obvious financial benefits to a couple of West Coast nerds and the odd German engineer? The point of this kind of technological innovation is to improve our control over individual cars in particular and traffic in general. Talk to anybody working in or around this sector, and they will explain to you how much more quickly, accurately, softly, and—most importantly of all—safely some basic bit of software can brake than Sebastian Vettel or Lewis Hamilton. Actually, they will explain to you that, despite what you think, if your car was built this century, it was actually the car doing it on your behalf—the automobile industry stopped trusting drivers much earlier than drivers stopped trusting car companies.

Whether your current vehicle ought to be already labeled "autonomous" or not, the point is control: who would want less control over their vehicle? If engineers can really set up your car so you will never again brake too late, then most people would be more than happy to pay a premium on that—call it a *control premium*. After all, you and yours will be safer and the car will last longer or look better (for longer). So it's a win-win for both the driving populace and the engineers.

However, there is a price to pursuing this promise of safer drivers, safer pedestrians, and, generally, more coordinated traffic—which supposedly means fewer accidents, fewer traffic jams, and shorter commuting times. The price is neither the odd software defect nor the much-publicized AI dilemma between sacrificing driver and pedestrian (basically because neither is new or interesting);[1] rather, the cost of safer and better-functioning traffic is that we must cede (at least some) control to machines. In order to increase (or improve) control, we must cede it, and this is what I argue is paradoxical.

We must let go of the very thing we want more of (sounds a lot like relationships, I know). The reason for this is simple enough: software—whether it's installed on a car or, as we will see shortly, on many other things—is better than we are at controlling, so that if we really care about control, we must let software take care of it for us—and not just for software or cars.

What we have just said about self-driving cars can be applied to another fashionable gadget of our times: drones (and autonomous weapons). The promise is pretty much the same: the deployment of drones and autonomous weapons will allow us to have more and better control over our military activities to reduce both casualties among our own personnel and hopefully collateral damages. (I say "hopefully" because evidence from drone deployment by the Obama administration in Pakistan and elsewhere does not point to a substantial reduction in civilian deaths.)[2]

We can use the military example to show that the control paradox doesn't just apply to software and cars—for example, notice the difference between drones and autonomous weapons. Drones are not autonomous in any sense of that word because they are remotely controlled by human pilots. Autonomous weapons are not remotely controlled by human pilots but rather guided by preprogrammed software (possibly, but not necessarily, machine learning). Obviously the difference is more complicated than this, but the point is the following: while autonomous weapons are supposedly the parallel of self-driving cars, the way the control paradox applies to drones is different from how we have applied it to automobiles, but it still amounts to ceding control in order to increase/improve it.

After all, the weapon in question—drones—is miles away (often thousands of miles) rather than being in our hands, nor are we sitting inside it. We literally have to let go of it in order to use it. But by letting go of the weapon, we actually increase/improve our control over both the weapon itself and the battle space. A military drone can be much more accurate than both a rifle and a fighter jet—not *despite* being (thousands of) miles away but *because* of it. It can, for example, take risks that an infantry soldier or pilot could not reasonably take, often resulting in improved accuracy. Mission accomplished.

You might have noticed something missing from my discussion so far: no technological second coming, not even one apocalyptic thought, even though autonomous weapons and self-driving cars are big favorites when it comes to warning the distracted public about the machines taking over. (Speaking of paradoxes, you have to give it to Elon Musk for making disturbing amounts of money out of the very phenomenon he is constantly warning us against—recently it was AI and the third world war [Hern 2017]; his cars may not take you very far, but the guy knows a thing or two about marketing.)

Technological apocalypticism is feeding the control paradox: the basic worry is that we are ceding too much control to machines, robots, software, AI, machine learning, Silicon Valley, or whatever your placeholder of choice for current technological developments is. And there is nothing paradoxical about the worry itself; the paradox comes in when we notice that if we are ceding too much control, we are doing it in order to improve and increase the very thing we are worried about losing: control.

It is important to distinguish here between a stronger normative claim and a weaker descriptive claim: many people may be tempted by the former, but the paradox arises even if we only accept the latter weaker claim. You don't need to believe that we are ceding too much control to the robots (where "too much" is the normative bit); it is enough to notice that even if we are not ceding too much control, the way we are trying to increase and improve control through innovation is indeed by ceding some/more control to the relevant technology. The latter is admittedly not apocalyptic enough to interest Twitter or even the papers, but it has the advantage of being both more plausible and also free from normative assumptions.

To clarify this point, we could distinguish between a *normative control paradox* (we are ceding too much control to technology and, paradoxically, doing it for the very reason that we want more/better control) and a *descriptive control paradox* (in order to gain more/better control, we have to let go of the very thing we want more of).

FRIDGES AND PASSWORDS

There is at least one thing that urgently needs unpacking: this talk of "ceding" control. After all, no ceding, no paradox. But before I do that, I'd like to mention a few more developments that you might like to apply the paradox to: smart environments. An example is the intelligent fridge, which learns from your habits: it will order groceries preemptively so you will never run out of anything or have to throw out groceries past their expiry date; your fridge will always order just the right amount of food at just the right time. All it needs is your credit card details (not so scary) and so much access to your behavior that it will very soon know you better than you (or your partner) know yourself (scary).

Then there are passwords. Passwords are the control paradox par excellence. You set up passwords in order to protect something, but having a password between you and the thing you want to protect generates lots of new problems, the most typical of which is when you forget the password. As above, having something password protected gives you more/better control over the account or information in question, but it also alienates you from that information—so that you risk losing control over it.

And it's not just a matter of forgetting the password or having it hacked. Think of the much more banal case of the time it requires you to access your phone if it is password protected as opposed to when it is not; depending on the task at hand, time is control too. Think, further, of a well-known company (whose name you will have heard of even if you spent the last three decades on Alpha Centauri) that wants to make it supposedly easier for you to both protect your phone and have easy access to it, and thus has moved from passwords to fingerprints and to facial recognition—and that's just your telephone I am talking about.

That's the thing about the control paradox: you are not just a subject *to* the paradox; you are the enthusiastic agent *of* it, buying the very (expensive) thing the car salesman is telling you will (ultimately) kill you. It's not ironic; it's more like making fun of customers but not doing it behind their backs because being made fun of is exactly the thing that will make customers pay the big bucks. Okay, maybe it is a bit ironic—but only if you are watching these developments from the safe distance of a few light-years away, and even then, it had better be before Elon Musk's great-granddaughter has broken the speed of light with her new Tesla.

DELEGATING CONTROL

To better understand the control paradox, we need to unpack the concept of "ceding control." Such unpacking, you will be relieved to hear, might even provide a possible solution to the control paradox. Are we really *ceding* control to self-driving cars, drones, fridges, and passwords? The idea of ceding control—or, if you are a monarchist, *abdicating* control—appears to imply that afterward you no longer have control. But that would be self-defeating, since the very point of the exercise is to improve/increase control. That's why it's a paradox, you'll object. Not so fast. There is conceptual room between controlling and abdicating/ceding control: being in control or having control are two ways of talking of the logical room between the activity of controlling and losing control.

That's because being in control does not always require the activity of controlling; we are way more effective than that. Think of your bike—or mine, if you haven't got one (get one!); it is—as I type—locked outside. The lock's key is in my pocket. I am in control of my bike—I hope—even though I am not *directly* controlling it. Imagine if I had to spend my whole working day looking out of the window in order to directly control my bike; I wouldn't get any work done (no jokes here; philosophers do work, in their own very special way). More to the point, I can't always park my bike where I can see it from my office window.

What a brilliant little invention, the bike lock. I don't need to spend my whole life watching over my bike. But who is doing the controlling that allows me to be in control while doing something else? Well, the bike lock's doing the controlling. More precisely, I have delegated control to the bike lock; that means I am not myself actively or consciously—*directly*, as the rest of this book refers to it—controlling, but at the same time I have not lost, ceded, or abdicated control. I am in control without controlling. That's the power of delegation; that's the beauty of bike locks—and perhaps technology in general.

One more thing about bike locks: they do a better job at protecting and controlling my bike than I could ever do myself. So it is not just a matter of sparing time and other resources that would otherwise have to be invested in controlling my bike (as in staring out of the window all day long); it is also that even if I were to invest (waste) such resources, my bike would be much more exposed than with a simple bike lock. So you can now see that delegating control has two distinct advantages: I spare resources while improving performance. These correspond to what I call, respectively, the *economic* and *strategic* character of delegation.[3]

Notice how bike locks work exactly like passwords: if there were no lock on my bike, anybody could use it; similarly, if there were no password on my phone (there isn't) or my email account (there is), anybody could use it. On the other hand, the fact that there is a lock on my bike makes it paramount that I don't lose the lock's key, just as I'd better not forget my password. The point is banal, but it illustrates how delegation works. In virtue of having delegated control, I might have achieved better/more control, but there is also a related risk of loss of control that wasn't there before: without the bike lock, anyone could access my bike, but at least I myself am also one of those anyones; with the bike lock in place and after I have lost or misplaced my key, nobody can access my bike, and that includes me.

Is delegation the solution to the control paradox then? Before answering this crucial question, let us take stock of a few important bits of progress we have made. We have introduced the control paradox as the idea that, while trying to improve/increase our control over the environment, we put at risk the very thing we want more of, namely, control. We have emphasized the way the control paradox applies to technological innovation, specifying the way it does not uniquely rely on software or any particular kind of technology—indeed, something as basic as a bike lock provided an example of how the control paradox does not even depend on particularly complex technology. Finally, we have introduced the practice of delegation as a way of illustrating the difference between directly controlling something (or someone) and being in control of (or having control over) something (or someone). Before further analyzing how delegation works, let me introduce three further applications of the control paradox that show it is not even restricted only to technology—it goes much deeper than that.

AUTOMATIC ACTIONS

We are not always conscious of what we do. Often, we act automatically or without thinking, with skillful movements such as in driving, sport, music, or even cooking.[4] A lot of the time your body "knows" what to do without getting the consciousness involved. Indeed, sometimes that may be counter-productive: next time you go down a flight of stairs, try to look at every step you take; you will very likely fall down the stairs. It's not just that conscious attention is not always required; it often gets in the way of successful task completion. Another such case—at least for me—is if I try to remember my pin number before typing it in; I get confused (contactless payments have been such a relief!). But I have no problem with just mindlessly typing it in every time.

Are we controlling our movements on those occasions? Yes and no. Yes, we are in control; indeed, when we act habitually or skillfully, we are often more in control than when we have to pay attention to what we do because, for example, we are executing a novel task. No, we are not consciously controlling our activity because there is no need for that, or even because consciously controlling the activity would interfere with successful completion—as when you walk down a familiar flight of stairs.

You will have noticed that with these kinds of automatic actions, you find yourself in the same kind of in-between logical space as in earlier examples, where you are in control while not actively or consciously controlling your movements. It is not clear who or what you are delegating to—your body? The unconscious or subconscious? Is system 2 delegating control to system 1?

Here again, feel free to pick your placeholder of choice; the important thing is just that once again we have identified a difference between controlling and being in control. And this difference has many of the same features that we have previously identified; for example, it is economical—in terms of cognitive resources—not to have to think of or pay attention to the relevant movements or activities; you can rather deploy those cognitive resources somewhere else. Think of chatting to the person in the passenger seat while driving, for example.

Another similarity is that, on top of being economical, being able to do something automatically often means you are better at completing the task (this would be the *strategic* element, to use the language I have introduced to analyze delegation). While you are learning how to do something, you are paying attention to every step and making mistakes; once you have learned, you are quicker and less prone to mistakes. This is again something that automatic actions have in common with delegating control to technological devices. You improve/increase control by not having to actively do the controlling yourself anymore (even though, admittedly, in this particular case "yourself" may turn out to be little more than a metaphor).

Where's the paradox with automatic actions, you may ask? I think here the dialectic is again one of, on the one hand, economizing resources and improving performance and, on the other hand, allowing for new or increased risks. A common occurrence is to take the wrong turn because you are on a familiar route, even though you want to go somewhere else. You are so much at home on that route that you become absentminded and forget that—this time—your destination was a different one. Let's call this a *familiar mistake*: familiar in the first instance because we have all been there and made such mistakes, and familiar also because *familiarity* is exactly what explains the mistake.

Had you not become so familiar with a certain route, then when your route is similar but not identical you would make no mistake, but on the other hand, if you weren't so familiar with the original route, every time you took that route you'd have to invest more resources, time, and energy in accomplishing such a simple task. It is a trade-off: habits and automatic actions mean fewer invested resources, but they also mean more mistakes; you could cut down on those mistakes by resisting the power of habit, but that would be a waste of time.[5]

It is the control paradox again in the case of automatic actions: by performing certain tasks automatically, you have more/better control over those tasks while at the same time exposing yourself to novel risks. Even the much-discussed phenomena on implicit bias can be understood along those lines. After all, implicit bias is also the result of cognitive economizing on your part: the world is so diverse that you just have to cut some corners; otherwise, you wouldn't get anything done. Biases are cognitive shortcuts, just as are habits, skills, and other automatic actions.[6]

There is an important distinction somewhere along this continuum but one that will not necessarily affect my application of the control paradox. Some unconscious (or less than conscious) phenomena you still have some form of supervisory control over; other unconscious phenomena you have no control over, even if you become aware of them. Take the difference between familiar mistakes and implicit bias: you may absentmindedly take the wrong turn when on a familiar route, but this kind of mistake can be either avoided—if you remember that, today, the route is a bit different—or corrected, if you notice the mistake before it's too late. That's not the case with implicit bias: yes, I am aware that the relevant psychological literature and data are subject to some controversy, but at least in principle the idea is that you are subject to the bias even if you are aware of it and are actively trying to avoid it.

This distinction is important in many respects, for example, when it comes to questions of intentionality and responsibility. But as far as the control paradox is concerned, the distinction makes little difference: both familiar mistakes and implicit bias can be understood as novel or as increased risks of control loss that are the result of the kind of cognitive streamlining actually meant to improve and increase control over both your own body and the environment.

COMPLEX ORGANIZATIONS

Finally, I will examine two more cases: complex organizations and political power, which are phenomena to which we can apply the control paradox. Let us start with organizations; it is important to add this example because, in contrast to the previous cases, organizations delegate control to other people, rather than just to more or less complex machinery. While even delegating to technology raises questions of responsibility (see the debate on the so-called responsibility gap[7]), issues of responsibility are even more urgent—and more obvious—when it comes to delegating to other people, because while a drone or self-driving car cannot be itself morally responsible, people are (normally) capable of moral responsibility.

When I talk of delegating control within organizations, think, for example, of a boss giving some task to one of her employees—that does indeed often involve delegating control, even though, depending on the task and the organizational structure, the line manager in question may or may not still have supervisory control over the task. Still, there are obvious advantages in delegating control—and these are the obvious advantages of *division of labor*, actually.

So there is no need to overwork this simple observation. An example will do: Imagine your boss sends you to a foreign country for an important commercial meeting; she could have gone herself, but she decides that the most effective strategy is for her to take care of business at the office and for you to go on the trip. These kinds of decisions probably take place just about every second within organizations the world over. Your manager has delegated control to you, but she has not completely abdicated control: she will not be physically in the room during your negotiation, but she can still give you directions—before the trip or by phone during the trip, for example. She will not be able to control everything the way she could have had she gone herself: whether you address your counterpart by first or second name, for instance, or whether you accept or decline their offer of coffee, and hundreds of other little things that might or might not affect successful completion of the deal. There are other things she will want to keep a close eye on from a distance, such as the right price or delivery schedule.

This is, I realize, all very banal, but it is just a simple way to show how control delegation routinely happens in every organization—and how that does involve at least the same dialectic as the control paradox. In order to optimize performance, we delegate control to something or someone else; this involves risks that have to do precisely with control loss. Whether those risks are worth taking is a strategic decision that has to be made about the particular cases, and that is beyond the scope here.

The manager–subordinate relationship is not the only paradigm though: there is at least one other, different kind of relationship that needs addressing. This is particularly interesting because, while in the manager–subordinate relationship it is the more powerful partner that delegates control to the less powerful partner, the other kind of relationship I am thinking of is an example of the reverse: the less powerful delegate to the more powerful (who was already more powerful before being delegated to and now has been further empowered by the delegation). This other kind of relationship is a good model for the final application I will discuss: political power.

CONSENT AND THE DOCTOR–PATIENT RELATIONSHIP

The second example I wish to examine is the doctor–patient relationship, where usually (but not always) patients delegate control to doctors; so, for example, when patients consent to some form of treatment, they are delegating control to their physician, even though it will be important to specify what exactly they are delegating control of: a body part, some disease, or treatment. Indeed, the whole idea of consent as empowering patients only makes sense against a background of control delegation from patients to doctors. And it is interesting to note that whatever you think about consent— you may, for example, be skeptical about the way healthcare systems the world over are outsourcing a lot of treatment and decision-making to patients themselves under the pretense of consent—control delegation is happening regardless of whether consent has been obtained.

Here matters are delicate, so it is worth being more precise: one could actually argue that whether consent has been obtained is what distinguishes ceding or abdicating control from delegating control, namely, that in a legitimate doctor–patient relationship in which voluntary and informed consent has been obtained, the patient has merely delegated control, but in a doctor–patient interaction in which—for whatever reason—consent has not been legitimately obtained, the patient has not just delegated control but has actually ceded or abdicated—namely, lost—control.[8]

How does the control paradox apply to the doctor–patient relationship? By delegating control to doctors, patients improve their chances of, say, curing some disease so that they gain better control over their disease through control delegation—at least in the successful case anyhow. On the other hand, the whole issue of and debate on informed consent is there exactly to guard against the risks of delegating (too much) control to doctors, thereby losing or abdicating control in some significant way.[9] So we have again found the same dialectic of the control paradox, and—interestingly— we have identified it in a case in which the less powerful is delegating to the more powerful.

Indeed, when thinking big about the philosophy of technology and the relationship between humans and machines, one question will surely be whether the more powerful partners are delegating to the less powerful or whether that's just an illusion and the roles have already been reversed, and the related question is whether the preexisting balance of power—whatever it was—is altered by delegating control (just in case this was a bit obscure, it's just another way of asking the much-beloved question by the media of whether machines are taking over).

POLITICAL POWER

Political power is more controversial, and I won't provide an actual argument, just some thoughts about similarities between the phenomena I have been discussing so far and political power (refer to part IV of this book and chapter 11 in particular for more details and arguments). I now already have a structure to talk about political power, having just shown that control can also be delegated by the less powerful to the more powerful, which is what happens within democratic regimes: voters delegate control to their elected representatives, on the understanding that these politicians will then make decisions on their behalf and in their (the voters') best interest.

You may argue that the difference between direct democracy and representative democracy is exactly whether control is delegated, and you may further argue that the difference between representative democratic regimes and nondemocratic regimes is whether the people merely delegate or cede/ abdicate control. Still, even in the successful cases of control delegation within functioning representative democracies, delegating control to politicians carries obvious risks that the elected representatives will then abuse the power they have gained through delegation. On the other hand—following the dialectic of the control paradox—there are obvious advantages in delegating control to politicians: you can then get on with life, instead of worrying about boring policy details. This is the equivalent of the bike lock. But you also hope that professional politicians are better qualified and more skilled than you are at dealing with boring policy details—that's, after all, their job. So again you have—at least in successful cases—the double advantage of sparing resources that can be invested elsewhere while at the same time boosting performance.

FURTHER APPLICATIONS?

There are a few more things that are interesting to test against the control paradox, for example, social media and maybe sex (the book is full of further cases; just read on). Here I rather want to look at an objection I am sure you have already thought of by now: can the control paradox be applied to pretty much anything? That would make it meaningless. To show that's not the case, let us test it with another plausible candidate that, in the end, will turn out not to be a good fit: the increasingly ever-present (and growing in size) monsters otherwise known as headphones.

Headphones, one could try to argue, represent another example of the control paradox on the grounds that, on the one hand, you put them on in order to have more and better control of what you hear, so that you bike to work with headphones on because—instead of hearing the random noise of the city—you can decide exactly which five songs you are going to hear during those twenty or so minutes. That's a triumph of control and choice over randomness, music over noise.

So the one side of the control paradox dialectic is there for headphones as well. And you could argue that the other side is also secured just by noting that having headphones on is more dangerous than not having headphones on because you are less perceptive of the traffic—and relative traffic risks—around you. So in order to gain more control—over what you hear—you end up increasing the risk of losing control, over your bike and the surrounding traffic. Isn't that just another great example of the control paradox?

I don't think it is actually. Because the control gain you are aiming at through headphones—selected music over random noise—has nothing to do with the increased risks, which are rather about personal injury to either yourself or others. Yes, there may be a trade-off in this case just as there are trade-offs in genuine cases of the control paradox, but you are trading two different things: auditory aesthetics against personal safety. In genuine cases of the control paradox, by trying to increase/improve control you raise the risk of losing control over the very thing you were trying to increase/improve control over—that is not the case with the headphones scenario. And that's why headphones are not an example of a genuine control paradox even though they might also involve interesting technological trade-offs.

Headphones have been really helpful to you, though, because now you can more precisely say what characterizes the control paradox: it's not just trade-offs; it is the increased risk of loss of control over the very thing or phenomenon you were aiming to gain more/better control over. This book's task then will be to identify genuine applications of the control paradox and distinguish them from merely apparent applications, such as headphones.

CONCLUSION

I will now conclude by looking at how the concept of delegation can offer a possible solution to the control paradox. Before that I would like to briefly summarize the topics I have covered in this introduction, many of which will be developed in depth in the rest of the book:

- Self-driving cars
- Drones and autonomous weapons
- Passwords
- Smart environments
- Bike locks
- Organizations and the manager–employee relationship
- Healthcare and the doctor–patient relationship
- Political power

The basic idea is that if successful control delegation means not having to do any direct controlling while remaining in control, then when you successfully delegate control you do not lose control, and therefore there needs to be no paradox because, at least in principle, control losses are not the necessary consequence of control delegation.

Indeed, we may even go as far as arguing that the control paradox is only a subjective appearance to those who delegate; because they are no longer directly or consciously controlling, they may have the impression that there has been loss of control or an increased risk for loss of control—but that's just the subjective result of no longer doing any direct or conscious controlling. What is actually happening—at least in the successful cases of delegation—is that control has been increased or enhanced, and the delegating agents—in their right mind—should know that, because control enhancement was the very reason for delegation in the first place.

I can't discuss this in any detail here, but at least two considerations deserve further attention:

- First, as opposed to thinking of the paradox as some misguided subjective impression resulting from the absence of active controlling, it may be that there is a theory–practice gap here: in principle, there is no paradox at least when delegation is successful, but the paradox is a practical one, especially given the ever-increasing complexity of information technologies.
- Second, what the paradox may be pointing to is that the widespread practice of delegating control—which is only growing through technological innovation—often results in unsuccessful or less than fully successful del-

egation, and that is what generates control loss or increased risk for control loss.

What both considerations point to is the need for a full-blown account of
delegation, and in particular of delegating control, one that will allow you,
for example, to distinguish between successful delegation and unsuccessful
or less-than-successful delegation. Once we have such a full-blown account
of the practice of delegation—and this need not be restricted to control, as we
delegate other things as well, such as choice (think of nudges and Sunstein's
Choosing Not to Choose [2015])—I may be able to offer a solution to the
control paradox. An account of delegation and a solution to the control
paradox are what I aim to deliver in this book, but you will have to read on
for that.

Part One

Introducing the Paradox

Chapter One

The Paradox

You might have heard of the *happiness paradox*,[1] which says the more you try to be happy, the less happy you are. My *control paradox* has the same structure: the more control-enhancing technologies we develop, the less control we end up having.

Think of the no-longer small gadget in your pocket: wasn't it supposed to be empowering and liberating, allowing you to check up on all sorts of things and get things done from just about anywhere in the world? As it turns out, those devices are also very good at tracking and manipulating those who carry them.

Alternatively, you needn't be as old as I am to have already faced the following problem multiple times: passwords are supposed to protect you and your data; they are supposed to give you more and better *control*. But if you forget your password (in fact, more plausibly, *when* you forget your password), you will have less control than if you hadn't had a password in the first place.

That is an example of the control paradox. And it recently resulted in separating me from my own money, because my bank *increased* security. Even though passwords can be very annoying, I guarantee you that by the end of this book, you will come to see them as the least scary application of the paradox—quite a comforting one, actually, because all you need to do is remember them. Things are going to get more complex than passwords. I will present the control paradox and then answer the following four questions:

1. Is it real?
2. Is it really paradoxical?
3. Is it just about passwords?

4. Is there a solution?

The answers are, basically, yes, yes, no, and yes. But it is going to take us an entire book to get there. As is often the case with philosophy, it is mostly the questions that will make trouble for us. Once those four questions and a lot of other questions related to those four have been properly analyzed and understood, the answers will turn out to be quite obvious and (obviously) true.

The first thing I should say—and this is very much question 3—is that it is definitely not just passwords, and in fact, it is not just technology either, so that the original tech formulation of the paradox should be understood generously, as follows: the more control-enhancing technologies *and practices* we develop, the less control we end up having.

As I am not interested in a metaphysical or a postmodern (or whatever other fancy word folks associate with philosophy) discussion about the nature of tech, I will just take this above shortcut of adding the all-encompassing concept of "practice," so that almost anything goes.

WHERE THINGS GET POLITICAL

And when I say anything, I mean anything. Think radically, please (or just read the book's title): the control paradox can also be applied to political representation, or so I will argue in this book—that's where, by the end of it, populism will have come into the picture. And in fact, why wait? The idea of the *political control paradox* is that the kinds of practices of political representation that we develop within *representative* democracy—as opposed to *direct* democracy, for example—are subject to the control paradox too.

We develop representative institutions based on expertise that is supposed to deliver better governance—that is how they are supposed to be control enhancing in my original terminology from the paradox's definition—and end up wanting to *take back control* from these institutions. Crazy, right? Well, not quite crazy, just paradoxical. But all will be explained—and all will be well—by the end of the book; just bear with me.

Do you still need examples? *Taking back control* is code for Brexit, Trump, and all the other populisms.[2] Don't worry, there will be plenty of examples to come—both technological and political (and some other ones too, especially from healthcare).

Having started with a rough and ready definition of the control paradox modeled on the happiness paradox, I have now already refined it to be more inclusive, so that I can apply it more widely than just control-enhancing *technologies*. Still, the control-enhancing bit is crucial, so that whether a practice will be able to qualify as an application of the paradox will depend, among other things, on whether it is plausibly control enhancing—even though sometimes that plausibility will turn out to be only a promise rather than a reality.

In philosophy-speak I should say the following: control enhancing, as far as the definition of the paradox is concerned, should be understood *intentionally* and not *extensionally*, as in, as long as there is a plausible control-enhancing intention behind the practice's (or technology's) development, that might be enough to meet the control-enhancing necessary condition of the paradox, even though that intention might not be ultimately fulfilled.

I am sure you now want to know how to understand "control enhancing." Fair enough, but you should not be greedy, dear reader, and you must learn patience, because this is a book, not a tweet. I will have a great deal to say about what "control enhancing" means and even more about the concept of control in general. If this means anything to you, let me tell you that I trained as a philosopher of action, so that control, intentional action, and responsibility are my bread and butter, which is to say, yes, things will get boring and technical. Sometimes boring is good though; just look at Trump.

For now it will suffice for our purposes to provisionally state here that this technical term *control enhancing* has been chosen for the very purpose of its inclusivity; take it as a placeholder for "more or better control" (as opposed to "more and better control"), because more is not always better. And in fact, as the paradox shows, more is not always more either, when it comes to control anyway.

INTERPRETATIONS OF THE PARADOX

There is another aspect of my initial definition that will deserve a closer look: what is the paradox exactly about?

1. Is the paradox that you end up with *less control*?
2. Or is the paradox rather that you end up with an increased *risk* of control loss—as in, an increased risk of less control but not necessarily less control?
3. Or is it instead that you end up with increased *fear* of loss of control?

Those three versions are importantly different, and we will have to decide between them, or at least I will have to explain the differences between these three possible interpretations of the paradox. For now, think of them as decreasing in strength:

Strongest **control paradox:** The more control-enhancing technologies and practices we develop, the less control we end up having.

Stronger **control paradox:** The more control-enhancing technologies and practices we develop, the more we risk losing control.

***Strong* control paradox:** The more control-enhancing technologies and practices we develop, the more we worry about losing control.

As we will see, this last interpretation—the *strong* control paradox about fears of control loss—must itself be divided into two different versions, one normative and the other descriptive (or psychological):

Normative *strong* control paradox: The more control-enhancing technologies and practices we develop, the more reasonable fears about losing control we end up having.

Psychological *strong* control paradox: The more control-enhancing technologies and practices we develop, the more we end up worrying about losing control.

The difference between these two alternative versions of the *strong* interpretation of the paradox is basically that the latter psychological version says nothing about whether those fears of losing control are in any way justified.

If you don't like the terminology above, send me an email to complain (ezio@sund.ku.dk). But basically I chose it to emphasize that each version of the paradox must be taken seriously, although we must not mix up the different versions. To call the *strong* control paradox "weak," for example, would have had the consequence of failing to acknowledge the seriousness of user attitudes (which, remember, in my framework also includes voters) when it comes to the development, implementation, and sustainability of technological and nontechnological practices.

There is a fourth interpretation of the paradox that will be kept, for now, off the above scale, but it is useful to have it in our toolbox from the beginning, so here it goes:

OTHER control paradox: When we develop a technology or practice to enhance our control of A, that will also result in control loss over B.

The reason I want to keep this further interpretation off the scale for now is that it is more about question 2 than it is about question 1, namely, it is about the challenging question of whether what we have here is a genuine paradox or just some common tension or trade-off between different kinds of control or control over different domains. This is a standard objection to my account that I will have to deal with in due time—which means, not quite yet.

ARTIFICIAL INTELLIGENCE

I know what you are thinking: I have mentioned the "control paradox"—tick. I have mentioned "populism"—tick. But there is another part of the title of this book that has been conspicuously absent so far: artificial intelligence (AI). What does AI have to do with anything? Good question. I am myself very skeptical of the AI label. As someone (wise) used to say: AI is whatever hasn't been done yet (Tesler's Theorem; see Hofstadter 1980). And in fact in this book, whenever I speak of AI, what I will mostly mean are so-called *machine learning algorithms* (Domingos 2015), and it might well be that machine learning algorithms do not actually deserve the AI label—they have already been done, after all (Di Nucci 2019).

This note of caution to one side, I will follow current fashion and use the label AI—it is nice and short, after all (and that might be the secret of its success—it's definitely the reason it made the book's subtitle, I can tell you that much). So you have been warned. The reason AI is relevant and important to my overall argument is that it increases *complexity*, and complexity is a crucial part of the paradox. In fact, it might turn out that some technologies and other practices that we would be very tempted to understand in terms of the paradox will ultimately fail to qualify, for lack of complexity.

Even apart from control, complexity might be the price (and side effect) of enhancement. We enhance by increasing complexity, and that has serious side effects. That's the basic idea; after that, occurrences of increased complexity that generate genuine control paradoxes will have to be established on a case-by-case basis. And that is what this book does for you in the chapters to follow, especially in parts III and IV.

In fact, complexity also does another job for my argument: by the end of this volume you will hopefully have been reassured that there is nothing apocalyptic about the control paradox. It is all about managing complex systems, so that—past all the talk of *singularity* and the like (Bostrom 2014; Wajcman 2017)—technology introduces no fundamentally new challenges. It is just that more and new complex systems are introduced through technological innovation. And complexity is the key to understand how to bridge the gap between technological systems and nontechnological systems and practices.

This leads me back to the AI terminology and what I have in the past called the techno-apocalypse (Di Nucci 2019). Namely, AI terminology mustn't be thought of as normatively neutral: if you are going to make a *elonmuskesque* argument about how fancy and therefore scary some new gadget is, then call it AI and you have already accomplished half the job; folks will be impressed and terrified at once.

More academically now, we must carefully analyze and try to understand whether AI systems introduce novel problems, including ethical, social, political, and legal problems. This book makes a contribution to that task. In this respect, being too quick in labeling something as AI might actually constitute an obstacle for our analytic endeavor.

Here one helpful distinction that has established itself is the one between so-called *narrow* AI and so-called *general* AI (Brockman 2019). So the kind of computer systems that can successfully complete discrete tasks—for example, machine learning algorithms helping us rank therapeutic options in cancer treatment—would count as narrow AI, while the kind of humanlike artificial intelligence that can think for itself would count as general AI. The irony of this distinction is that it begs the question of why we would even think of referring to narrow AI as any kind of AI—and in fact I am not a historian, but my impression is that the current tech-driven AI boom has mostly to do with calling things "AI" (albeit narrow) that we previously just called "computers" or "software." Still, this distinction might be a start.

There is something perverse here: both the tech community and the critical community might have a vested interest in overplaying complexity through the AI label. That's the elonmuskesque bit of the dialectic: on the one side of the debate, the tech community wants to impress us through complexity, and on the other side, the critical community—including academics and the media—wants to scare us through complexity. So the AI label serves both. In between is this book, which emphasizes both promises and risks of technological innovation through its control paradox and its analysis of the practice of delegating tasks to human and nonhuman systems.

IS THERE A SOLUTION TO THE PARADOX?

This leads me to question 4—most of what I said so far, you must have noticed, referred to questions 1 to 3. Is there a solution to the control paradox, and if so, what is the solution? Basically, the solution is the old-fashioned practice of delegating a task or, for short, *delegation*. I will offer a philosophical analysis of the practice of delegation, and hopefully by the end you will have discovered both how the paradox is supposed to work and how you can deal with it—no panic, no apocalypse. The end of the world will have to wait; sorry, Elon.

Basically, the argument goes like this: when you delegate a task, including when you delegate control itself, you give up *direct control* over that task, but that does not mean that you give up control altogether. Think of when an employer, supervisor, or manager delegates to her subordinates or employees. The fact that you give up direct control while not giving up control altogether is what generates not only the control paradox but also the starting point of our solution: successful delegation is when despite the loss of direct control you keep or increase overall control.

So successful delegation avoids the control paradox, even though it requires loss of direct control—and in fact, as you will see, that's the whole point of delegation, to spare the resources that would be otherwise invested in direct control and use them somewhere else more efficiently. That is, in a nutshell, the argument that I will put forward in this book: both an explanation and a possible solution to the control paradox. One important element within the argument is that you are, as an agent, biased toward direct and conscious control—and you must free yourself from that particular prejudice; let go of direct control and embrace delegation, in tech as much as in politics.

RESPONSIBILITY AND WHAT'S TO COME

There is also a normative element within my argument that must be emphasized from the outset: as control is crucial to responsibility, you don't need to have read much philosophy to ask yourself what the paradox means for responsibility. And in fact complex technological systems have been over the last decade or so increasingly throwing up the question of what happens to responsibility attributions, given all the complexity. Who is responsible for what the AI does or decides? And isn't there the risk of so-called responsibility gaps? (See, for example, Di Nucci 2017; Di Nucci & Santoni de Sio 2016; Matthias 2004; Nyholm & Smids 2016; Santoni de Sio & van den Hoven 2018; and Sparrow 2007.)

My short answer to the question about the consequences from the control paradox for responsibility is not short enough to be summarized here, but I do want to highlight a driving hypothesis of this book: there is no such thing as *delegating responsibility*—that's just a category mistake, because responsibility cannot be delegated.

Whether you are talking about technological systems and practices or, indeed, human systems and practices (and mostly we are talking about both at the same time, intertwined), when you delegate control you do not also delegate responsibility. You remain responsible when you delegate control, because, in a slogan, *responsibility is not a cake*—as in, it cannot be divided, only shared.

CONCLUSION

Most philosophy books pompously announce at the outset: this is *not* a self-help book. In other words, this is a serious book, and for god's sake do not confuse it with that airport rubbish with a similar title.[3] That's a sorry state our profession is in, if help has become something to be ashamed of. So, here it comes: this *is* a self-help book in at least one important respect. This book is meant to help you understand recent technological and political developments from two important points of view: that new complexity is both real and serious—and it generates paradoxes—and that the new complexity can be dealt with; *disruption* is only temporary at best.

This is why I focus on both tech and politics: not just because the control paradox happens to apply to both technological and political systems and practices but also because analyzing the paradox across these two distinct domains helps me explain how the paradox itself can ultimately be solved.

Namely, there is nothing special about technology. Or, we have been dealing with complexity since at least the Stone Age, so keep calm and carry on—AI is not going to take over. At the very least, read this book to find out how to avoid the mistakes that might ultimately lead to AI taking over.

I don't want to simplify things too much—this is, after all, a book about complexity. But I can say this much: the idea of the paradox is that there is a "more control" aspect and a "less control" aspect, there is a tension between the two, and the tension is paradoxical because both are about control. And here I just want to emphasize that one element of this paradox is that at least from the outset we should not and ultimately probably also cannot weigh the two elements—more control versus less control—against each other and prioritize one over the other.

Both the "more control" element and the "less control" element must be taken seriously; both are an important development and will keep us busy for at least the rest of the century. Nor should we underestimate the control-enhancing promises that come with technological innovation—we can, after all, do such amazing things, and I don't just mean those small gadgets in your pockets;[4] I mean, for example, the clinical potential of so-called medical AI (see, for example, Di Nucci 2019; Elmore et al. 2015; Esteva et al. 2017; Fry 2018; Gulshan et al. 2016; McDougall 2019b; Mittelstadt & Floridi 2016; and Obermeyer & Emanuel 2016); nor should we obviously underestimate the risks, whether it is defense and the military, the justice system, politics, the media, or indeed healthcare (see, for example, Coeckelbergh 2013; Enemark 2013; Pasquale 2015; Robillard 2018; Strawser 2010, 2013; and Susskind & Susskind 2015).

One final question that this first chapter must at least address if not answer is the following: is the control paradox—in all its different variants—supposed to be an empirical paradox? That is, are the control gains and control losses empirically verifiable? Whether the paradox is supposed to be empirically verifiable is a crucial question, and I can't get around it by pointing to the philosophical nature of this book or even to the conceptual intricacies about control and delegation that the next few chapters will illustrate. The answer to this question turns out to be relatively easy: yes, the paradox is supposed to be empirical, and the simultaneous control losses and gains that the paradox points to are real and measurable. It will be important to remember the empirical nature of my claim when I evaluate, especially in parts III and IV, the application of the paradox to different technological systems and political practices. The empirical nature of the paradox will inevitably make a difference to the various claims about whether a particular technological system or practice does in fact give rise to the paradox or not.

Okay, enough of the preliminaries. In the next chapter we will make further progress on understanding the control paradox and see how it comes to bear on recent social and political developments.

Chapter Two

Control and the Empowerment Illusion

There is indeed a dangerous link between developments in information technologies and recent populist successes across Western democracies (Brexit, Trump, Italy's populist government). But it is not what you think, and neither is it the second one you thought of. The link is not, namely, Trump's and his imitators' undeniable social media skills. But neither is the link Russia's cyberwar or Cambridge Analytica.

Those have certainly been important factors, but the larger phenomenon is a different one: recent technological development has given voters the *illusion of empowerment*, so that they ended up forgetting the advantages (or even necessity?) of delegating to experts in general and of *representative—* instead of *direct—*democracy in particular. This, I contend, is the basic reason—given certain background economic conditions—that populists have been so successful of late. To understand this hypothesis, let's go back to the *control paradox*—the subject matter of this book.

THE CONTROL PARADOX, AGAIN

Take killer robots and their predecessors, military drones (more on these particular technologies in chapter 6). On the one hand, there is the scary prospect of decisions to kill being outsourced to merciless algorithmic machines. On the other hand, there is the promise of fewer collateral damages—because those machines are supposedly more precise than human soldiers—and fewer casualties among one's own military or intelligence personnel, because there is no longer the need for boots on the ground (in theory anyway).[1]

Similarly, take self-driving cars. You have, on the one hand, again the scary prospect of a self-driving car programmed to protect its passengers at all costs, which might opt for running over schoolchildren instead of crashing into a wall. On the other hand, there is the promise of safer driving—algorithms don't drink or get tired behind the wheel, after all—fewer accidents, and less traffic.

Both of the above are possible examples of the control paradox: autonomous technologies such as killer robots and self-driving cars promise more and better control over the task at hand—killing, driving—while at the same time threatening the very thing they were supposed to improve on, namely, control. In developing those and similar technologies, we aim for more control while at the same time being terrified that those algorithms will end up taking over (control).

Within healthcare, something similar can be said of Watson and other algorithmic systems used within pathology, radiology, and oncology (the list grows longer every day; see in particular chapter 10). We aim for more precise diagnosis and therapeutic solutions while at the same time fearing that Watson will end up deciding—over both doctors and patients—who lives and who dies.

I will analyze in later chapters the above applications of the control paradox in detail. And once you have understood how the dialectic of the control paradox works, this book will help you find your own applications; a particularly relevant one in the context of this chapter is the idea that social media platforms such as Facebook were supposed to give us more control over who we interacted with and which news we consumed—instead of the randomness of analog life—while we have ended up being manipulated by data brokers and blinded to alternative points of view. (Cass Sunstein makes a version of this argument in some detail in one of his most recent books, *#Republic* [2018]; see chapter 9 for more.)

THE POLITICAL CONTROL PARADOX

Going back to this book's overall hypothesis, notice the similarity between the control paradox as I have just applied it to various recent technological developments and the distinction between *representative* democracy and *direct* democracy. Indeed, we may speak of a *political* control paradox that is structurally similar to the original—*technological*—control paradox with which I started: We delegate power to politicians and bureaucrats because they are supposed to have the skills, expertise, and resources (time, education) to run the country better than we ever could, individually or collectively—the average voter is, after all, busy trying to make a living (see chapter 11). But with delegating power comes an increased risk of *abuse of power* (and therefore control) and loss of power (and therefore, again, control— don't let me say that power is control, but control is definitely power), if those politicians and bureaucrats we delegated turn out to be incompetent or greedy.

And even if those politicians—surprise, surprise—turn out to be competent puritans, they are still in charge, for good or bad; that is, loss of overall control might be a *risk* of representative democracy, but loss of direct control is the *point* of representative democracy. The *political* control paradox is the idea that representative democracy is supposed to deliver people better control in terms of a country that is run more professionally and efficiently (than under direct democracy). But the price is giving up direct control and also potentially losing overall control due to incompetence, greed, and all those other common virtues of politicians (and bureaucrats;[2] never forget those—they're elite par excellence).

In fact it wasn't that long ago that the internet was still being praised, sold, and marketed as the holy grail of direct democracy. Who still needs delegated power, hierarchical structures, and division of labor in the internet age—after all, haven't we got the world at our fingertips? This once compelling argument has turned sour very quickly.[3] Within this narrative it really should be no surprise that many of the populist successes of recent years are due to a referendum, in many ways the purest form of direct democracy. I am thinking of you, Britain, but it's not just Brexit; the origins of Italy's populist government of 2018–2019 between the Five Start Movement and the Lega can also be traced back to an ill-advised constitutional referendum called and then lost by then prime minister Matteo Renzi, for example.

DIRECT CONTROL AND DIRECT DEMOCRACY

Can you now see the structural similarity between the *technological* control paradox and the *political* control paradox? In both cases, you give up *direct* control because an alternative arrangement promises to deliver better outcomes and ultimately an overall improvement or enhancement of control. But in giving up direct control, you expose yourself to the risk of losing control altogether, or at least to reasonable fears that algorithms and politicians will end up taking over.

You let go of direct control because indirect systems of control (either technological or political) are supposed to be superior. But no longer being in direct control is hard, at least from an epistemic (and also psychological) point of view. So you understandably become anxious that you have lost control altogether to these systems. That's where technophobia, especially in the media and public opinion but also in academic and scientific debates, comes into play—as a consequence of the technological control paradox.

And that's where you see populism—as a consequence of the political control paradox. Within this analogy, technophobia is to the technological control paradox what populism is to the political control paradox: both, if you like, are a reaction to (at least the perception of) too much delegation. And the scary machines that will take over the world in the technophobic reaction to the technological control paradox are the "crooked" politicians (technocrats) who, according to the populist mantra, abuse their power and have forgotten the little people (political control paradox).

It is important to distinguish two elements in this analysis that might appear similar. The idea that as a result of ceding direct control you might become anxious about having lost control altogether should not be merged, for multiple reasons: First, as I will argue, if we delegate successfully, ceding direct control ought not to result in epistemic anxieties about having lost control altogether (that's a normative claim, obviously, because in one version of the paradox, *fear* is exactly what the development of control-enhancing technologies and practices gives rise to).

Second, even if loss of direct control does result in "control anxieties," those are still two separate phenomena. Finally, there is an obvious gap between perceived loss of control and actual loss of control. And that's the difference between the different interpretations of the control paradox that I have already emphasized in the last chapter.

VACCINATING AGAINST POPULISM?

As you will see, populism should be understood not as a purely electoral phenomenon but rather as a broader cultural one; just think of medical fake news and growing vaccination skepticism (see figure 2.1[4]). Indeed, it does not take a very wild hypothesis to see a link (see figure 2.2[5]) between the electoral success of populism and movements such as vaccination skepticism (or "hesitancy," as the WHO cowardly called it in 2019 while declaring it one of the top ten health threats of the year[6]).

More interesting would be the question of the direction of causation between those two, namely, whether it is populism's electoral successes that have contributed to growing scientific skepticism or rather the other way around, with movements such as vaccination skepticism enabling populism at the ballot box (very likely the two have fed each other in a vicious circle).[7]

I can now introduce a third version of this paradox: the *medical* control paradox, in which we give up direct control over our own—and our children's—health to medical experts (and technologies, such as drugs and algorithms) because, supposedly, those healthcare professionals can better control our health (prevent and cure disease, avoid and delay death, improve health and well-being, etc.) than we could ourselves. By now you know the dialectic of the control paradox and you can see for yourself how this further

Europe has had more measles cases in 2018 than any other year this century

Reported measles cases, WHO Europe region

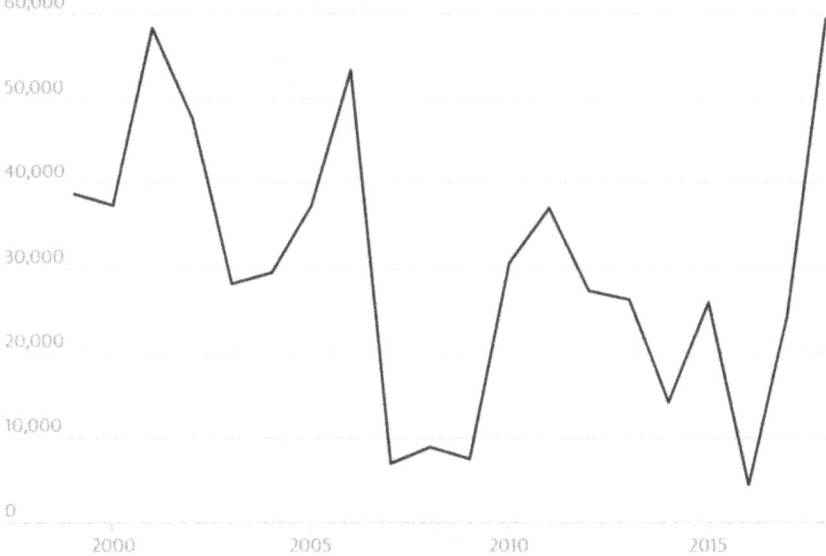

Figure 2.1.   Graph of measles in Europe. *Source: WHO*.

version plausibly ends up with vaccine skepticism and similar anti-scientific side effects.

THREE PARADOXES?

What a deal you're getting! The book's title promises a single control paradox, but after a few pages, you already have three different ones (not to speak of all the different interpretations of each from the last chapter, adding up to at least twelve combinations and counting):

1. The *technological* control paradox
2. The *political* control paradox
3. The *medical* control paradox

You might start to worry that I am overapplying the paradox, seeing it everywhere—thereby making it ultimately meaningless as an analytic tool. But there is a simple reason the control paradox is so widespread: our society is fundamentally still based on the old Smithian (Adam) principle of division of

D   J.   p 🔵   (Follow)   ⌄

Healthy young child goes to doctor, gets pumped with massive shot of many vaccines, doesn't feel good and changes - AUTISM. Many such cases!

5:35 AM - 28 Mar 2014

13,438 Retweets **12,267** Likes   🔵🔵🔵🔵🔵🔵🔵🔵🔵

💬 4.9K   🔁 13K   ♡ 12K

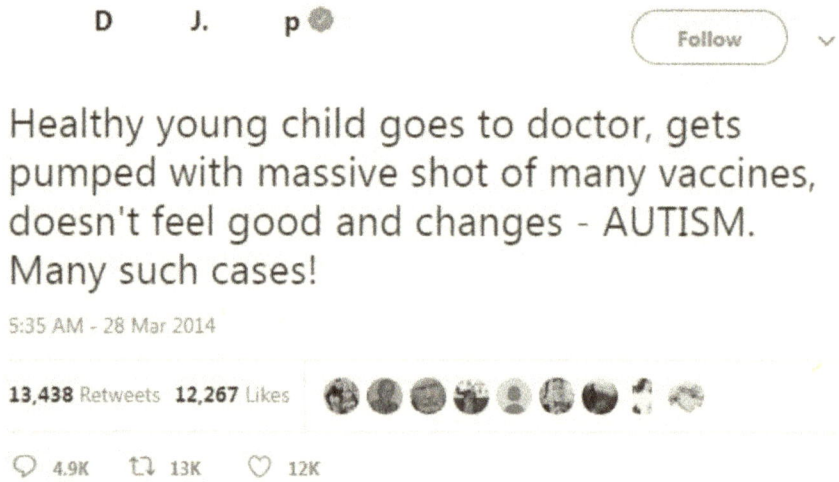

Figure 2.2.   Populist tweet about vaccines.

labor (even though there are some new variables in the equation, such as algorithms), and our control paradox naturally feeds off good old-fashioned division of labor—plus human cognitive limitations (what others might call ignorance, bias, and irrationality).

Do you notice something peculiar about the cases of division of labor that, according to my preliminary analysis, give rise to the control paradox? In the case of both the political paradox and the medical one, direct control is being given up by the less powerful party (voter, patient) toward the more powerful party (politician, doctor). Two points here: First, this directionality in the power asymmetry might indeed provide a criterion for which cases of division of labor result in the control paradox and which do not. In contrast, consider the employer–employee relationship (or, in its more classic version, Hegel's master–slave dialectic, even though the master–slave dialectic might well turn out to be another version of the control paradox in the end). Second, the power asymmetries in play here between patients and doctors and between voters and politicians highlight the crucial question of what we ought to say about the original technological control paradox in which humans give up direct control to technological systems. Which way does the power asymmetry break in that case? Well, a boring but plausible answer might well turn out to be that, throughout history, humans have increasingly lost to technology the role of master, so that now, when it comes to information technologies and so-called autonomous or intelligent technologies, the relationship does end up mirroring the other two versions of the paradox, with the less powerful party ceding direct control to the more powerful party.

This relationship would then be fluid not just in the sense of changing through history and over the course of technological progress but also in the sense—applicable across each of the three versions of the paradox—that every time the less powerful party cedes direct control to the more powerful party, the power asymmetry widens. But surely we must be careful with this quick conclusion, because wouldn't a widening of the power asymmetry be inconsistent with the other horn of the paradox, in which by giving up on direct control we improve or enhance overall control?

BACK TO BASICS

So far, it's been only wild hypotheses and questions answered with more questions; luckily, it's still just part I of the book, and hopefully I will make some progress as I go along. On the topic of early disappointments, you might be puzzled by the provincialism of my approach. After all, both information technologies and populism are very much first-world obsessions and problems. What about the fundamentals? Big problems such as poverty, climate change, and basic access to healthcare and education?

Who cares about populist strides in a bunch of (privileged) Western democracies when even Chinese regional politics affects more people, let alone the whole of Asia? And yes, mobile phones are everywhere even in the so-called third world, but it is still the case that only about half of the world's population has internet access—against, say, more than 90 percent of the world population having access to old-fashioned technologies such as electricity, according to the most recent World Bank estimates.[8] So shouldn't I rather focus on the good old basics, when it comes to both politics and technology?

There are various ways to answer this challenge. More defensively, I could point out that, actually, once you understand populism as a broader cultural phenomenon encompassing anti-scientific prejudices against vaccines experts/elites more in general, then it becomes a challenge well beyond the privileged minority—and indeed even more dangerous for the world's most vulnerable. Basic vaccination is estimated to save between one and three million lives every year (WHO estimates).[9] Or again, defensively, I could point out that by the time this book comes out, internet access will probably be just as widespread as electricity, if not more.[10]

The point about the risks of vaccination skepticism being much greater for poorer countries is symptomatic of a wider dialectic: even if we granted just for the sake of argument that populism as an anti-globalization movement might deliver not just a voice but also better conditions for the forgotten majorities within rich Western democracy (the unemployed and underemployed, rural voters, working- and lower-middle-class voters), still the real forgotten majority (the billions remaining in the Rust Belt, Northern England, or Southern Italy) ends up being worse off because of it. The other obvious example of this dialectic is clearly immigration.

THE SCOPE OF DEMOCRACY

There is a more important reply here though. The control paradox is at the core of a fundamental philosophical question about how to run our societies and live our lives—which is universal: what ought to be up for democratic deliberation and what should be beyond its reach—things such as scientific truths or human rights. What is fair game and what is nonnegotiable?

Populism can be interpreted as a movement to widen the scope of what is up for grabs. This apparent inclusiveness is at the same time why populism is so tempting, even on the left, but it is also at the core of its illusion of empowerment. The control paradox reminds us that there is good reason some things are beyond electoral reach: we should not even *try* to control them.

What is this *illusion of empowerment* that I am accusing tech and populism of? Basically, it's a lie; according to this lie, there is no price, no side effects, to an improvement of our general control mechanisms over ourselves and the environment. It's as if labor no longer needed to be divided, because technology will have torn down those barriers. To understand this, you just need to imagine what our world would look like if indeed there were no paradox—and there might well not be, although the rest of the book will demonstrate that there is, but don't believe it until you see it.

Without the paradox, you would give up direct control to technology and not lose anything, either ontologically (actual risks) or epistemologically (*perceived* risks). Or—because there are always two horns to a dilemma—you wouldn't even need to give up direct control. That would be the case, for example, of *direct* democracy within the political control paradox. So the illusion of empowerment can take two different forms:

1. No-paradox *first* horn: Giving up direct control does not result in increased actual or perceived risks.
2. No-paradox *second* horn: Better overall control comes through more direct control (or, division of labor is overrated!).

No paradox basically means a free lunch—and indeed the rhetorical force of technological progress is often cashed out in terms of previously unimaginable free lunches that technology suddenly makes possible.

Another aspect of the populist illusion of empowerment has to do with its perversion of egalitarianism: It is indeed true that historically there has been a contraposition between economic and political theories based on division of labor, such as market capitalism, and egalitarian theories such as socialism. But egalitarianism does not negate an economy based on the division of labor, given a certain set of rights and distributive rules.

Marx (1891) himself recognized this; just think of the classic "from each according to his ability, to each according to his needs." Admittedly, even the latter part of the principle (the distributive part) is compatible with nonegalitarian distributions, but the reason I am emphasizing it here is rather that there is a former nondistributive part that allows, for example, for delegating direct control to experts—regardless of the slice of the distributive pie experts will ultimately get.[11]

There is, then, an important sense in which the control paradox is not politically neutral—because it might feed populist temptations. But there is a more important sense in which the control paradox *is* politically neutral: it does not support any particular distributive principle. And even though this might be true in theory, it would be myopic to deny—in practice—the connection between populist temptations and distributive principles: If I no longer need to delegate to experts—not human ones anyway—should I not be entitled to a bigger slice of pie? Doesn't more direct control also mean a bigger distributive share?

That's another question that is beyond the scope just yet—even though it is tempting to say that the whole point of the control paradox is that more direct control means, first of all, a smaller overall pie, whatever distributive principles will end up applying. That is, delegation (division of labor) is more productive, more efficient, or economically more advantageous than nondelegation (direct control).

IS THE PARADOX REAL?

We have already encountered this question as one of four fundamental questions in the last chapter—it was question 1. My seven readers now have three options:

1. There is no such thing as the control paradox.
2. The paradox is real and unresolvable.
3. The paradox is real, but we've got an antidote.

To those who endorse (1), all I have to say is read on, which come to think of it is my answer to (2) and (3) as well—bullet points really are useless. Seriously, the main argument of this book is to establish the control paradox and show how it applies and can be applied to diverse domains and sectors such as tech, politics, and medicine (and there is more . . . if you read on). So by the end of the book I hope to have proven that (1) is false. As to (2) and (3), I will put forward a possible resolution to the paradox that, if it works and if theory does matter in practice (which it might not), could also provide an antidote to populism.

My resolution of the paradox—briefly—consists of an account of what it means to successfully delegate a task in general and delegating control in particular. If control is properly delegated, we can avoid the paradox; that does not mean there is no need for giving up on direct control. But it might mean we can successfully enhance overall control by giving up on direct control, under certain conditions. And it means that when we delegate successfully, at least in theory we do not increase *actual* risks. Perceived risks are more difficult, but they are, luckily, no business of philosophy.

So my proposed solution is a particular version of the no-paradox first horn, in which giving up direct control results at the same time in enhanced overall control and no increase in actual risk; it's then up to politicians (and maybe also the media) to make sure this is reflected in perceived risk as well. Whether this is a genuine resolution of the paradox—and whether it applies to all the different versions of the paradox presented in this volume—is one more thing the rest of the book will have to find out.

"ASYMMETRISCHE DEMOBILISIERUNG"

So far, I have talked quite a bit about populism, so I'd like to make some clarifications. First, populism is not the subject matter of this book—only the control paradox is. Populism is just an illustration of one of the most prominent ways, I believe, the control paradox currently manifests itself in our societies. This isn't a book about Brexit or Trump (and in fact, only one further chapter will feature these phenomena prominently, namely, chapter 11).

Second, readers might rightly point out that populism is only one-half of the political control paradox—if at all; it's too much direct democracy as a reaction to (perceived) too much representative democracy. But what about not enough direct democracy? Don't the populists have a point after all?

Here is an example: Angela Merkel has been accused of so-called *asymmetrische Demobilisierung*, a strategy explicitly meant to lower turnout by avoiding fundamental debates and controversial topics. And even within political philosophy, there are voices that worry about too much instead of too little political involvement and participation: I am thinking, for example, of the book *Against Democracy* by Jason Brennan, which suggests that voters should be subject to some kind of epistemic vetting before being allowed to influence the political process. [12] If populism is supposed to be one extreme of the political control paradox—too much direct democracy/control—these could be examples of the other extreme—too much representative democracy/delegation.

Whether it is technology, politics, or indeed healthcare, the question is always the same: how much control should each party have? It is only the relevant actors who change:

humans—algorithms
bosses—workers
voters—politicians
patients—doctors

After which point has delegation gone too far? More boringly, WHAT tasks should be delegated to WHOM under WHICH conditions?

The complexity of these sets of questions gives rise to the control paradox, and it is by answering these questions that I can put forward a resolution of the paradox. So another way of establishing whether this volume will have been successful is whether it can provide an answer to the complex question above for each of its many applications of the paradox.

Another important clarification is the following: it is not just populism that is *not* the subject of this book; neither is the initial political hypothesis according to which information technologies have given an illusion of empowerment that, together with the control paradox, has led to the rise of populism. This is, after all, a philosophy book, which could hardly be expected to give a full argument for the above hypothesis, given that such a full argument would be, at least to some extent, empirical. So again, that hypothesis will remain in the background, motivating an analysis of the control paradox.

THE EMPOWERMENT ILLUSION

Still, are there any plausible reasons to entertain my illusion-of-empowerment hypothesis? Here's one: there has been a gap in recent decades between technological innovations on the one hand and progress broadly conceived on the other hand, at least for the lower socioeconomic "classes" in Western democracies. Interestingly, that gap might stand in contrast to a correlation between technological innovation and progress broadly conceived at the global level (poverty, starvation, sanitation, healthcare, basic education, etc.).

Working-class and (lower) middle-class voters across Western democracies have in recent decades experienced stagnating wages. Figure 2.3 shows the wage growth in the United States in the last half century (Desilver 2018). If you can't read this kind of economic data, I will summarize it for you: *no real wage growth over the last forty years*; then people called Trump a surprise. In some cases even more fundamental indicators such as life expectancy are declining: life expectancy in the United States was marginally down in 2017 compared to 2016, as shown in figure 2.4 (Murphy et al. 2018). You might think this is a one-off statistical anomaly, but as other studies show, this trend is neither only U.S.-based nor does it concern only the year 2017 (see, for example, Ho & Hendi 2018).

Aren't these material indicators much better explanations of recent events than illusions and paradoxes? This would be, in principle, a powerful objection; the good news is that I do not need to resist it because my argument is that this material decline, together with superficial technological innovations such as mobile internet, have contributed to the empowerment illusion. So wage stagnation and decline in life expectancy are not an alternative explanation to the one my empowerment illusion hypothesis offers; rather, those material conditions are essential elements of my explanation, which goes like this: superficial technological innovations such as the internet and the mobile phone might have had a chance of really empowering people, if they hadn't happened at the same time as material indicators were showing downward curves.

From a philosophy of technology point of view, we can say that, rather than technophobia, the problem has been that voters are technophiles, mistaking small technological steps (iPhones, anybody?) for easy solutions to fundamental trends.

There is a dualistic way of thinking of material conditions as opposed to emotional or otherwise immaterial factors that we ought to resist: on the one

Americans' paychecks are bigger than 40 years ago, but their purchasing power has hardly budged

Average hourly wages in the U.S., seasonally adjusted

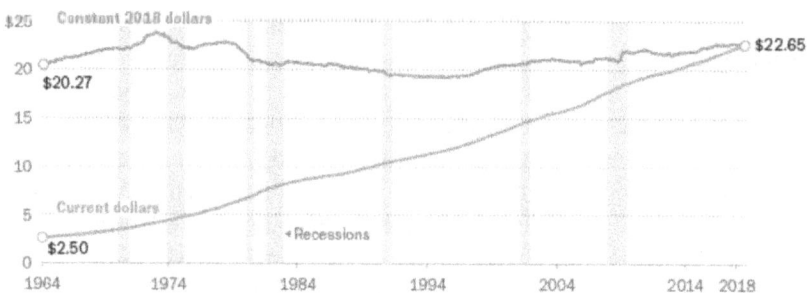

Note: Data for wages of production and non-supervisory employees on private non-farm payrolls. "Constant 2018 dollars" describes wages adjusted for inflation. "Current dollars" describes wages reported in the value of the currency when received. "Purchasing power" refers to the amount of goods or services that can be bought per unit of currency.
Source: U.S. Bureau of Labor Statistics.

Figure 2.3.   Wage growth in the U.S., 1964–2018. *Source: PEW Research Center.*

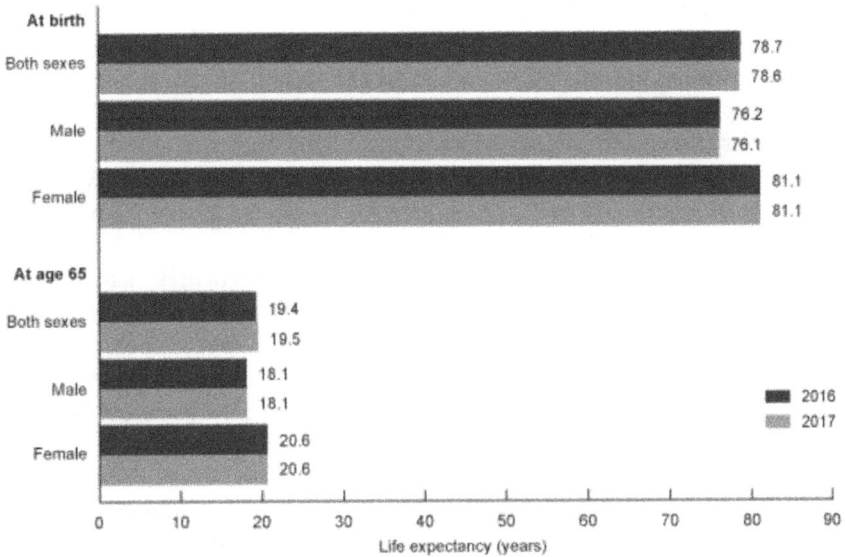

Figure 2.4.   Life expectancy in the U.S. for 2016 and 2017.

hand, wages, health, and the like; on the other, issues of identity, for example. You can see this kind of dualism in current debates about identity politics on the left. Those are interesting and important questions, but it is a mistake to think that material and symbolic considerations are alternative to each other, and the two examples I have selected above—stagnant wages and declining life expectancy—are a good example of this dialectic.

What's the point of delegating power to bosses and politicians—the average worker-voter will plausibly think—if my wages are lower than forty years ago in real terms (inflation adjusted)? If this is the best experts can deliver, I might as well give it a go myself and otherwise trust a self-declared nonexpert, whether by the name of Berlusconi or Trump. What's the point of doing what my doctor tells me if I am not even going to live longer than my folks, who never even went to the doctor? So instead of a mistaken dualism between Marxism and identity politics, we ought to recognize that processes of identification happen as a direct result of changes in workers' material conditions—or is that just Marxism winning out?

TAKING BACK CONTROL

Another mistake here, by the way, is to think that populist skepticism toward expertise is an issue of trust—as in, why should I trust experts? Trust isn't the point; power and control are: the argument for delegating power and control to expert elites—whether to your line manager, local MP, or GP—is that they are supposed to deliver better outcomes than you could yourself. So the crucial *t* word is not trust, it is *trade*; you are trading off direct control over something important to you—time, governance, health, whatever—in exchange for an expected higher return. If there is no higher return, the result is not lack of trust; the result is a poor trade or bad deal. And then no wonder if someone promises you to "take back control"—as the Leave Campaign in the UK Brexit referendum did—you might be tempted.

In fact, "taking back control" is a perfect antithetical slogan for this book's argument, as long as I specify that it is "direct control" that I am talking about—but then "taking back direct control" makes for uglier posters—trust experts to always spoil a good story with the truth, right?

What the control paradox points to, at its core, is a trade-off between direct control and delegated control: we are delegating control to experts—both human and nonhuman—because they are supposed to do a better job of controlling our car, society, health, and so forth. The price is giving up direct control, and the question is whether that is worth it. So if we don't think we got a good deal out of it, then we understandably want to take back (direct) control. And the obvious irony of the control paradox is that, unsurprisingly, taking back (direct) control won't actually give us better overall control, as the Brexit mess so graphically demonstrates.

There is something else that the Brexit case illustrates well: when there isn't enough delegation or the wrong task is delegated—as when something that, because of its complexity, ought to plausibly belong to parliamentary deliberation is instead put to a referendum—that ends up creating even more complexity, which is then even more difficult for nonexperts to navigate.

You would be forgiven for thinking that this is itself an argument for the benefit or even inevitability of delegating to experts: if you don't delegate some control to experts at T1 but rather try to directly solve the problem yourself (or trust some amateur, call him Nigel or Boris, who speaks like you do at the bar), you might end up having to delegate even more control to experts at T2. A simpler way of saying this is that trying to take back direct control could well backfire and you could end up with less control than you previously had, which seems to me to be a very accurate description of Brexit.

This also allows me to clarify that the control paradox should not be misunderstood for some sort of technophile (technological paradox) or authoritarian (political paradox) argument in favor of delegating more to algorithms and experts. In fact, as the previous point shows, there is a genuine danger for representative democracy of losing too much control—and that is an essential part of the paradox, that through delegation we expose ourselves, becoming more vulnerable (at least epistemically).

So one of the reasons it is important to answer this complex question—
what tasks to *whom* under *which* conditions—is exactly the vulnerability of
giving up on direct control: if we delegate the wrong tasks to the wrong
people, we will end up violating the minimum oversight requirement that is a
condition of democratic life—and which in my argument is the equivalent,
when it comes to technology, to so-called *meaningful human control* (you
will read a lot more on meaningful human control, or MHC, in parts II and III
of this book).

How much delegation is legitimate and efficient without losing meaningful human control? That's one of the main questions I will have to answer.
And I am emphasizing it here so it is clear that, whether I am talking of the
technological or the political paradox (and indeed the medical one as well),
we should not underestimate the risk of giving up too much oversight.

For example, many people would be understandably uncomfortable with
delegating the killing decision to a drone, while it might be legitimate to
allow the drone to independently identify possible targets. Similarly, it might
be legitimate to allow Watson to come up with a ranked set of therapeutic
alternatives, but you might still want a human doctor to provide advice and
decision-making based on those algorithmically predetermined alternatives.
Again, *what tasks to whom under which conditions?*

Does that mean the populists have a point after all? If you wanted to be
particularly sympathetic, you could say they have identified an important
question—that delegation is not a free lunch—while at the same time often
answering it with the implausible simplification of suggesting that you don't
need to delegate at all, such as with vaccines or referendums.

Speaking of populism and experts, I am sure populism experts will be
horrified by how loosely I am applying "their" concept. In fact, I am not
interested in providing a definition of populism, nor am I too bothered by
having to respect the populism landscape in current literature. I am only
using the term to identify some phenomena that, I believe, are interestingly
and tightly related to philosophical questions about control and delegation
that drive this book.

It might turn out that talking of "direct democratic movements" instead of
talking of populism would be more appropriate, given the structure of the
paradox, but as you have seen, the questions at stake go way beyond a
particular form of government. Having said that, if we take the influential
modern definition of populism put forward by the so-called ideational approach, I think my own use of the concept here is legitimate:

> Agreement is general that all forms of populism include some kind of appeal
> to "the people" and a denunciation of "the elite." Accordingly, it is not overly
> contentious to state that populism always involves a critique of the establish-
> ment and an adulation of the common people. More concretely, we define

populism as *a thin-centered ideology that considers society to be ultimately separated into two homogeneous and antagonistic camps, "the pure people" versus "the corrupt elite," and which argues that politics should be the expression of the* volonté générale *(general will) of the people.* (Mudde & Kaltwasser 2017, 5–6; emphasis in original)

CONCLUSION

Summing up, I have identified a relationship between ethics of technology questions about how much control we ought to give to algorithms and political questions about how much control we ought to give to experts and politicians. I have structured both kinds of questions following the control paradox, according to which in trying to enhance control we risk losing it—and suggested that the control paradox can be applied to other domains, such as healthcare. I emphasized how in both cases the crucial question is what tasks we ought to delegate to whom under which conditions. At the same time, I have shown how the promises and risks of the control paradox might be linked to the success of recent populist movements such as Brexit, Trump, and the 2018–2019 populist government in Italy.

There haven't been many answers in this chapter—that's what the rest of the book is for. I will analyze in detail both the structure and some exemplary applications of the control paradox in both its technological and its political versions. But first, I need to say more about the philosophy of control and delegation, to which I now turn in part II of the book (chapters 3, 4, and 5).

Part Two

Control and Delegation

Chapter Three

The Concept of Control
and Direct Control

You cannot understand the control paradox without first understanding the concept of control. So this chapter is about control in its many different manifestations, with a special focus on the difference between *direct control* and (overall) control. The control paradox makes at least two claims, both of which have to do with control:

1. New technologies and practices (innovation, basically) can give us *enhanced control* (remember, I am for the moment understanding "enhanced control" as "more or better control," but by the end of this chapter I will have a more precise definition of what ought to count as "enhanced control").
2. At the same time, these very same new technologies and practices can also result in loss of control (or, according to the different interpretations from chapter 1, increased risk of loss of control—that would be the *stronger* paradox as opposed to the *strongest*—or increased fear of loss of control, which would be the merely *strong* paradox in my taxonomy).

I therefore need a good working understanding of control if I am to evaluate those two claims above, about enhanced control and loss of control. This is what this chapter aims to deliver. When philosophers discuss control, what they normally mean is "human control" as a condition for responsibility, raising questions such as whether control is necessary for responsibility—or indeed sufficient (let alone necessary *and* sufficient).

Control—especially in the context of this book—is not necessarily just control over actions; an agent's control over her actions is also the paradigmatic case in the philosophical literature. So we—philosophers—normally think in terms of human control of an agent over her actions and whether that is necessary or sufficient (inclusive disjunctive) for responsibility (less often the same questions are raised for intentional action).

Given the subject matter of this book, my discussion of control will transcend what is paradigmatic in the philosophical literature, because I am primarily interested in control over technological systems and control within interhuman practices, including groups, organizations, and whole societies or political systems—that's where delegation comes in.

While this chapter is not specifically about delegation—that will come later (see especially chapter 5)—the practice of delegating a task and specifically control delegation will already be crucial here because it informs our conception of control, especially when it comes to distinctions between *direct* or *conscious* control and other forms of control.

The reason I stress this "paradigmatic" use of control within the philosophical literature as opposed to "technological" and "social" control (see the next chapter, chapter 4) is simply that we cannot assume we are talking about the same phenomena and the same concept—and that will in fact be one of the questions I will try to answer, whether the conditions for (human) control (over our actions) can also be useful when thinking in terms of control over technological systems or control within organizations and between agents, as in the political case.

For this reason and for the purposes of my argument in this chapter and beyond, we should therefore think in terms of the following three categories:

1. The interaction between a human agent and her actions (and relative control of a human agent over her actions) or "human control";
2. The interaction between different human agents (and relative control of one or more human agents over other human agents) or "social control"; and
3. The interaction between human agents and nonhuman agents or technological systems (whether intelligent ones such as AI or simpler ones such as tools and machines—here again, the same category can be understood in terms of control, either of the human agent over the nonhuman agent or also of the nonhuman agent over the human agent)[1] or "technological control."

In terms of the structure of my argument, this chapter will be mostly about control in general and especially number 1, *human control*, while the next chapter will deal with number 2, *social control*, and 3, *technological control*. And clearly the overall question is whether there is some basic form or unified notion of control that spans across the three domains.

ACTION THEORY FOR DUMMIES

Let me start from the action-theoretical basics about control: whether some event counts as an action or not can plausibly be said to depend on whether there was some kind of agential control over that event, which would otherwise have to be considered a *mere happening*. The very same movement might or might not count as an action depending on whether I was in control; that's the difference between jumping and being pushed, for example. My body might in both cases move in exactly the same way, but in the former case I am in control of how my body moves, while in the latter case someone else is. At least, I am not in control; the one pushing me might want to exercise some form of control over my fall, for example, if they aim to use my body to crash something. Or they might alternatively be satisfied with my free fall, for example, if I am on top of a mountain and all they want is to kill me. In either case, I am not in control. In the former case, the other agent has some degree of control, and in the latter case, nobody has any control once I have been pushed.

The first philosopher of action, Aristotle, has a nice case of being carried by the wind to illustrate this kind of *involuntary action* in his *Nicomachean Ethics*—more than two thousand years ago. I submit that, to this day, there's still no better way of characterizing lack of control than being carried by the wind.

> Those things, then, are thought involuntary, which take place by force or owing to ignorance; and that is compulsory of which the moving principle is outside, being a principle in which nothing is contributed by the person who acts—or, rather, is acted upon, e.g., *if he were to be carried somewhere by a wind*, or by men who had him in their power. (Aristotle 1998, book III, I, p. 48; my own emphasis)

Also notice Aristotle's useful comparison between being carried by a wind and being in someone's power: if you have lost control, does it matter who is in control? Here it is standard—and important—to distinguish between causing some event and being in control of some event, so that, for example, the one who pushes me down the mountain causes me to fall, but once they have pushed me they no longer have any control over my fall—and that matters, because they cannot save me . . . it's simply too late. And that's the difference between being a mere cause of an event and (still) being in control of some event, a difference that is indeed morally crucial.

Often these action-theoretical distinctions are made in terms of the agent's attitudes: Did the agent want, desire, or intend the outcome? Then she must have jumped. And if the agent did not want, desire, or intend the outcome, then she must have been pushed. And in fact standard accounts in the philosophy of action define what an action is and what counts as an intentional action in terms of whether the "right" attitude caused the relevant movement; see Donald Davidson (especially his 1980 collection, *Essays on Actions and Events*) for the most influential example of a causal account of intentional action.

What action theory is aiming at then, when pairing the "right" intention (or belief-desire pair—that's the difference between Davidson's reductive account of intentional action and nonreductive accounts such as Michael Bratman's [1984, 1987]), is really to give an account of control, because if you have the "right" intention but no causal link, there is no evidence of control. And the same goes for a causal link with the "wrong" intention or belief-desire pair. Just to be clear, here "right" and "wrong" refer to the link between the content of the intention and the content of the action, the link between "I want to jump" and the action of jumping, for example.

There are classic ways of showing that the "right" attitude plus the causal link cannot be sufficient, so-called deviant causal chains—but this is beyond the scope here (see Davidson himself again [1980], as well as my own work on deviant causal chains [Di Nucci 2008]). All I want to illustrate is the basic relationship between the concept of control and the idea of acting intentionally and for a reason.

What can we learn from the basic case of human action about interactions between different human agents and interactions between humans and intelligent machines (which are the two cases that primarily interest us here)? First and foremost, we can learn that the basic question is really the same: can we trace some event back to some agent? In this way, we are in the position to ask why that event took place (Anscombe 1957).

Starting from the basic case of human agency, then, allows us to recognize that the questions are the same—that the reason we are interested in control in the first place is to find out why something happened and who is behind some event. And that does not change whether we are talking of individual human agents, interactions between human agents, or indeed interactions between human agents and nonhuman agents or machines. It is too early here to settle the question of what criteria must be fulfilled in order to qualify as an agent, but we should certainly not rule out at the outset the possibility that nonhuman systems might qualify as agents.

Here I should clarify that, obviously, there are at least two different things that one might be after when asking the question "why?" and that explanations and rationalizations are not the same. Namely, while rationalizations might always be explanations (even if not always true ones), not all explanations are rationalizations, simply because not all explanations point to reasons; some simply point to causes.

This distinction between reasons and causes (even if one accepts that reasons are causes, as Davidson [1980] famously claims) is easily applicable to the difference between natural phenomena and human actions, for example. But, importantly, the other two phenomena I am interested in here, namely, social control and technological control, also call for reasons and not just for causes, because neither is a natural phenomenon. So I have already identified a fundamental similarity between these three domains: *all three domains are domains of reasons.*

The fact that I have here started from the basic case of human actions to illustrate the concept of control might give you the wrong impression, namely, that when it comes to human actions there is no question of control. But there are at least two different standard "control" problems with human actions that must be highlighted here, even though I won't have time to go into much detail.

The first is causal determinism: This is the idea that the physical world is causally determined and that, if human actions are part of the physical world, then human actions must be causally determined as well. And that has famously been thought to be incompatible with free will and moral responsibility—one of philosophy's oldest and most classic problems. Here the problem of free will is relevant because you could just as well worry that the fact that actions and events are causally determined is incompatible with the idea that some agent—human or otherwise—has control over those actions and events in any meaningful sense.

I will come back to free will and determinism and how that debate is linked to the concept of control later on in this chapter, where you will see that accounts of control from the determinism debate have already made their way to the debate about technological control, for example, Fischer and Ravizza's (1998) idea of *guidance control*. First though, I will look at the other problem of control for human action.

Before moving on to this second case, let me take this opportunity to stress that I am using the language of "actions and events" because we ought not to assume from the outset any specific link between the question of control and the question of when an event qualifies as an action; it is plausible to think that we might have control over events that still do not qualify as actions, for example, and that therefore our agency and our control are not necessarily coextensive.

AUTOMATICITY AND HABITS

The second complicated case, when it comes to control and human action, is automaticity (Di Nucci 2008, 2011, 2012, 2013), and this will be my focus in this section. The interesting thing about automaticity is that it goes both ways: on the one hand, when we act automatically, we sometimes throw up the question of whether we were in control of what we did. In fact, sometimes we say that we did something automatically to explain or even *excuse* ourselves.

As I discussed earlier, I am sure the following has already happened to you: You are on a familiar route and only once you took the usual turn did you realize that, on this particular occasion, you are actually going somewhere else. For instance, when you have an appointment that is on your way to work but not quite at the same location, you might inadvertently turn left toward your office even though you were supposed to keep going till the next junction to your appointment.

You turned left toward your office *out of habit* or *automatically*. It is not surprising, in this particular case, that your habit fooled you, given the familiarity of the route. Sometimes people in these kinds of cases speak of being on "automatic pilot," but given the overall subject matter of this book, I find that particular metaphor and expression not very helpful, so I will try to steer clear of it—but I'm sure you know what I mean (and I will have much more to say about "autopilot" and related systems in the coming chapters on planes and cars).

And there are other cases of automaticity when we might challenge whether we were in control, such as when we instinctively lower our head or close our eyes to avoid some object or to protect ourselves. Cases of so-called implicit bias (Gendler 2011; Holroyd et al. 2017; and especially Saul 2012, 2013a, 2013b) are also automatic actions where the question of control is crucial. If it turns out that, without realizing it, John speaks slower to people whose skin is darker, is John a racist? Probably. But more importantly for my purposes, is John in control of his actions in this particular instance? And also, can we even claim that John is a racist if he is not in control of his actions? Those are important questions—and these are questions about control.

I have said that automaticity cuts both ways when it comes to control. As we have just seen, on the one hand there are cases in which we seem to have *less control* in virtue of the fact that we are acting automatically—or at least we claim as much to make excuses. But there are also cases in which we seem to have *more control* in virtue of the fact that we are acting automatically. Think of the kinds of skills involved in sports or music and, in general, think of what it takes to learn some practice. It is part of learning to do something that we increasingly become better at it, bringing it more under our control. And part of that consists of actually having to pay less attention, no longer having to think through each step.

There are some now famous experiments by Beilock and colleagues (Beilock & Carr 2001; Beilock et al. 2002; Beilock & Gonso 2008—I summarize and discuss much of this evidence in Di Nucci [2013]) that speak very vividly to this. In those studies, professional golfers are compared to amateurs not just in terms of performance but also in terms of effort, attention, and the ability to deal with distractions. The results of these studies are fascinating and very much in line with what I have sketched above: professional golfers not only do not need to concentrate or pay attention as much as beginners (which we would have expected given some reasonable assumptions about how practices are learned). Professional golfers are also better, performance-wise, when they cannot pay attention or are under time pressure than when they are given more time or less distracting conditions in which to perform.

Forgive me for slightly laboring this point, but I want to be precise, for once, as these issues will be relevant again in later chapters: those studies do not just show that, as could have been expected, professionals (*experts*, anybody? Can we still use the word?) might need fewer attention resources than nonexperts. That we might be able to spare resources with time and experience is an important aspect of expertise, but again a predictable one.

Those studies do not just show that, in stormy conditions where attention resources are scarce (maybe because it is difficult to focus, such as when someone follows you around the world shouting, "You are the man, Tiger!" before every shot?), experts are better than nonexperts. Again, that experts might be able to deal with the scarcity of attention resources better than nonexperts is a predictable—if important—aspect of what it means to be an expert. After all, there will only be a market for experts if somehow they end up generating efficiencies, and experts might well achieve that, in the first instance, through attention economizing.

So, big deal, experts need less attention resources than nonexperts and experts can deal better than nonexperts with situations where attention resources are scarce, and the latter probably follows from the former, actually. If all the Beilock studies had shown would be these important but predictable features of expertise, we might end up being underwhelmed. But the added twist is that the Beilock studies purport to also show that attention resources—when it comes to experts—might actually be counterproductive. And, crucially for the purposes of this book, attention would be then counterproductive to control, when you are an expert.

Below you can see the radical interpretation of these results that is relevant to my argument about the control paradox:

Expert: More attention → less control; less attention → more control
Amateur: More attention → more control; less attention → less control

CONTROL AND AUTOMATICITY

These results suggest that, when learning a practice (or at least when *mastering* a practice, if you think there is an important difference there, which there might well be), we improve control while actually paying less attention. This is the dialectic of automaticity:

Control is enhanced by paying less attention.
Less attention is the consequence of control enhancement.

Given what you already know about the control paradox, I am sure you can already begin to see what I am getting at.

Still, for now my purpose is just to emphasize that the basic case with which I have started—human agents' control over their own actions—is less simple than it might have initially appeared. But that's a good thing, because it means we can learn from this initial case important insights to bring to bear on the case of control between human agents and control between human and nonhuman agents such as technological systems, whether intelligent ones such as AI systems or less intelligent ones such as tools and machines.

The following claim, though, is just too tempting to be left unclaimed, namely, that automaticity itself represents a case of the control paradox. Think about the scenario earlier: you are on your habitual route, but you are not supposed to turn left to your office but to continue to the next junction to your appointment. As it happens, you inadvertently (and automatically) turn left toward your office anyway.

Was that the control paradox getting in your way? Let us look at it more closely, remembering that for a case to count as an application of the control paradox, we need both control enhancement and control loss (even though there are different interpretations of what might actually count as control loss, as we have already seen).

The control loss bit is, on the face of it, obvious: you made a mistake and missed your appointment. You were not supposed to turn left toward your office but to continue until the next junction. Still, even assuming your intention to make the appointment in time, it's unclear whether you wanted to turn left or go straight, at least at the precise time when you turned left. It might be argued that, given the familiar route, you simply forgot that you were not going to your office, so that at the time of the turn you in fact did want to turn even though that was incompatible with your overall intention.

There is an old distinction by James Reason (Reason 1990, 2000) between two kinds of human errors, slips and mistakes, which could help us here: a "slip" is when you didn't mean to make that particular erroneous move, while a "mistake" is when you did mean to make that particular erroneous move but did not realize that it wasn't strategically conducive to your overall strategy.

So was your turning left, on that particular day when you were not going to the office but had an appointment nearby, a slip or a mistake? It definitely looks like a slip, because it's not as if you thought that by turning left you would have gotten to the appointment more quickly—that would have instead qualified as a "mistake" according to Reason. It's rather that your habit of going to the office took over because of the route similarity between the two different destinations.

We might assume, just for clarity's sake, that 95 percent of the route to your appointment was the same as your daily route to the office. So it's an understandable error. Even though, depending on what's at stake, 95 percent might be good enough or not good enough. A commercial pilot cannot get away with a 95 percent successful landing, for example. But you are a philosopher, so you have it easier.

So this is the control-loss part of the paradox: you lost control because of your habits and the familiarity of the route; you made a mistake and took a wrong turn, which in turn meant you missed your appointment. Tough luck, but nobody died, given the low-stakes philosophy nature of your appointment. And still it was a regrettable loss of control. But was it avoidable?

Here we get to the interesting part: was the control loss related to the control enhancement? That's what is crucial in order to determine whether we are looking at another case of the control paradox. In order to answer this question, we must first establish whether there was any control enhancement to begin with. And the crucial element here is your daily habit of going to work along the same route.

It could in fact be argued that you know your habitual daily route to the office so well that, once you are on it, you stop paying as much attention as you did previously (when the route was less familiar, as if you had just gotten the job, say) or as much attention as you pay to a less familiar or wholly unfamiliar route. You are feeling confident, namely, *in control*. And as a result you don't pay as much attention. This understanding of familiarity is quite plausible even beyond these kinds of cases; it is a sense of being at home, of relaxing, of no longer being on guard.

That's the value of familiarity, and that's the value of habits—that's also why they are so difficult to break (see the new book on habits by Wendy Wood [2019], a psychologist who is one of the leading empirical experts on the topic; see also Neal et al. [2013] and my own Di Nucci [2013]).[2] The basic idea being that habits and skills are good for control; learning a skill and developing a habit boost our control over the relevant performance; in fact, it's such a boost that we no longer need to pay attention, and as Beilock's studies show, attention can even become a problem for performance.[3]

Habits, skills, and automaticity are, then, control enhancing. But that can come at a price, as my little thought experiment shows—and that price is also in terms of control. Here it might be helpful to introduce another influential behavioral psychologist of our time, economics Nobel Prize–winner Daniel Kahneman, of *Thinking, Fast and Slow* fame (2011).

What that book popularized was the idea of a dual-system theory, where there is a conscious system and an automatic system. Here's a rough simplification for our own purposes: the conscious system plays a supervisory role and does not always have to be active or intervene. And in fact the automatic system is better at some things, but it needs to be kept in check by the conscious system, or we have the same difficulty of my thought experiment, as well as the nastiness of implicit bias, for example—we have, in short, control loss.

It is a trade-off between the kinds of efficiencies that we can make through habits, skills, and automatic actions (Kahneman's automatic system) by sparing the cognitive resources otherwise invested in paying attention to our performances (what I am here referring to as "attention resources"), and the kinds of risks—or do we want to call them *collateral damages*?—that such efficiencies bring with them, for example, the fact that, if we turn off[4] the conscious system on a familiar route to spare cognitive resources (maybe in order to listen to some highbrow podcast, say), then we might miss the slight difference between today's route and our daily route.

Obviously—but let's say it anyhow—we should not think of the interaction between the two systems as being itself necessarily active; we should rather think in terms of these efficiencies and accompanying risks creeping in. This more nuanced way of conceptualizing the interaction between what we do and think consciously and what we do (and think?) automatically will also be much more realistic and useful once we apply these theoretical insights to the interaction between different human agents and the interaction between human and nonhuman agents (such as technological systems).

Here we can make a distinction that will turn out to be useful in order to establish whether these kinds of automatic action cases might qualify for the control paradox, and later a similar kind of distinction will be useful to make similar evaluations about other cases—so it has dialectic value for the whole book, if you like.

Holding on to the control-enhancing power of habits for now, the distinction I am thinking of is between on the one hand the idea that control loss in this case is represented by the risks emphasized by my familiar route example, namely, risks that narrowly apply to the very case to which we want to predicate control enhancement. On the other hand, one could think of control loss more broadly in terms of the risks involved in letting Kahneman's automatic system take over too much control and resulting, for example, in our cognitive biases and the nastiness of implicit bias.

Simplifying, if the case is one of automatically cycling or driving (or walking, why does nobody ever use *walking* examples?) to the office, one example is when the control loss is specific to the case, with the risk of taking a wrong turn. A different example would be when the control loss is more general, such as too much heuristics might help you with your daily route to work but also get you in trouble with implicit bias, discrimination, and prejudice (here see, again, Di Nucci [forthcoming] on implicit bias).

This distinction plays an important role in the overall argument of this book, because it leads to the following alternative interpretation (and maybe ultimately even possible solution?) of the control paradox:

Local control enhancement → global control loss
Global control enhancement → local control loss

We will come back to these distinctions between local and global control, but as this is not a crime novel, there is no point holding on to important stuff until the end—just keep it in mind for now because it will matter later on.

I do not want to necessarily decide between these two different control-loss risks for this scenario. I am only using the distinction to illustrate two different ways of thinking of the control paradox. In fact, it could be argued that there is a genuine control paradox only if the control loss is specific to the very scenario or case of which we are also predicating control enhancement. Otherwise it's not a paradox, just a control trade-off between different domains. According to this way of thinking, then, we would only end up with a genuine control paradox if we found cases of the paradox that could not be "resolved" through, for example, the local/global distinction. Even then, though, it would still be a big deal if our capacity for switching off attention on our way to work turns out to make us into racists too.

Before moving on, there is an obvious objection to this argument that is screaming to be dealt with: people do not normally think of habits as control enhancing; people normally think of habits as control problems. Basically, if something is a habit, I no longer control it. Call this the "addictive" view of habits; already its name should tell you what I make of it, namely, that it has a tendency to reduce habits to addictions. It might in fact be true that some of the phenomena that we think and talk of in terms of "habits" are in fact addictions—smoking, for example—or at least turn into addictions. But the fact that some habits might turn into addictions or that some habits might not actually be habits but rather addictions does not mean that habits are necessarily addictive.

Take the following definition of habit, which I once heard attributed to the philosopher Anthony Kenny (but I can't find the actual source): actions are habitual if they are easier to perform than not to perform.[5] This way of thinking of habits does not directly reference control, nor does it have any obvious implications for our control over habits. In fact, this definition could be taken to speak to the other control side, because if something is easier to perform than not to perform, that might say something about our ability to perform and skills in performing the relevant action—namely, it might say something about how good we are at it, how much control we have over the performance when we do it.

This issue is too complex for me to do justice to it here: I just wanted to mention the objection and point out that we should not assume the "addictive" theory of habits. To make further progress I would then probably have to distinguish between control over some performance during the performance and control over initiating that performance. It could, for example, be the case that—with habits—we have enhanced control over the performance once it has been initiated, but we have reduced control over whether to initiate the performance. That would speak to Kenny's idea that it is easier to light up than not to light up, for example, but once we have started we might be very good at it—we might be fully in control. Whether that might itself be a paradox of sorts, I will let you decide for yourself, my dear reader.

BACK TO CONTROL

Internalizing a practice or getting habituated to something is a form of control enhancement, but it brings with it its own control-loss risks, just as the control paradox predicts. And even Kahneman's dual-system theory can be interpreted in terms of a conscious system of control and an automatic system of control, where the former has a supervisory function and does not have to intervene or even be active all the time. This allows for some efficiencies, but it also carries risks, like our thought experiment about mistakenly taking a turn toward the office shows.

Still, have we learned anything about control by looking at automaticity? I think we have: for example, that control does not need to be conscious, otherwise it would be difficult to argue that automatic actions are under our control, given the dual-system theory and the idea that automatic actions no longer require our attention and in fact work better without it.

Automatic actions allow us to make a distinction that will turn out to be crucial for the overall argument of this book (yes, one more crucial distinction—hope you are keeping count):

> When we act automatically, we are **in control**,
> but we do not **consciously control** our actions.

Further,

> When we act automatically, we are **in control**, but we do not control.
> For example, we don't do any **controlling**.

With those two claims taken together—and please take them as claims for now, even though the previous section was an argument of sorts for these two claims—allow me to make the following two distinctions:

> Being in Control—Conscious Control
> Being in Control—Controlling

You might think it is a waste of paper to make two distinctions here instead of just one, but I do not want to assume there is an equivalence between "conscious control" and the activity of "controlling" for now because it might be that, for example, the activity of "controlling" could itself be carried out automatically or less than consciously. So you will have to bear with me there.

When you take the two distinctions together, you learn two important things about control: that control does not have to be conscious and that control does not have to be an activity or action. So we might not have said yet quite what control is (that's philosophers; get used to it), but we have just said two important things about what control is *not*.

And neither of those two claims is obvious, actually, because the fact that control does not need to be conscious (because of the relationship analyzed above between attention and control) says something substantial about the epistemic conditions for control, and because the fact that control does not require any activity of controlling means that our understanding of control cannot be purely agential. *Control, in short, is not an action.*

The reason I have emphasized these two distinctions can now be stated in full: conscious control and controlling (as an activity) are two ways of understanding *direct* control. So having shown that control does not have to be conscious or agential was a way of showing there is a difference between control and *direct* control. And this further distinction will turn out to be crucial to both the paradox and its solution.

Allow me to summarize the progress in this chapter, even though I am not finished, by combining two crucial elements:

1. On the one hand, the tripartite distinction among a human agent's control over her actions, human agents controlling other human agents, and human agents controlling nonhuman systems (technological ones, for example)
2. On the other hand, the idea that control does not have to be direct

Those two elements combine to give us the following preliminary conclusion: if control would have been necessarily direct, it would have been difficult to even begin to apply the concept of control to relationships between different human agents and also to the interaction between humans and nonhuman systems, because most of these latter relationships and interactions do not even allow for direct control. So if there is control between different human agents and also between human agents and nonhuman systems, that control can only be less than direct. That is why it was so important to establish that control does not need to be direct—which is the first preliminary but important conclusion of this chapter.

Now I have a way—at least in theory—to apply this conventional concept of control to those relationships and interactions that go beyond the basic case of individual human agency. Still, the big question has not been answered yet: what does it mean to have control over something or someone? In philosophy-speak, what are the necessary and sufficient conditions for control? This is the question that the rest of this chapter must address.

THE CONDITIONS FOR CONTROL

In looking at what conditions must be satisfied in order to claim that an agent or system has control over something, we should first go back to an element of my argument that was left behind by this chapter's discussion. I introduced two control "problems" for human action, but then I only really went on to discuss the latter of those, automaticity. What about causal determinism?

As I mentioned, this is too big an issue to deal with in just one section of one chapter of one book—whole libraries can and in fact have been filled by the problem of free will and determinism.[6] But there are some specific aspects of the problem of free will that are extremely relevant to our understanding of control for the purposes of this paradox and this book, so that is what I will focus on here.

Basically, the problem of free will is that given the causal closure of the physical world, everything is causally determined (that is, predetermined by events that have occurred at earlier times going back to the beginning or infinity). If you accept the causal closure of the physical world, and you additionally accept that human actions are part of the causally closed physical world, then you have the consequence that human actions too are causally determined—predetermined by events going back to, for example, before the agent was even born.

And if actions are predetermined in this particular sense, then you might think such predetermination is not compatible with things we hold dear such as free will, responsibility, or indeed our own good old control. (Predetermination by the way is different from fatalism, which holds that whatever you do, some event X in the future will inevitably occur, while determinism only holds that some event X is predetermined but that predetermination is not independent of what you do—the causal chain is crucial.)

Now, let us not focus on those famous premises or the even more famous question of whether those premises have significant consequences for what we hold dear (that would take us way too far off). Let us rather focus on what the "free will" worry—if we can call it that—says about our concept of control. Why would one think that predetermination is a problem for control?

If something is under our control, then supposedly we can influence (causally or otherwise) what happens to it—we can influence, for example, the direction of its movement. And if something is outside of our control, then supposedly we cannot influence (causally or otherwise) what happens to it—we cannot influence, for example, the direction of its movement.

Call this the *street definition of control*, because it is—may I say it—unrefined. Is the street definition of control incompatible with determinism? Not necessarily. It's just that our influence or noninfluence would itself be causally determined by previous events. In fact, as the great modern philosophers (Locke and Hume, I mean) already noticed, the real question might not be whether determinism is compatible with control; the real question could actually be whether there can be control without determinism. Because how else are we going to understand our capacity to influence what happens to the thing that is supposedly within our control?

The relation of cause and effect, causation for short, is a natural way of understanding such influence. Without causation, there might be no determinism. But without causation there might well be no control either. Still, we should not understand this as the strong claim that control must necessarily be causal—the latter claim turns out to be a close relative of a claim that I have already rejected, namely, that control must necessarily be direct.

The problem of determinism has led me to the street definition of control, and it doesn't matter, for the purposes of this book, whether the street definition of control or some more refined definition of control is compatible (or indeed dependent upon) causal determinism—that is beyond the scope. I just needed causal determinism to get to the definition, and now I can move on to assess and refine the definition of control by comparing it with two other accounts of control in the philosophy literature.

Meaningful Human Control and Guidance Control

Let me start by comparing my street definition of control with an account of *meaningful human control* that has been recently developed by Filippo Santoni de Sio and Jeroen van den Hoven for the very purpose of applying it to what they refer to as "autonomous systems" (Santoni de Sio & van den Hoven 2018). Their account of meaningful human control identifies two necessary conditions (which are presumably to be thought of as jointly sufficient):

> *First necessary condition of meaningful human control.* In order to be under meaningful human control, a decision-making system should demonstrably and verifiably be *responsive* to the *human* moral reasons relevant in the circumstances—no matter how many system levels, models, software, or devices of whatever nature separate a human being from the ultimate effects in the world, some of which may be lethal. That is, decision-making systems should *track* (relevant) human moral reasons. (Santoni de Sio & van den Hoven 2018, 7)

Second necessary condition of meaningful human control. In order for a system to be under meaningful human control, its actions/states should be traceable to a proper moral understanding on the part of one or more relevant human persons who design or interact with the system, meaning that there is at least one human agent in the design history or use context involved in designing, programming, operating and deploying the autonomous system who (a) understands or is in the position to understand the capabilities of the system and the possible effects in the world of the its use; (b) understands or is in the position to understand that others may have legitimate moral reactions toward them because of how the system affects the world and the role they occupy. (Santoni de Sio & van den Hoven 2018, 9)

In brief, the authors identify a necessary *tracking* condition and a necessary *tracing* condition for meaningful human control. The first thing I should say is that this is not supposed to be an account of control itself, but just of meaningful human control—and this cannot be ignored in the comparison with my street definition of control. On the other hand, given that my street definition of control in the context of this book on the control paradox is meant to be applicable beyond human agency to technological systems, then my task is similar to the one for which the above account of meaningful human control has been developed.

This account of meaningful human control heavily builds on the notion of "guidance control" developed in the nineties by Fischer and Ravizza (1998). Fischer and Ravizza's account of guidance control also consists of two conditions, and each of the two conditions of the above meaningful human control account corresponds to one of the two conditions of the guidance control account. So you will see below how the tracking condition is based on Fischer and Ravizza's reason-responsiveness, while the tracing condition is based on the ownership condition of guidance control.

Let me now go directly to the source:[7] guidance control is presented in section 3 of chapter 2 of Fisher and Ravizza's influential book from 1998, *Responsibility and Control*. There guidance control is presented as follows: "An agent exhibits guidance control of an action insofar as the mechanism that actually issues in the action is his own, reason-responsive mechanism" (Fischer & Ravizza 1998, 39).

Sorry for complicating things (and for the two long quotations to follow), but given that I am looking for definitions of control, here I must also mention that Fischer and Ravizza distinguish "guidance control" from "regulative control," and for that purpose use a thought experiment that will turn out to be very useful for my overall discussion in this book, so that I will quote it in full, as follows:

Let us suppose that Sally is driving her car. It is functioning well, and Sally wishes to make a right turn. As a result of her intention to turn right, she signals, turns the steering wheel, and carefully guides the car to the right. Further, we here assume that Sally was able to form the intention not to turn the car to the right but to turn the car to the left instead. (We are thus not making any special assumption, such as that causal determinism is true.) Also, we assume that, had she formed such an intention, she would have turned the steering wheel to the left and the car would have gone to the left. In this ordinary case, Sally guides the car to the right, but she could have guided it to the left. She controls the car, and also she has a certain sort of control over the car's movements. Insofar as Sally actually guides the car in a certain way, we shall say that she has "guidance control." Further, insofar as Sally also has the power to guide the car in a different way, we shall say that she has "regulative control." (Fischer & Ravizza 1998, 30–31)

To develop these notions of control (and their relationship), imagine a second case. In this analogue of the Frankfurt-type case presented earlier, Sally again guides her car in the normal way to the right. But here Sally's car is a "driver instruction" automobile with dual controls. We can further imagine that the instructor is quite happy to allow Sally to steer the car to the right, but that if Sally had shown any inclination to cause the car to go in some other direction, the instructor would have intervened and caused the car to go to the right (just as it actually goes). Here, as in the first car case, it appears that Sally controls the movement of the car in the sense of guiding it (in a certain way) to the right. Thus, she has guidance control of the car. But she cannot cause it to go anywhere other than where it actually goes. Thus, she lacks regulative control of the car. (The instructor has regulative control over the car.) *Sally controls the car, but she does not have control over the car (or the car's movements).* (Fisher & Ravizza 1998, 32; emphasis mine)

Fischer and Ravizza's two conditions on guidance control, as Santoni de Sio and van den Hoven correctly identify, are *reason-responsiveness* (specifically, *moderate* reason-responsiveness) and *ownership*. Other commentators (Todd & Tognazzini 2008, 685) have helpfully summarized this by providing the following definitions of both "guidance control" (GC) and "moderate reason-responsiveness" (MRR):

GC. An agent exercises *guidance control* of an action if and only if that action issues from the agent's own moderately reason-response mechanism. (Todd & Tognazzini 2008, 685)

MRR. An actually operative kind of mechanism is *moderately reason-responsive* if and only if (1) it is at least regularly receptive to reasons, some of which are moral reasons; (2) it is at least weakly reactive to reasons (but not necessarily moral reasons). (Todd & Tognazzini 2008, 685)

In order to better understand the other condition, *ownership*, we can instead look at the way Fischer himself summarized it in a later work:

> One has control of one's behavior at least in part in virtue of having taken control of the mechanisms that produce it. One takes control by taking responsibility. Taking responsibility involves three elements. First, the agent must see that his choices have certain effects in the world—that is, he must see himself as the source of consequences in the world (in certain circumstances). Second, the individual must see that he is a fair target for the reactive attitudes as a result of how he affects the world. Third, the views specified in the first two conditions—that the individual can affect the external world in certain characteristic ways through his choices, and that he can be fairly praised and/ or blamed for so exercising his agency—must be based on his evidence in an appropriate way. (Fischer 2004, 146)

This is helpful because it also clarifies that Fischer thinks of his (and Ravizza's) account of guidance control as an account of control proper, as starting the above summary with "one has control of" suggests. Here are some of the cases that Fischer and Ravizza themselves identify as being ruled out by their theory of guidance control:

> Agents who perform actions produced by powerful forms of brainwashing and indoctrination, potent drugs, and certain sorts of direct manipulation of the brain are not reasonably to be held morally responsible for their actions insofar as they lack the relevant sort of control. . . . Also, if we discover that a piece of behavior is attributable to a significant brain lesion or a neurological disorder, we do not believe that the agent has guidance control of his behavior. . . . Also, certain coercive threats (and perhaps offers) rule out moral responsibility. The bank teller who is told that he will be shot unless he hands over the money might have an overwhelming and irresistible desire to comply with the threat. Insofar as he acts from such an impulse, it is plausible to suppose that he does not have guidance control of his action. (Fischer & Ravizza 1998, 35)

Looking at these cases absolves two different tasks: it gives a clear idea of what kind of cases do not supposedly qualify for guidance control according to the very authors of this account of "guidance control," but it also emphasizes that this account of "guidance control" has been developed for the very purpose of dealing with cases in which, intuitively, agents cannot be held morally responsible. This close link between control and moral responsibility, which I have already emphasized, is both important and dangerous, as it could cloud the analysis.

This tight link between responsibility and control is actually a welcome feature of these accounts, given the overall purpose in this book when it comes to the consequences of the control paradox for responsibility, which could be stated as simply as follows: no control without responsibility, no responsibility without control. These authors might think this statement is so obvious that there is no point making it; after all, in the examples above, Fischer and Ravizza use control and responsibility interchangeably.

That should not fool us, though, because in this book we have to deal with the idea that we can (and in fact do) *delegate control but that we cannot delegate responsibility*. So control and responsibility might be as closely related as I claim above, but they are not overlapping concepts, otherwise one could not delegate control without delegating responsibility (before you complain, I know this is unsatisfactory, but you will have to wait until the end for the full account ... it's called b-o-o-k-s).

Summarizing, I have identified three different accounts of control (the *street definition of control, meaningful human control*, and *guidance control*), going all the way from the free will and determinism debate to so-called autonomous systems.

There are at least two things to notice when I compare the different accounts: First, there is no reference to an agent's reasons in the street definition of control while reason-responsiveness plays a big role in the other two accounts. Second, while loss of control should be easily accounted for by these accounts—if the conditions for control are no longer met, then there is loss of control, basically—it is not as obvious how these different accounts can make logical room for "more or better control"; after all, the conditions for control are either met (then there is control) or not met (then there is no control). But how can you have more control or better control (our "control enhancement") according to the control conditions on these three accounts?

Let me start from the first worry, which is basically that the street definition of control needs refining. Specifically, let me compare the street definition of control with the difference between "regulative control" and "guidance control" identified by Fischer and Ravizza (1998), specifically their claim that "Sally controls the car, but she does not have control over the car (or the car's movements)" (Fischer & Ravizza 1998, 32). "Control over the car" should, here, represent "regulative control" while "controlling the car" should represent "guidance control." And Fisher and Ravizza's idea is that regulative control is not necessary for responsibility, only guidance control is.

On the one hand, regulative control being Fisher and Ravizza's place-holder for alternative possibilities—and this not being a metaphysics book about free will and determinism—I could just ignore regulative control. But it is not as easy to ignore their distinction between "controlling the car" and having "control over the car" because it sounds a lot like the kind of distinction between direct control and overall control that I made earlier in this chapter.

My claim was that control does not have to be direct, that is, we can have control without "controlling"—we might have, in short, the sort of control that the driving instructor has over Sally's car. And this is in fact compatible with Fischer and Ravizza's account, since they themselves claim that "the instructor has regulative control over the car" (Fischer & Ravizza 1998, 32). I must distinguish two claims here:

1. There is Fischer and Ravizza's claim that control does not need to be regulative (not to qualify for moral responsibility anyway); in a slogan, guidance control is genuine control too.
2. There is my claim that control does not need to be direct; we might be in control without doing any controlling, as the instructor does in Fischer and Ravizza's thought experiment; in a slogan, regulative control is genuine control too.

Fischer and Ravizza are not interested in claim 2 because they are interested in free will and determinism. But that does not mean they reject claim 2; in fact, their effort is precisely to try to make the case that not just regulative control is genuine control but guidance control too. So there is no danger for my distinction between "direct control" and "overall control" coming from Fischer and Ravizza—it's just that they are interested in something else, namely, the free will debate.

The main aim of this chapter—apart from a better understanding of the concept of control—was to establish a difference between direct control and overall control and to argue that we can be in control even without direct control. So, in Fischer and Ravizza's terms, as long as we recognize that regulative control is genuine control, whether guidance control too qualifies as genuine control is beyond the scope of this chapter.

So for now there is no great rush to refine my street definition of control, as long as we hold on to the following features:

- Through the street definition, I have only formulated necessary conditions and not also sufficient conditions for control, so it isn't, strictly speaking, a definition (that's the *street* aspect).
- It is only a provisional account that will be refined as we move forward.
- Our influence—whether or not it is causal—will have to be reason-responsive in some relevant way, following the other two accounts of control that I have presented here.

Given that I am not refining the account just yet, there is also no problem so far for the idea that we can have "more or better control," since we can easily have more or less influence on some other person or system.

SALLY AND THE DRIVING INSTRUCTOR

There is one specific aspect of Fischer and Ravizza's argument that will be worth discussing in some detail for the purposes of the control paradox: they argue that although the instructor *has control over* the car (their "regulative control," my "being in control"), Sally is genuinely *controlling* the car (their "guidance control," my "direct control")—as long as the instructor does not intervene, that is. And they go on to give an account of Sally's guidance control being a form of genuine control (the kind that qualifies her for moral responsibility) in terms of the two conditions of ownership and moderate reason-responsiveness.

What does the relationship between Sally and her instructor look like, when I analyze it from the point of view of this book and specifically delegation and delegating control? Is the instructor delegating control to Sally even though the instructor keeps having control over the car? And what about responsibility? Fischer and Ravizza claim that Sally is morally responsible, because guidance control is enough for responsibility. But what about the responsibility of the instructor? And what about the technological equivalents of Sally, would those systems qualify for responsibility too?

To put these questions in focus, imagine a variation of Sally's case in which everything is as Fischer and Ravizza describe their original case, plus the car runs over a pedestrian. As Sally is herself driving the car, you would normally think that Sally is also morally responsible for running over the pedestrian—it was, after all, her action. But how do we square this intuitive responsibility claim with Fisher and Ravizza's idea that *Sally does not have control over the car*? Their idea is that guidance control is enough for responsibility—and that might be so. But what about the driving instructor? Shouldn't the instructor have stopped Sally and prevented the accident? So the instructor is morally responsible too, it would appear, but does that make a difference to Sally's responsibility?

There is at least some intuitive appeal for the idea that in this modified scenario the instructor is responsible and Sally is not responsible, given that Sally does not have control over the car while the instructor does—even though it is in fact Sally who is driving.

Fischer and Ravizza were not interested in these further questions because their focus was on a compatibilist account of responsibility; their focus was on Sally alone and whether she could be at all morally responsible even though she could not have done otherwise. But given my focus in this book, whether the instructor is responsible and what kind of control I can attribute to the instructor matters, and it also matters what kind of difference that makes to Sally's control and responsibility.

Does Sally have less control because the instructor can intervene? Fischer and Ravizza seem to think so, when they distinguish between regulative control and guidance control and claim that Sally does not have control over the car. But does that result in Sally also being less responsible? Does that even make sense as a concept, this idea of reduced responsibility? To answer all these questions, I need to take at least three further steps:

- Include in my discussion of control also the cases of control between different agents—what I am calling "social control"—and control over nonhuman systems—what I am calling "technological control." This is what chapter 4 does.
- Look at these issues from the point of view of the practice of delegation, and delegating control in particular. This is what chapter 5 does.
- Finally, bring to bear the work from these three chapters on issues of responsibility, by applying the control paradox to specific technological systems or practices—this is what part III, "The Technological Paradox," and part IV, "The Political Paradox," do.

In the next chapter, I will continue to discuss the concept of control by bringing it to bear on "social control"—control between human agents—and "technological control," control between human agents and technological systems. And my starting point in the next chapter will be again the little story of Sally and her driving instructor that I am borrowing from Fischer and Ravizza (1998).

To conclude this chapter, let me provide a bold and substantial answer to the question that has been left hanging about who is responsible if, in the original Fischer and Ravizza scenario, Sally runs over a pedestrian. The answer that I will provide here can also be a summary of this book's overall argument already: if Sally, while she is driving the dual-control car with the instructor sitting next to her, runs over a pedestrian, the instructor is morally responsible for the pedestrian being run over and Sally is not morally responsible for the pedestrian being run over. This is my (bold?) claim, and the rest of the book constitutes my (boring?) argument (for more details specifically on the responsibility aspect of my argument, see the book's final chapter). To be sure, Fischer and Ravizza would not accept this claim, because it runs counter to the compatibilist conclusion that their account was supposed to achieve, namely, that guidance control (what Sally has) is enough for responsibility. It ain't.

Chapter Four

Social Control and
Technological Control

I spent most of chapter 3 talking about control in the context of human action. But most of this book is actually about technological systems and human collective practices (like politics and organizations), so what happens to the concept of control when we move away from individual agents to groups (what I am calling "social control") and technological systems (what I am calling "technological control")? This is what you will find out in this chapter, applying the insights into control from the previous chapter to groups and technological systems.

Reenter our friend Sally and her driving instructor. That scenario—originally developed by Fischer and Ravizza (1998) in the context of a compatibilist argument for free will—turns out to be very useful for me because it has all three domains that this account—and this book—needs:

1. the individual agent (Sally, but also the driving instructor);
2. the interaction between different human agents (Sally and her driving instructor—maybe we should give her a name, btw, for shortness's sake; Fischer and Ravizza won't mind—so let's call Sally's driving instructor Lola and be done with it);
3. and the interaction between human agents—again both Sally and Lola—and technological systems and practices (the car obviously, but also traffic signs, traffic rules, traffic itself? You get the idea)—
4. and in fact there is a fourth level, possibly the most important and interesting, namely, where the complexity adds up and multiplies, because it is not just one agent Sally; it is not just two agents Sally and Lola; and it is not just one agent Sally or Lola interacting with a technological system—it is two agents Sally and Lola interacting both

51

with each other and also, individually and together, with multiple technological systems and practices, most of it *simultaneously.*

It is exactly this kind of exponential, multilevel complexity, where human control, social control, and technological control are all intertwined, that is the focus of this book. And here please again do not underestimate the point I made in the first chapter that, even though I will often be talking of technology cases, what I actually mean is technological systems and practices, where the practices might also be nontechnological ones, such as political representation. Such practices are represented in the Sally/Lola scenario by traffic signs, rules, customs, and the like.

Further, also please do not underestimate the difference between an individual agent interacting with a technological system and multiple agents interacting with each other and also with multiple technological systems simultaneously. It is easy to see how complexity goes viral even before we bring AI into the picture. But the good thing is this: a lot of these kinds of innovations—like machine learning algorithms—are supposed to help us deal with this kind of multilayer complexity, by—paradoxically—adding a further layer.[1]

Once we introduce social control and technological control, the questions that used to be about the criteria for a human agent's control over her actions become, basically:

1. Can human agents control other human agents? Namely, does the concept of control apply to interactions between human agents, or am I using the wrong concept there?
2. Can human agents control technological systems?

Interestingly, you might be tempted to answer, "Oh my god I hope not!" to the first question and, "Oh my god I hope so!" to the second. As in, the prospect of some human agents controlling other human agents is horrifying, and horrifying also is the prospect of human agents failing to control technological systems—think plane crashes or, more to the point for this book, think Stanislav Petrov, September 26, 1983.

Losing control over technology scares the living shit out of us—and maybe one of the few prospects that is just as terrifying is humans controlling other humans. So there is a relationship between social control and technological control, but it's not a straightforward one: in one case we want control, and in the other case we don't. But both have to do with autonomy: we cherish autonomy so much that we are scared of losing it to other humans or, in fact, of giving it—which does not necessarily mean losing it, by the way—to technological systems.

STANISLAV PETROV

The story of what Stanislav Petrov did on September 26, 1983, is so good—and so paradigmatic for my argument in this book—that I will in fact tell it with the words of his *New York Times* obituary in 2017:

> Early on the morning of Sept. 26, 1983, Stanislav Petrov helped prevent the outbreak of nuclear war. A 44-year-old lieutenant colonel in the Soviet Air Defense Forces, he was a few hours into his shift as the duty officer at Serpukhov-15, the secret command center outside Moscow where the Soviet military monitored its early-warning satellites over the United States, when alarms went off. Computers warned that five Minuteman intercontinental ballistic missiles had been launched from an American base. . . . As the computer systems in front of him changed their alert from "launch" to "missile strike," and insisted that the reliability of the information was at the "highest" level, Colonel Petrov had to figure out what to do. . . . After five nerve-racking minutes—electronic maps and screens were flashing as he held a phone in one hand and an intercom in the other, trying to absorb streams of incoming information—Colonel Petrov decided that the launch reports were probably a false alarm. . . . The false alarm was apparently set off when the satellite mistook the sun's reflection off the tops of clouds for a missile launch. The computer program that was supposed to filter out such information had to be rewritten. (Chan 2017)[2]

A computer-based decision-support system—an eighties version of the kinds of AI systems I discuss at some length in this book, like IBM Watson for Oncology (McDougall 2019a and 2019b; Di Nucci 2019; Di Nucci et al. 2020) in healthcare—suggested to Colonel Petrov that the United States had launched a nuclear attack against the Soviet Union. With today's eyes, it might seem hard to believe that the threat suggested by the computer should be taken seriously. But the early 1980s where a different time politically, and the Cold War was experiencing a "final" high, if you like. Just a few days earlier in September 1983, the Soviets had shot down a Korean commercial flight, killing all 269 people on board, including a U.S. congressman, Representative Lawrence Patton "Larry" McDonald, a Georgia Democrat.[3]

The unthinkable was not unthinkable back then—and maybe it isn't anymore today, with Putin, Trump, and the rest of them "strongmen." Even less so if you were Colonel Petrov, especially if a computer-based defense system rates the reliability of the threat at the "highest" level. In a book about losing control over technology while trying to develop systems that are supposed to enhance control through technology, this story is too good to be true—and too good not to be retold: one human being—against all political and technological odds and pressure from above—takes a skeptical stance toward the automated advice, thereby saving our little planet.

As this is a philosophy book, it is worth reconstructing Petrov's reasoning here, at least as he himself later reported it: If the Americans are really coming after us—Petrov reflected—why would they only launch five nuclear warheads? After all, the Americans knew what Soviet retaliation would look like: had, for example, Petrov not resisted the automated advice, the Soviet Union would have been capable of exterminating more than half of the U.S. population, according to estimates based on the number and range of Soviet nuclear weapons in the early 1980s.[4]

That's pretty sound reasoning, if you ask me: if the United States were actually going for it, they would have gone all in—that's what Petrov must have been thinking in those decisive few minutes. Five nuclear missiles would have caused a lot of damage and suffering, but nowhere near what the United States would have required in order to avoid a counterstrike that could have killed between 82 and 180 million Americans (the U.S. population in 1983 was around 230 million, just for context). It might be worth noting here that Petrov's reasoning—sensible as it was—could be itself implemented in a computer-based decision-support system (maybe already back then and certainly today).

There is nothing necessarily irreducible about such a premise—or step in the algorithm—according to which nuclear threats from the United States in 1983 should only be taken seriously if above a certain magnitude, and that premise would have its own risks and side effects, so that you could easily imagine that had the Soviets implemented such an extra step in their protocols and algorithms—and had U.S. spies found out—then a contained attack would not have been detected in time by the Soviet satellites and computer-based defense systems.

This aspect is important to my argument because it speaks directly to the question of which tasks should be assigned (delegated?—see the next chapter) to technological systems and which tasks reserved for human agents alone. Remember, through the paradox I want to try to answer this general question:

What tasks should be delegated to *whom* under *which* conditions?

Another important clarification that the story of Colonel Petrov allows me to make is of a more conceptual nature: what does it mean for a human agent to have control over a technological system?

Imagine our driving instructor Lola is a police officer teaching police trainee Sally so-called advanced driving. Lola, like every responsible officer, locks her weapon away when she is at home so that it is out of reach of her children. In this sense Lola certainly has control over the technological system represented by her firearm, because she controls access to it—through a key, code, or password. And there are other independent ways you can talk of control over a weapon: if, for example, Lola's weapon were not locked away,

Lola would lack a certain degree of control over it because she could not regulate access to it as strictly, but she would still have some control over it, through her training, for example. She would still have more control over her weapon through her police training than, say, her children or partner.

It is important for my purposes to distinguish between different ways human agents can be said to have control over technological systems, because in the case of Colonel Petrov, for example, there is both an important way Petrov did *not* have control over the computer-based decision-support system and an important way he *did* have control over it.

On the one hand, there was nothing that Petrov could have done to prevent the system from making the potential world-ending mistake it did make. There might have been others within the ranks of the Soviet Union's defense establishment who might have had that kind of control (engineers and developers who worked on that particular system, say), but once the system was developed, implemented, and in use, all Petrov could do was either accept the system's advice or not accept the system's advice.

Crucially, while this represents a clear limitation to Petrov's control over the system, you can agree that Petrov had control over the crucial element in the process, namely, whether the system's advice resulted in a Soviet nuclear counterstrike. And while you may not characterize that level of control as control over the particular technological system, it is still a crucial kind of control to have on the overall process that the system is part of. When I discuss control and technological systems, then, you again see that "direct control" is not necessarily what you should be after, as long as you have overall control over the processes to which the computer system feeds information, and this preliminary conclusion should no longer come as a surprise, given my arguments in chapter 3.

Go back to the "street definition" of control and apply it to Colonel Petrov's predicament: Petrov was, crucially and luckily, in a position to influence what would happen as a result of the computer-based advice. And that was the case, importantly, even though Petrov was lacking other crucial forms of direct control over the computer system itself, for example:

1. preventing the system from giving the wrong advice
2. shutting down the system (I presume)
3. stopping its implementation in the first place

Those three possibilities represent three ways to directly control technological systems, none of which was available to Petrov. These three possibilities also represent other roles within the chain of command: (1) represents the engineers, (2) represents Petrov's superiors within the military, and (3) represents politicians and other decision-makers further up than Petrov's military superiors. This analysis obviously oversimplifies the empirical realities, but it is still useful in understanding what control expectations are even fair for different stakeholders.

Still, something crucial was left to Colonel Petrov and within his sphere of influence—and that's why we are here, able to write about it after almost forty years. The reason I am emphasizing at the same time how *limited* Petrov's control was, and how *crucial* it was, is that I have picked this scenario precisely to show that neither more control nor direct control is necessary. Rather, what we should aim for are reliable and sustainable structures of delegation, where individual stakeholders are given precisely the degree of control and authority that they can cope with; no more but also no less.

For example, perhaps it was good that Petrov didn't have a stake in the decision-support system whose advice he had to decide whether to accept or not (if he was, say, one of the engineers tasked with developing the system), and perhaps it would have been bad if Petrov was, say, a member of the particular soviet that decided to deploy that system. Both of these situations would have given Petrov more and better control over the decision-support system. But such direct involvement in the decision-support system might have ended up clouding Petrov's judgment in those crucial minutes. Reliable and sustainable systems of successful delegation are important in *containing* control for particular stakeholders.

WHAT IF COLONEL PETROV HAD BEEN AUTOMATED AWAY . . .

Now replace Petrov with a further computer system or a further step in the algorithm and imagine the following scenario: what would have happened if instead of a human evaluating the computer-based decision-support system's advice there was instead another computer? As you might anticipate, you do not have to suppose that the further machine or further step in the algorithm would be incapable of detecting the mistake the way Petrov did. Petrov's reasoning or his premise about the likely size of a U.S. nuclear strike could have been incorporated into the system by the Soviets, so that the machine replacing Petrov could also have stopped the Soviet Union's counterstrike.

Just as well, you can imagine a different officer, call him Colonel Putin, who might have been on shift that morning instead of Colonel Petrov and might have been less skeptical of the computer system's advice—maybe because Colonel Putin was less familiar with the inner workings of the system, and he would have tended to trust it more; or maybe the opposite: because Colonel Putin was more familiar with the system—let's say he is himself an engineer—he would have gone along with its advice (is it, empirically speaking, more or less likely, actually?). Or maybe Colonel Putin had a computer scientist daughter and was therefore partial to such systems.

I am posing these alternative scenarios to emphasize that, as I have antici-pated above, you cannot say that more human control would have been more or less likely to result in nuclear catastrophe. You have to analyze the pecu-liarities of the actual case in order to make that judgment. This means that the counterfactual "Had Petrov not been working that morning . . ."—whether the alternative is that his role has been replaced by a further computer or by a different officer—cannot be resolved without knowing the specifics of both the actual chain of events and the alternative chains of events. Still, it is easy to imagine that if the Soviet engineers programmed that computer system so poorly that it confused the sun's reflection off the clouds for nuclear missiles, they might have just as well also programmed the further computer system tasked with evaluating the first system's advice just as poorly, resulting in the first system's advice being waved through all the way to a Soviet nuclear counterstrike and the resulting end of the world.

To be clear, I am not claiming here that, historically speaking, it was plausible in 1983 for the Soviet Union to have a fully automated nuclear defense program in which no human oversight or intervention was necessary for a nuclear counterstrike. That is hopefully not true for both 1983 and today. At the same time, we should not underestimate the way, especially with developments in military technologies, speed plays an important role (see later chapters, such as chapter 6, on drones and so-called autonomous weapons).

When I get to drones and autonomous weapons, you will see how the pressure to automate more and more steps within the system comes from the speed at which the enemy's attack can be carried out. And in fact, that too many steps in a chain of command can be counterproductive is probably true independent of technological innovation, but it might become an even more important factor in virtue of it (technological innovation, that is).

Surely that played a role in the Soviet Union's development of a comput-er-based decision-support system already in 1983: basically, the speed at which a nuclear attack could be detected was crucial—and it is not implau-sible to suppose that speed generates trade-offs in terms of the reliability of the advice received. So it is important, not just for these Petrov scenarios but for the whole book, to emphasize the role that speed and reaction time play in the development of technological systems within the military and beyond, especially with regard to the supposed unstoppable character of automation. And even though some of you readers might actually associate complexity with the opposite of speed, you will come to see throughout this book how speed adds to complexity.

Pause for a moment to ask yourself the following question: having spent so much time on Petrov saving the world, why have I not applied the control paradox to the story of Stanislav Petrov? There is a simple reason: this book wants to show that the control paradox results from technological innovation functioning as it is meant to function, not just from technological systems malfunctioning.

It might well be that I can interpret Colonel Petrov's story in terms of the control paradox, but it would not be that interesting to do so, because it is a story of system malfunction. My aim is to interpret the proper functioning of technological systems (and, don't forget, other nontechnological practices) as generating control paradoxes. We all know we are fucked when things go wrong; the real worry is that we might be fucked even when things work out, so to speak and pardon my French. That's the book's main thesis if you were to rap it. On a more positive note: there is hope; just ask Stanislav Petrov.

TECHNOLOGICAL CONTROL

I didn't, then, introduce Colonel Petrov to offer another example of the control paradox. Let me now tell you why I *did* introduce his uplifting story of a human saving the world from technological malfunction: it was to show how the conceptual work about control done in the previous chapter could be applied to the complexities of the socio-technological world, where you've got pressure from bosses and superiors at the same time as computers misfiring (almost literally, in this case). Still, the story also shows that if you have the rights processes and people in place, control is not necessarily lost.

What does it then mean to have control over a technological system or, as I am calling it, technological control? So far I have gained two important insights: that driving instructor Lola can be in control of the car (technological system) even though it is Sally who is driving, and that Colonel Petrov can be in control of (the advice produced by) the computer-based decision-support system, even though he was not able to stop the system's implementation, nor prevent the system from providing the wrong advice, nor shut down the system. All sorts of ways of controlling machines, then, seem to be unnecessary in order to have the kind of influence *we care about*.

What do Lola and Stanislav Petrov have in common, then? Quite simply, they are both *in charge*. And through these two cases, we learn two important features of technological control:

1. In order to have technological control, you do not actually need to do anything (see Lola), as long as other conditions apply (naturally).
2. In order to have technological control, you do not need to control the technology itself (see Stanislav Petrov), as long as other conditions apply (naturally).

Both (1) and (2) mention features that you might expect to be required but that you do not actually need in order to have technological control. What *do* you need, then? Let Lola and Sally swap places. Lola takes her new place behind the wheel while Sally sits next to her in the dual-control passenger seat. Lola, to be sure, is still the driving instructor and Sally is still learning, but now Lola is actually driving.

The question to ask yourself is whether now, in this new scenario, Sally is in control of the car in the same way Lola was in the original scenario. I believe the answer to this question is that Sally does not have the same control Lola had when in her seat—and the reason she doesn't will explain how technological control works and which conditions must be met in order for some agent to have technological control.

Now Sally, for example, can—in principle—stop the car or prevent Lola from taking a turn, because she is seated where the dual controls are. But will Sally know how to operate the dual controls? And will Sally know when and in which circumstances to operate the dual controls? This scenario shows that what matters is not just *physical access*—as in, being physically able to operate the controls. It is also a question of *epistemic access*, namely, knowing how to operate the controls and when it is appropriate to operate them. I might distinguish between the *possibility* to intervene and the *capacity* to intervene—and that capacity depends on epistemic considerations. So I can say that Lola, when at the dual controls, had both the possibility of intervening and also the capacity for intervening, while Sally at the dual controls only has the possibility of intervening and not the capacity. And the possibility alone—you can now agree—does not give control.

This is where my street definition needs refining: not any influence can and should count as control. This is also where you see that it might make sense to reject the dichotomy "either you have control or you lack it." Imagine the dual controls in Lola's car consist of four buttons, each with a different function. Sally—now sitting at the dual controls—does not know which functions are activated by the different buttons, but if we suppose that one of the four will stop the car, we can also imagine that if Sally were to just push all four together the car would still stop (and probably do some other weird stuff). Does the fact that Sally stopped the car by pushing four buttons, one of which was the stop button, mean that she had control over the car? I don't think so: she didn't know enough about the technological system in question to be attributed control.

Still, the limited amount of influence Sally does have on the car could be said to put a limit on how much control Lola, behind the wheel, has. She can be comfortable in her knowledge that Sally is not familiar with the dual-control system; still, Lola also knows that if Sally really wants to, she can cause trouble—as she does by pushing all the buttons at once.

This is interesting, if you think about, because it shows that control is not a zero-sum game. Control is non–zero sum because, as you have just seen, Sally's influence might limit Lola's control without itself resulting in any (additional) control on her part, so in sum there is actually a loss of control because Lola has less without Sally having (necessarily) any more. This is a further important provisional result of my analysis that I will have to keep in mind as I move forward in analyzing the different complex interactions between agents and technological systems.

Now you might think that a dual-control car is not a good analogy for all technological systems and practices, both because it is by now a quite old-fashioned system (we have, after all, self-driving cars now; who needs dual controls anymore? Lola, just like Petrov, has been automated away—one more thing that they have in common) and more importantly because this kind of sharing of control—it might be argued—is pretty unique.

I respectfully disagree. In fact, the very reason I chose this old dual-control case is that it mirrors the relationship between human agents and technological systems and also the relationships between different human agents. Sally and Lola could just as well be an employee and her line manager, for example—and the car could be the project that line manager Lola has tasked her employee Sally with. Sally is running the project (driving the car), but Lola is in charge (of both the project and the car). It is a simple and prima facie perfect analogy of the way relationships within complex organizations look.

Also, do in fact think of self-driving cars, because they are again analogous to Sally and Lola—the only question is who between Sally and Lola is the Uber algorithm within the analogy and who is the human sitting inside the driverless car. No, seriously, the analogy should surely be that Sally is the algorithm and Lola is the person inside the driverless/self-driving car (but, as you will see in later chapters, things can get more complicated).

FROM TECH CONTROL TO SOCIAL CONTROL

I am sure that even the more sympathetic readers here—those willing, for example, to go along with my account of technological control—will wonder how on earth one human agent is supposed to control another human agent? Humans, after all, are not machines: they have free will and can decide for themselves. Or, in Kantian language, they are ends in themselves, autonomous agents. Fair enough, but, first of all, let us not confuse the normative with the descriptive. Namely, it could be that "social control" is a horrible thing, but that does not mean that it doesn't exist—think slavery. And so the fact that—in order to describe the complexities of today's world—I might need an account of social control (control of human agents over other human agents) does not mean that I would endorse such practice.

Also, I don't think I need to go all the way to slavery in order to recognize the reality of social control. It is, for better or worse, much more common than that. Just go back to employee Sally and line manger Lola and their project. Even if Sally and Lola live in the most emancipated democracy (I don't know, maybe Denmark?) and even if they work for the most emancipated of employers, it is very difficult to imagine that there is no sense in which Lola has some degree of control over what Sally does: after all, it is part of Lola's job description to tell Sally what to do (on this, see Anderson [2017]). Sure, we could imagine a world in which there is no employer–employee relationship (only, could we, really?). But we don't need to do that, as long as we remember that discussing the ways control is true of relationships between human agents in our world does not mean endorsing it.

The important thing—if you allow me to simplify—is the following: talking of control between human agents—and even making comparisons and analogies between that and the control human agents have over machines—does not mean reducing human agents to machines. That's because those kinds of analogies are compatible with human agents keeping their free will and even liberty. In fact, that is exactly the problem: we can be free and still be subject to another person's control.

At the same time—and this is as important as the above—talking of control of human agents over machines and comparing this to the relationships between different human agents does not even begin to "humanize" AI systems or make them responsible or capable of acting for reasons. That's a separate question and, as you have just seen, it does not necessarily have any bearing on the question of the human agent's control over the technological system, given that control is compatible with the controlled being free in both the (common) metaphysical and political senses.

As the last two paragraphs are both important and complex, let me put things a bit more clearly and technically: *technological control and social control are both compatible with the controlee* (which is the system—human or otherwise—being controlled) *not performing all and only the controller's* (which is the system—human or otherwise—controlling) *instructions.*

In fact—going back to my street definition of control—you will find the above to be true of control in general. An account of control in which the controlee does all and only the controller's instructions would miss, I submit, most real instances of control, even more real instances of control of human agents over their actions—limited cognitive agents like ourselves are simply not that precise, to be honest, to meet such a strict definition of control.

What have I learned so far by applying the conceptual work on control from the last chapter to technological innovations and social practices? Quite a bit, actually. I have learned, for example, that the street definition of control does a decent enough job and might not need as much refinement as I initially thought. Crucially, though, random influence will not do (as the scenario with Sally at the dual controls shows)—and thinking in terms of reason-responsiveness along the lines of the previous chapter is in fact helpful, because I can then say that I have control only if I can influence outcomes in ways that are responsive to my aims or reasons—this refinement rules out, then, the kind of random interventions that Sally attempts when sitting in Lola's place. Being able to intervene as such is, then, not enough, but is the possibility of intervention necessary for control? Stay tuned for an answer to this decisive question, just not quite yet.

Reason-responsiveness here includes being able to meet some epistemic condition because, if I lack crucial knowledge or access to important facts, then my influence will not be reliably responsive to my reasons: so Sally does not know which button to push, which breaks the link between her aims and reasons and the kind of influence that she can exercise over the car's direction.

Another important lesson I have learned is that I can claim control over some technology—for example—even if I do not control the technology itself, as with Colonel Petrov and the computer-based decision-support system that was, itself, not being controlled by Petrov. Still Petrov was in control—including in control of the technological system—in virtue of being in control of the overall process leading up to the crucial decision of whether to counterstrike or not. And here you can easily imagine that the structure of the chain of command both above and below Colonel Petrov would in fact be crucial to a specific assessment of whether Petrov was in control and how much control Petrov actually had. So, for example, if Petrov's commanding officer was in a position to easily overrule or just skip Petrov's judgment, then it would no longer be clear that Petrov was in control of the overall process leading up to the crucial decision whether to strike back.[5]

I have also learned—perhaps most importantly—that control is compatible with the controlee not "doing" all and only what the controller instructs "her" to do—and this is the way our account of control can be applied across the three domains of human agents and their actions, technological innovations, and social practices.

As I anticipate this being the part causing the most resistance to my argument, let me say a bit more about the idea that we can claim that A has control over B even though B may be a human being or otherwise in a position not only to "do" all and only what A instructs "her" to do—the language here is on purpose less than precise because I do not want to make metaphysical assumptions about the nature of B nor about whether B might be capable of acting or similar.

Again, I must keep the normative consequences of such a claim in terms of ethics and morality separate for now: the question is not whether a human being's control over another could ever be a good thing; the question is only whether I can ever say, meaningfully, that a human being is in control of another human being. That's an important question in itself, but it is clear that it also has widespread consequences for a book about control over intelligent technologies. Namely, if human beings can be said to control or be in control of other human beings, then the question of whether intelligent systems can ever be said to be autonomous loses some of its edge, at least for the question of control. If human beings can be said to control other human beings, then human beings can be said to control nonhuman intelligent systems such as AI systems, whether those AI systems qualify as autonomous or not. And that's an important dialectical step in my argument. But, crucially, it does depend on this peculiar claim about human beings controlling other human beings. So let me turn to that claim now.

The structure of my claim is such that it depends in turn on the idea that the controlee does not need to be able to "do" all and only what the controller instructs in order to have a genuine instance of control—there is, in short, some flexibility. And given what I said about direct control in the previous chapter, this element of my claim should not be too surprising either.

Further, consider the following possible ways human agents could be said to be in control of other human agents: threats and irresistible offers.

Threat: If you don't do X, then Y.
Offer: If you do X, then Z.

In cases of threats and irresistible offers, you could also talk in terms of a controlee who does not need to do all and only what the controller instructs—after all, someone at gunpoint has the option of being shot alongside the option of giving up her belongings. And something similar can be said of prison, by the way.

It's a simple truth, really: we can make people do what we want them to do, including significant cases in which we can make people do what they don't want to do. This is, if you like, so obvious that it would be preposterous for me to claim any novelty or copyright, but at the same time it would be preposterous to deny its truth. The only aspect of it that might be both new and possibly controversial is whether this widespread social phenomenon in which people make other people do what they don't want to do should count as a genuine instance of control. That's my own contribution, if you like.

Going back to Sally and Lola, you can see a further aspect of my claim: all I am saying, really, is that in the original scenario, Lola is in control (of the car, if not of Sally). That should not be mistaken for a claim about Sally's control. As Fischer and Ravizza (1998) argue, for example, Sally—who is driving, remember—can be said to have guidance control. I am emphasizing this for the following reason: those resistant to my claim that human agents can be said to be in control of other human agents might want to argue in terms of the residual control that the controlee, being a human agent, still has. But once we have recognized the flexibility of control, the residual control of the controlee—call it guidance control or something else—is not a problem for my argument. My argument makes a claim about Lola, after all—not about Sally. And as long as Sally's residual control is not incompatible with Lola's control, I am fine. Obviously a different story applies to the corresponding responsibility attributions for both Lola and Sally—but it's too early in the book for that.

I am not, in other words, reducing human beings and human agents to machines or marionettes. Human beings can still keep their free will and even some control; it's just that often that happens within systems, processes, and organizations in which they are also being controlled—by other human beings. And in fact, given that I am putting normative ethical considerations aside, it doesn't really matter whether the controller is their employer, a prison guard, or a mugger holding them at gunpoint. All of these examples count as structures in which one or more human agents can be said to be in control of other human agents: such control relations might limit but do not deny or erase the agency of the controlee.

I am not, then, reducing human agents to machines. But am I going too far in the other direction? A reader could be worried about the following: if I use the same account of control both for relationships between human agents and nonhuman technological systems (again, I will not commit myself either way to the agency of nonhuman technological systems just yet) and also for relationships between human agents and other human agents, aren't I thereby admitting the autonomous character of some nonhuman technological system, such as AI? I said before that my holistic approach has the advantage of sidestepping the question of the autonomous character of intelligent systems, but could it be that by using the same account of control that I use for the relation between humans (by definition autonomous) I am granting autonomy to the machines through a back door?

That would be bad. Not because I have something against talk of "autonomous systems" (even though I do) but because the question of whether a system qualifies as autonomous is a big complex question in its own right and its answer cannot simply be derived from my account of control, because otherwise my account of control would, in an important respect, be question begging (given the close connection between the three concepts of autonomy, control, and responsibility).

This worry is misplaced, I believe: what my account does is show that control is not incompatible with the autonomous character of the controlee. You might object to this compatibility claim, but it must be recognized, at least, that this compatibility claim is logically different from a claim about the autonomous character of some technological system. Admittedly, if I had a different, more restrictive account of control, that account might not be applicable at the same time to social relations and human–machine interactions. But that could at best result in an objection against my account of control; it wouldn't amount to accusing my account of being committed to the autonomous character of technological systems, simply because I am agnostic about this latter point.

Finally, my flexible account of both tech control and social control allows me to include AI systems such as machine learning algorithms where some of the steps might not be anticipated or anticipatable either. Machine learning, then, would just be another controlee whose performance is not fully determined by the controller, just like any employee's performance would and should not be fully determined by the controller. And at the same time my flexible account of tech control and social control does leave some logical space for residual control on the part of the controlee—raising the interesting question, when it comes to AI systems, of whether we are actually giving these AI systems some degree of control.

The time has come, I believe, to introduce a concept that is crucial to control relationships both between different human beings and between human beings and technological systems: the concept of *delegation*. Through my analysis of the concept and practices of delegation in the next chapter, I will be able to answer some of the questions left outstanding in this chapter; I will get an insight into the inner workings of the control paradox; and finally I will start to see light at the end of the tunnel: delegation is, in fact, both the source of the paradox and also the beginning of its solution.

Chapter Five

Delegating Control and the Practice of Delegation

Whether a noun or a verb, the meaning of delegate is simple: a delegate is a person chosen to act in your place, or the act of choosing someone to act for you.[1]

We are *delegating* agents at least as much as we are social agents. Delegating is what bosses do when they ask us to do something. Delegating is what you and I do when we drop off our kids in kindergarten or at school. And you are also delegating when you go see your GP or employ a new cleaning person; you are delegating big-time when you order a taxi or pizza delivery on your phone. "Big-time" because you are, in those particular circumstances, delegating at least twice: to the device which does the ordering, and then to those who drive you or cook for you (the pizza delivery example in fact has at least three delegates involved: the app, the pizzeria, and finally the driver, who nowadays is "independent" of both the company behind the app and the establishment behind your pizza). And you are delegating when you set up a new password or just lock your bike. You are even delegating when you enter the electoral booth, as this book will go on to argue (in part IV).

As these examples should make clear, I must distinguish between those *delegated to* and those (doing the) *delegating*. Take Jane, who is John's boss. When Jane delegates to John the task of making her morning coffee (*ristretto*, black, no sugar, and the water better be bloody fresh too!), Jane is the *delegating party* and John is the *delegate*, the party Jane *delegates to*. Employees like John are, normally, delegated to and—thereby—delegates. Bosses like Jane are, normally, delegating parties: they delegate (more or less imperatively).

The above distinction between *delegating* party and *delegated to* party (delegate) should not be understood to imply a certain power structure: bosses are indeed more powerful than employees, but not all delegating parties are more powerful than their delegates. Two relevant examples here are the relationship between patient and healthcare professional and the relationship between voters and their political representatives. It is patients who delegate their healthcare and well-being to the healthcare professional,[2] but it is normally—especially inside the healthcare context—healthcare professionals who are "more powerful" than patients. Similarly, it is voters who delegate to politicians, but it is normally politicians who are more powerful than their voters.

Interestingly, in both cases it could be argued that delegation exacerbates the power asymmetry, so that politicians are already more powerful and gain even more power the moment we as voters delegate to them by electing them or anyway participating in the process that results in their election (the same could probably be said of healthcare professionals, even though the power distribution is probably even more complicated). There is, then, a distinction between delegating party and delegate, and there are also powerful differentials, and the latter can apparently go both ways—so let's not mix up delegation with power just yet.

So far, I have focused on people delegating to other people—as in, human agents delegating to other human agents. But a lot of delegation—as this book shows—takes place between human agents and artifacts (tools, machines, software, devices, etc.). When I lock my bike, I delegate *control over* and the *security of* my precious bicycle to the bike lock; in the same way, when I put a passcode on my device, I delegate control over and the security of my device to some bit of software. If I were posh enough, I might even consider having a human person protect my bike or device (call them, respectively, bike guard and device guard).[3]

This is a serious point: in adding to the mix delegating practices between human agents and artifacts, I must consider the economic reality of artifacts replacing human agents as the go-to delegates of choice (what people normally refer to as "automation"). You might think that history goes only one way, with machines increasingly replacing humans, but there is some evidence of developments going the other way around as well.[4]

In adding nonhuman variables to my analysis of delegating practices, I must also remember that artifacts need not only be delegates: they can sometimes take the role of delegating party, as when someone is assigned a task by some software or app. Uber drivers are an example here, but in general software is now so well integrated into most complex organizations that many employees receive their tasks from "computers" (what has recently been called "computer control").[5]

Here I don't just mean that you find out through a computer system what your task is—most of us do, given smartphones and computers. I mean the more substantial case in which some computer system or algorithm decides which task to assign to which employee, the way the Uber or Wolt algorithm might decide to give a certain ride to another driver even though you are closer because the algorithm takes into account not only location but also, say, customer satisfaction. This is a case in which whether you get a certain job is itself decided, it could be argued, by the algorithm.

I don't think I need to, for starters, precisely define the practice of delegation, but—having introduced artifacts—it will be helpful to at least distinguish between delegating to someone or something and using a tool, which I take to be a distinct practice. The difference is, basically, that when you delegate, the recipients act *on your behalf* (or *in our place*). This is the difference between cooking—using all the tools, instruments, and machines that this requires—and having someone cook for you (don't just think of restaurants and pizza deliveries but also wives in traditional patriarchal settings and servants in the old days—but actually I'm sure rich people still have cooks, don't they?).

As I move forward toward a more substantial account of delegation, you will see how the difference between *delegating to* something and *using* something has to do more precisely with control. Before I proceed in that direction, though, let me make a provisional distinction between what I call *strategic delegation* and *economic delegation*, which helps us understand both the rational justification and motivation for delegating.

Strategic delegation can be understood as the practice that aims to *improve outcomes* by delegating tasks to, for example, experts—as when you employ an accountant for your tax returns or a broker for your investments; the people you delegate to are supposed to be experts in their fields so that they will hopefully be able to deliver outcomes that would not have been accessible to amateurs like yourself. Here it is important to understand the category of strategic delegation as an *intentional* category (rather than an extensional one, to be sure), which does not depend on actual outcomes but only on intended outcomes or, alternatively, on reasonable-to-expect outcomes. This is because history is full of cases in which experts did not deliver: to stick to the financial example, just think of the "invention" of indexes that passively track the stock market, which often turn out to be more profitable—or equally profitable but cheaper—than so-called expert human brokers trying to outperform the stock market on behalf of their clients.

This example brings me directly to the alternative category of *economic delegation*, where you do not necessarily delegate a task in order to improve performance but rather to *spare resources* that you can then deploy elsewhere, as when you employ a cleaner, for example, or use a washing machine (this particular example also shows that often we get both strategic and economic delegation in a single system), or, at work, you might give an employee something to do. In these cases, you do not necessarily aim at or get a better performance than you would have yourself achieved, but the deal still makes sense because you can use your time and energy elsewhere. Here again, a lot of delegation to technological systems should probably be understood in terms of economic delegation, where the system does some menial task for a fraction of the time or money, relieving us of a burden.

In analyzing the concepts of strategic delegation and economic delegation and their application to technological innovation and especially algorithms, I will have to test the hypothesis that it is a necessary condition of the concept of delegation that you could have at least tried to complete the task yourself; otherwise there would not have been anything to delegate in the first place because you never could have done it yourself. Does this hypothesis limit the scope of applying delegation to technological innovation, given that new inventions and systems are often meant to make the previously impossible possible?

HOW DELEGATING WORKS

After one final clarification, I will now put forward my first claim about the nature of delegation. The clarification is that, even though I have focused a lot on control in this book, you should not understand my analysis of delegation as being limited to the practice of delegating control—it applies more generally to the practice of delegating a task; for example, you can also delegate choice (here see, for example, the already cited book by Cass Sunstein, *Choosing Not to Choose* [2015]). My claim—and this one does have to do with control—is *when you delegate, you cede (or give up) direct control.*

This should be understood as a necessary but not sufficient condition, so that, if you do not cede direct control, you have not really delegated. And this is, as I have anticipated, also what distinguishes the practice of delegating from the practice of using. Before I argue for the above claim, here's another: *when you delegate successfully, you keep overall control.* This should also be understood as a necessary but not sufficient condition, such that if you lose (or cede or give up) overall control, then you have not successfully delegated.

Delegation and control, then, are conceptually related in such a way that you give up direct control but keep overall control when you delegate successfully. The following will have to be worked out in some more detail before the end, but for now I can provisionally say that the above two conditions are individually necessary and jointly sufficient for (successful) delegation. And to be sure, the reason I am stressing "successful" delegation is that you can sometimes fail to properly delegate for exactly the two reasons above:

- You might set out to give up direct control but end up keeping it—this is like the bad guy in old cartoons complaining that he has to do everything himself for it to be done properly; does anybody remember Cruella de Vil and her two hopeless helpers?
- Alternatively, you might set out to keep overall control but end up losing it—a lot of the control paradox cases in this book will have to be analyzed as this kind of scenario, for example. It is only when you manage to genuinely give up (to someone or something else) direct control but also at the same time keep overall control that you have successfully delegated. I might be stating the obvious here, but given that I have in the space of a few pages introduced two crucial distinctions, let me emphasize that the following are two independent distinctions that ought not to be mixed up:

1. the distinction between economic delegation and strategic delegation; and
2. the distinction between the direct control condition and the overall control condition on delegation.

Delegation, with a few exceptions (see, for example, Collins and Kusch [1998] and also Sie [2009]), has hardly received any interest within philosophy—you need authors like Bruno Latour in science and technology studies (STS) and the subsequent development of actor–network theory (ANT) to find academic work on the theory and practice of delegating a task (Latour 1988, 1996) (see also Bohlin [2000] for a discussion that tries to bridge the gap between the little philosophy work on delegation and the STS and ANT traditions).[6]

There is, therefore, no such thing as a philosophy of delegation, not even at an embryonic level. And in fact, probably many colleagues would be outright suspicious of someone like myself, trained within analytic action theory, suggesting that there should be action-theoretical work on delegation and that delegation should not be left to those working within STS and similar fields. Their work is important, but as a colleague of mine put it recently, STS researchers do not operate with a substantial conception of agency, and that impacts their take on delegation.

You should not confuse the above point with the claim that there is no current work in philosophy that is relevant to a philosophical account of delegation. For example, there has been growing interest, over the last couple of decades, in social ontology, group agency, and related topics. Such work is relevant. But at the same time, it is symptomatic of the way philosophers have stayed away from delegation that the standard case of group agency and social ontology is collaboration rather than delegation; think of Margaret Gilbert's classic "Walking Together" (1990).

Comparing the cases of delegating and collaborating, both in the sense of doing things together, is helpful to my understanding of control, because it points, for example, to the idea of *sharing control*. So far, I have emphasized giving up direct control and keeping overall control—but what about sharing control between the delegating party and delegate? Is that an alternative way of thinking about delegation? There is a sense in which control is shared, but it might be a sense that is incompatible with the idea of shared control. Namely, in the delegating sense of working together—and simplifying things to two human agents for now—I have the following possibilities, taking the previous case in which boss Jane asks employee John to make her coffee:

* Jane gives up direct control while she keeps overall control—over the coffee making.
* John has direct control (as a consequence of successful delegation) but no overall control—over coffee making.

Clearly, here the description of the relevant actions will be crucial, but you can already see that even if I could, at a stretch, say that Jane and John are sharing control of "making coffee" for the simple reason that John directly controls "making coffee" while Jane has overall control over "making coffee," there is no genuine sense in which there is shared control. John is making coffee—on his own—and Jane is in charge. It is indeed joint agency, but it is joint agency of a particular, *hierarchical* kind.

Here you could object that, on the above description and in this particular case, it is not at all obvious that Jane has any control over making coffee. Whether or not Jane has any control will indeed depend on some details, including details about the working relationship between Jane and John. But I think it is plausible to imagine many instances of the broad scenario above in which Jane has control. If John is, for example, making Jane's *ristretto* in the next room and Jane can shout at him to stop if she needs him back to pick up the phone, then it sounds like Jane is in control of the coffee making (at least given some further assumptions about what Jane can be reasonably expected to ask and get from John, as in blind obedience, for example).

Obviously there are, like in the other cases I have dealt with, crucial epistemic conditions that need to be met in order for the claim that Jane is in control to be plausible: for example, John needs to know well the details of how Jane likes her coffee ("*ristretto*, black, no sugar, and the water better be bloody fresh too!"), and it additionally needs to be the case that I (and Jane) can reasonably expect John to act on those details and make the right kind of coffee. John's coffee making basically needs to be reason-responsive to the taste of Jane for coffee.

Given such epistemic considerations, and some crucial facts about the power dynamics in the working relationship between Jane and John, and finally some more basic physical conditions about what is actually possible, it is easy to imagine Jane being in control even after having delegated to John. And this—mutatis mutandis—applies across many different delegating relationships.

For the purposes of contrasting the above case in which Jane is still in control, I can imagine a case in which Jane sends John out to get her a *ristretto* from a "proper" barista around the corner (John is a slow learner, I guess, or maybe his barista training is scheduled for next week). Suppose additionally that John forgets his phone and that he gets the details of his order to the barista mixed up—no reminder about fresh water, say. This could be, I might argue, a case in which Jane tried to delegate but ended up losing overall control. So delegation was not successful, and Jane's coffee doesn't taste quite right.[7]

In fact, I think I can go even further than the conditions above.[8] Think of the following case: I delegate, to a significant extent anyway, the care and education of my three young children to others, their teachers and caregivers at school and kindergarten. The fact that I talk of "delegation" for this case—instead of, say, dropping them off at school—implies, according to my own account, the following two elements:

1. When I drop off my kids at school and kindergarten, I cede direct control over my kids to the institutions. As I said, if I still had direct control (what would that look like anyway?), then it would not be a case of delegation.
2. The second element of delegating care would then be that when I drop them off, even though I abdicate direct control to the relevant institutions, I still maintain or keep overall control of my kids' care and education. Again, if I lost overall control by dropping them off, then the case would not qualify as successful delegation.

You might disagree and say that this case should not be understood in terms of delegation, but even if you do, please bear with me for a little bit longer so that I can show you, my dear reader, what I take to be an interesting consequence of thinking of primary school education and childcare in terms of delegation. First of all, you can see both the strategic and economic argument for delegation, so that in this particular case I can say that there is both strategic delegation and economic delegation. After all, I delegate care to experts, who have been trained as caregivers and teachers and are now qualified to perform these roles. I can argue that they are better than I am at taking care of my own children.

I might want to resist this strategic delegation approach—after all, you could argue that even though teachers and caregivers might be better at taking care of children in general, they are not necessarily better than I am at taking care of *my own* children. But even if I granted you this objection—and I would not be so sure, dear helicopters—I still have economic delegation. Namely, the idea that I spare resources—primarily time—by delegating childcare to others so that I can go to work and earn more than it costs to pay for kindergarten.

That's only the theory, of course; in practice, there might be all sorts of obstacles that result in not being able to delegate, including the fact that if there are not enough subsidized places some private kindergartens might be so expensive that they negate the economic delegation argument. But again, here I am not interested in the question of whether we should delegate childcare or primary school education (even though I genuinely think that keeping kids at home or homeschooling is crazy). I am rather interested in the claim that if I do drop my kids off, this practice should be understood as a delegating practice, thereby resulting in loss of direct control without a loss of overall control.

Here's why this is relevant: when the kids are at school and in kindergarten, there is not much I can do. I can't, for all intents and purposes, intervene (this is, btw, where I answer that cliffhanger question about intervention and control from the previous chapter): I am too far away and I don't know what's going on. So neither physical nor epistemic conditions appear to be met. So how can I possibly speak of control? And if there is no control, then how can I speak of delegation?

On the one hand, it looks as though what I am doing is delegating—but on the other hand, it looks as though I don't keep any control, because I can neither intervene nor know what is happening while I am away. Does that mean that my account of delegation as giving up direct control while keeping overall control needs revision?

Not so quick: I actually think that there is a suitable sense of control at play even when I delegate childcare. And in fact, I just need to go back to my street definition of control to see it; namely, even if I am not there, I am in fact able to exercise influence on what happens, and I do. And that is basically why I still have overall control even though I don't have—nor do I want to have, that's the important part—direct control.

Small aside: I say that I don't want to have direct control and that this is important because in order to make the kinds of efficiencies that economic delegation aims at, something's got to give. And what I give up is direct control—that is how I spare resources. So I should not necessarily think of giving up or losing direct control as a nasty side effect, because it is actually the whole point of economic delegation. I will come back to this point when I apply my account of delegation to the control paradox, but it is important to emphasize already now the "cost" of losing or giving up direct control.

This is as good a place as any in this chapter to make a further crucial clarification about what it is that I delegate when I delegate control: I do not delegate direct control; I properly *give up* direct control—as in, I no longer have it. So what I delegate is control, and what that means is giving up direct control but keeping overall control. So the object of delegation is "control" itself, unanalyzed, and what that consists in is giving up (losing, abdicating, ceding, or whatever verb you find most helpful) direct control while at the same time keeping overall control.

Having said the above, I should also clarify that there is a clear difference between actively "giving up" direct control and passively losing direct control. But given that the loss of direct control is compatible both with the delegation of control and with keeping overall control, you should not think of the loss of direct control—whether active or passive—as necessarily problematic to begin with. Still, as I in later chapters apply these conceptual distinctions to the control paradox—where whether or not different parties have direct control might turn out to matter in some circumstances—it will be important to keep in mind this further distinction between actively and passively losing direct control—even though, again, both are compatible with keeping overall control and also with control delegation.

The reason the distinction between passively losing direct control and giving up direct control is important is clearly that the former makes the loss of direct control sound more like a nasty side effect, while the latter makes it sound more like one of the goals of delegation. So the way I frame the "loss" of direct control is crucial to what I will end up saying about it in the context of the control paradox.

DIRECT CONTROL IS OVERRATED

Okay, the aside was not that small, but now I go back to my argument about keeping overall control of delegated care. Where was I? The question is on what grounds I can claim that I keep overall control even though I am neither there to intervene nor know what's going on while I am away. So *direct control is overrated!* Namely, you aren't much help if you are not properly trained or you are busy on the phone. And knowing what's going on is, again, not much help if you can't do anything about it or you don't have the epistemic qualifications to evaluate what's happening.

You will probably know, dear reader—because I'm just going to assume that my readers know more about tech than I do, since I don't even have a bloody smartphone—that there are people who have an app on their phone that is connected to a camera so that they can check what's happening at home while they are away. I am sure there are much more fancy things than such an app these days, but this simple technology will be enough to make my point.

Now imagine that a couple both have such an app on their phone to check on their cat that they left back home while they went traveling—you can really tell that this is a fictional thought experiment and not an anecdote about my best friend, right? Anyway, so they have this app and multiple cameras in their flat, and those cameras rotate so they have a pretty good view of most corners of most rooms. And obviously cats can't normally open grown-up doors, so if you plan it right, you pretty much have an uninterrupted view of your cat—should you wish such a thing.

You guessed my next question already, right? Is the couple in control, given the app, the multiple cameras, and also the preparations before they left? They are certainly checking on their cat and—in that way, you could say that they are controlling the cat. But are they in control? And—mutatis mutandis—would you be in control if you sent your kid to a kindergarten that offered the same app-plus-camera service? I honestly hope that they don't exist, but I have certainly met parents who would sacrifice their inheritance to get a place in such an institution.

This not-so-fictional system would satisfy some plausible epistemic requirement for control, but would it be enough in order to be in control? You could certainly phone the institution to complain if you didn't like what you were seeing on the app, so in a sense you would have more control than if you didn't have the app. But, crucially for me, would you, really? And—also importantly for me—would that still be delegation?

It would not, because delegation requires sacrifices—in this case, giving up direct control. And if you insist on direct control, well, you can care for your bloody children your own bloody self, I guess. More to the point, I have generated an example in which parents certainly have more direct control than if there was no such system. But does the app give them more overall control? Not necessarily, and this is where my account of delegation meets the control paradox, because the idea is that through delegation you improve overall control—especially through strategic delegation.

You need to let go of direct control in order to improve overall control. This is the lesson of my little story and also the basic lesson of delegation. Because compare the cat's app with leaving the cat with someone you know will take good care of it—the way well-trained childcare providers take care of children. What's the difference between these two alternatives? Crucially, the difference is not just that only in one case can you be said to have direct control, if at all; only in one case do you retain overall control, and that happens not to be the same case in which we have direct control.

Just in case you are wondering, the crucial comparison is not between the case in which the cat is left alone at home for a week and the case in which the cat is left alone at home for a week but you have the app and the cameras—because in neither case do you have meaningful control nor instances of successful delegation. The relevant comparison is rather between the case in which you have the app and the case in which you leave the cat with someone you "trust" (more about that in a bit). Only the latter results in keeping overall control, and—importantly for the argument in this book— only the latter constitutes a case of delegating.

You are not delegating control of the cat to the cameras or the app. Why not? Simply because if you were successfully delegating to these technologies, you would still be in control, but you are not. If the cat does something stupid, all you can do is watch it suffer or even die. And yes, it's easy to imagine improving the app-camera system in such a way that it is also connected to someone local or even the vet, but apart from the fact that it might never be enough, the important theoretical point here is that in fact there might be technological solutions such that you are keeping overall control. The app alone just isn't one of them.

What have I learned? I have found out a bit more about how successful delegation, ceding direct control while keeping overall control, works. And also I have learned that as long as reliable practices are in place, neither the intervention condition nor the epistemic condition are necessary in order to exercise influence and keep control.

Still, there are at least two aspects of my argument so far that need further unpacking: the notion of "trust" and the idea that you can actually improve control through delegation. Let me start with the latter, because it is directly relevant to my formulation of the control paradox, given its reference to improving control. Can and do I improve control through delegation?

The answer to this question, it turns out, is pretty obvious, at least given the delegation framework I have set up so far. Just ask yourself the question, "Why do you delegate?" Or—if you are worried that the answer to that empirical-psychological question might be something like "because you are lazy" or even "because you are a power fanatic" or something—ask yourself, "Why does it make rational sense to delegate?" The answer is that there are two rational explanations for the practice of delegation, which I have been using throughout to distinguish strategic delegation from economic delegation.

It is possible to imagine economic delegation without performance improvement, but—by definition—successful strategic delegation requires performance improvement. Now you might be delegating some task other than control, and you might do that strategically, and then the performance improvement might not be an improvement in control. But if the task that you delegate strategically is indeed control, then the performance improvement must also be in terms of control. So in fact the idea that you improve control through delegation just follows from my conception of strategic delegation, at least in the cases in which what you delegate is control. Still, you might delegate control only to achieve some efficiencies, and then—in the case of economic delegation—you would not necessarily achieve improved control through delegation.

The technological systems or human agents to which you delegate strategically are normally—and that's the crucial bit—*experts* in their fields, or anyway they have more expertise with the relevant task than you possess. And that is how you achieve improved performance. Just think of when you employ an accountant or even just go to the doctor: those are experts who take care of stuff on your behalf.

Here one distinction is in order, though: whether or not what you delegate is control might make a difference to whether or not you give up direct control and retain overall control. So my opponent could argue as follows: Ezio, your account of delegation as giving up direct control while retaining overall control only works for a particular delegated task, namely, control itself. When someone delegates different tasks—like taxes and medicine— then they might have true and successful delegation but not necessarily give up direct control or keep overall control.

AN ALTERNATIVE ACCOUNT OF DELEGATION

This is an interesting challenge that I want to engage with, because it points to a plausible alternative to my own account of delegation: according to this alternative, delegation only necessarily consists of giving up direct control (as I also claim) but not of retaining overall control (different from my account). Below I will ultimately reject this alternative account of delegation, but it is important here to illustrate it as a legitimate alternative to what I have put forward so far.

Let's test the two accounts by looking at the cases of taxes and healthcare, which I am choosing because in both, supposedly, what is delegated is not control but some other task (Cass Sunstein [2015] talks in this context of "choosing not to choose," namely, delegating *choice*, and he explicitly uses the tax example): filling out your tax returns (or should we just use its proper name, paying less taxes?) and having some symptom checked.

Given your lack of training on this side and the professional expertise on the other side (accountant, doctor), it is plausible to argue that you give up direct control to the professionals (for a time and only relative to a specific domain, to be sure), but for the same reason it could be argued that it is not plausible—given the gap in knowledge between client and accountant and patient and doctor—that you retain overall control.

The tension here is between the strategic character of delegation and retaining overall control, because it could be argued that the more strategic and effective the delegation is (and expensive! because we have an excellent accountant or a world-famous doctor), the less plausible it is to argue that you are still in control. Quick aside: the "expensive" bit is also important to emphasize, because you might delegate to spare resources or you might invest resources in order to delegate—and in fact you might do both at the same time, if the resources are different, as when we pay money to someone (or for something) in order to save time; that's economic delegation, and it costs money.

Take the following correlation: the more experienced your doctor is, the more you will feel the pressure to go along with her recommendations. And maybe even the more expensive your accountant is, the more pressure you will be under to accept her advice. Here things are genuinely complex, because even just the question of whether what these experts give you is their advice is a difficult one to answer. Would it even be a case of delegation if all you were getting was advice? And then maybe—if I frame things in terms of advice—you actually keep direct control and there is no delegation, let alone loss of overall control.

What you normally get isn't just advice, though, is it? Because doctors make diagnoses, and based on those you receive treatment—and very often you are not left to self-medicate but are medicated or intervened upon. So it is delegation, and there is some loss of direct control and, possibly, of overall control. And in fact, to think that there is a correlation between how good the doctor or accountant is and whether you will lose overall control is just to mix up direct control with overall control. Because there likely is a correlation between the quality of the expertise and whether you have much direct control or even involvement: if they are good, they will not ask you too many questions or let you decide things that you don't understand or choose between alternatives that you can't even tell apart. That's direct control, but that only happens with amateurs. The good ones will know from experience what to ask you and, especially, what not to ask you.

After all, your involvement is bound to decrease the overall quality of the outcome: that's the whole point of delegating to experts—that I don't have a (fuckin') clue. And still some involvement is important; just think of informed consent within healthcare (here I am assuming that most of you, dear readers, don't need any explanation—but if you want to brush up on informed consent in healthcare, you are welcome to check out my ethics textbook for medical students, *Ethics in Healthcare* [Di Nucci 2018]). Informed consent is also a good way of showing that, at least in principle, strategic delegation should not threaten overall control.

I might be able to resist the objection according to which there is a loss of overall control with the strategic delegation of tasks other than control itself, like delegating your tax returns to an experienced and expensive accountant. But what about an *improvement* in overall control when you delegate to an experienced and expensive accountant (or an experienced and expensive doctor—but I'm in Denmark, so it's "free," just with the world's highest tax rate)?

Well, this one is easy: I don't need to argue that there is an enhancement of overall control when you strategically delegate the choices involved in paying taxes—simply because the reason you delegate strategically is not control but paying the "right" amount of taxes. So you don't aim to enhance control, just your wallet—and therefore whether or not you end up having enhanced control is beside the point, and it is not a problem for my account of strategic delegation, as long as you retain overall control.

It is time to consider some consequences of my account of delegation. For example, one consequence is that the delegate (the person or system delegated to) gets some direct control over the task from the delegating party—such as John the secretary from Jane the boss. Now you might think that this is a very idealistic and unrealistic way of thinking of power structures, but don't forget that, after all, Jane keeps overall control—as in, *it's a short leash* (I'm sure you have had enough of my stupid slogans already, but sorry, I'm enjoying myself too much to stop).

Thinking in terms of a more or less short leash is actually really helpful, I believe, because the dog has some flexibility through the leash—there are things that the dog can do on the leash and that the owner cannot stop the dog from doing given a certain leash length. But on the other hand, the leash is there to *rein in* the dog if necessary—and also the length of the leash is never infinite. So there are also things that the dog cannot do. Therefore, think of the interactive relationship between a delegating party and a delegated-to party and its dialectic of direct control and overall control in terms of a flexible but finite leash.

This is possibly controversial but at least conceivable when it comes to human agents. But you might worry that once I apply my account of delegation to technological systems I will get one implication too many: how would it work, even from a purely conceptual point of view, to have to ascribe direct control to machines? This is an important question indeed, but you got lucky again, because it has been asked and answered already in the previous chapter; see under *technological control*.

Still, one aspect must be discussed here in some depth because it is not covered by the previous chapters on control. I talked of technological control primarily in terms of human agents controlling nonhuman technological systems. And indeed even in the cases in which through delegation the nonhuman technological system gets direct control, the human agent keeps overall control. So these cases do qualify as technological control in the sense I developed in the previous chapter.

The further objection that my account of technological control from the previous chapter does not cover, though, is the basic idea that technological systems—no matter how complex, intelligent, or autonomous—cannot be the bearers of direct control. This objection would then be founded on some metaphysical premise according to which any form of control requires some human-only capacity that you could call "free will," "autonomy," or "liberty" or some such big deal.

I hate talking shortcuts, but I might have to here. It is not clear that I can satisfy those kinds of metaphysical heights in the context of a book about the control paradox in tech and politics. Also, it could be argued that, given the premise on which the above objection is founded, the burden of proof is actually on the claim according to which any form of control requires some fancy human-only capacity such as free will—you could just as well call it the good old "soul" and be done with it, the name doesn't matter, but its metaphysical status will be difficult to get around.

Also—and possibly more to the point given my argument—whatever the merits of the metaphysical premise above, it might be overestimating my conception of "direct control." After all, direct control is both compatible with some master having overall control and also with a dog on the leash having some direct control. So assigning direct control in my account to nonhuman technological systems is really neither that complicated nor, given who keeps overall control, that scary either.

What would it mean, though, for a nonhuman technological system to have some direct control once a task has been delegated to it? I will have plenty of occasions in this book to discuss cutting-edge complexity such as AI systems. So I will start with something very simple here: Imagine you are some well-to-do lady in eighteenth-century England with plenty of staff. Every evening, when you go to bed, you either ask your maid to wake you at a certain time the next morning—say 8 a.m.—or you don't say anything, whereby the maid knows that you don't want to be disturbed and you will just ring the bell when you wake up.

What you do, in this scenario, is delegate the task to wake you up to someone else. There are multiple and significant ways you keep overall control in this situation:

- You decide whether or not to delegate in the first place, and in fact sometimes you don't delegate.
- You decide the time at which you should be woken up.
- You still keep the possibility of making alternative arrangements: you might recall the maid to tell her you changed your mind; you might wake up before the maid comes; you might even ask another maid as well just to make sure, in case the first maid forgets; you might tell the maid to go away when she comes and go back to sleep; and so on.
- You have reasonable expectations about being in fact woken up at exactly the time you ask.

- Finally, you are in charge: you can punish the maid or even sack her, without much reason, really—it is the eighteenth century after all (and in fact things haven't changed much). This last point also explains the previous point about your reasonable expectations that the maid will do as told.

The above list represents some of the significant ways you retain overall control, not just in general but over the practice of waking up in particular. Still, even accepting all the considerations above, it looks as though you have given some direct control to the maid when you delegated the task of waking you up to her. She might herself not wake up; she might run away during the night; she might get the time mixed up. Above all, she now—after the delegation—needs to do something in order for you to be woken up; it won't happen without her intervention. That's the whole point of the delegation, that you spare yourself an action that now needs to be performed by someone else.

Why have I told you this little old-fashioned story? I am sure you will have guessed where I was going long ago: think of a modern alarm clock, which these days pretty much everybody has on their phone—even I do, and my phone isn't smart. Without getting too far into the details, the alarm function/app in modern mobile phones does what alarm clocks were already doing before there were any mobile phones or even phones. Personal alarm clocks as we know them—as in, not water ones nor ones on top of church towers—existed at the time for the fictional lady in my little story; some people date them to Levi Hutchins in 1787 (Russo 2016). The mechanism makes a certain noise at a certain time, where both the noise in question and the time can be adjusted the evening before.

My account of delegation is compatible with delegating the task of being woken up to both an eighteenth-century maid and a twenty-first-century alarm app on a mobile phone (and in fact, perhaps most controversially, most other methods in between). As you now know, this implies both that the delegating agent keeps overall control and that the system to which the task is delegated gets direct control, which the agent no longer has.

These conditions rule out unreliable staff, malfunctioning systems, but also unsuccessful delegation, as when you set up the alarm on a phone that needs to stay on for the alarm to work and then—unaware of this requirement (or is it a Freudian slip?)—turn off the phone and sleep in the following morning. That would be a case in which you did not delegate successfully because you lost overall control. A case in which you did not delegate successfully because, on the other hand, you did not give up direct control is perhaps one in which you can't sleep (or wake up too early) because you are worried the alarm won't work or, more likely, that you won't hear it. Both of those fuck-ups, you will be unsurprised to hear, happen to me on a regular basis. There is such a thing as *too much control*, and there is such a thing as *not being able to let go*. That's the whole (self-therapeutic) point of this book, in fact.

I can still imagine my opponent being uncomfortable with one of the consequences—or is it itself a claim?—of my account, namely, the idea that simple technological systems such as alarm clocks should be assigned direct control. Doesn't this water down the concept of control to an extent that it is no longer useful? After all, for example, nobody would even consider assigning responsibility to an alarm clock. Things might get more complicated with some cutting-edge AI systems, but alarm clocks surely are not the right bearers of responsibility—and that much I agree with.

Here my account generates a little complexity: delegating parties who successfully delegate are always responsible in virtue of their intentional delegation plus overall control. If delegation is unsuccessful, then the story is more complicated, but in the normal case of successful intentional delegation where you retain overall control, you are responsible. The only difference that delegating to technological systems or human agents make is that only human agents—and possibly some AI systems that will be developed in the future—are possible bearers of responsibility. But that makes no difference to the responsibility of the delegating party. That some delegates are capable of bearing responsibility for direct control and some others are not makes no difference to the responsibility of the delegating party, because *responsibility is not a cake* (another slogan, after all). And also remember that it was Lola and not Sally who was responsible for running over the pedestrian while Sally was driving.

I will have plenty of time to discuss issues of responsibility in some detail in later chapters; here I just wanted to clarify some basics so you understand what I mean in claiming direct control for delegates who are technological systems. One more important clarification: even if you resist this idea that technological systems can be assigned direct control, that's not incompatible with my claim that when you delegate successfully you give up direct control but retain overall control, independent of whether you have delegated to another human agent—which then has direct control—or to a technological system, to which you might not assign direct control. So the crucial element for my account here is that the delegating party gives up direct control without giving up overall control.

DELEGATION AND THE PARADOX

What have I achieved so far? I have put forward an account of the practice of delegating a task according to which one delegates either for strategic reasons or for economic reasons. When you delegate successfully, you give up direct control while maintaining overall control. And I have shown that my account of delegation is applicable both to delegating relationships between human agents and also to human agents delegating to technological systems.

What's remains for this chapter is an explanation of what happens to the control paradox now that I have introduced my account of delegation. Two things, basically:

- Delegating practices generate the paradox.
- Delegation could also be the solution to the paradox.

So delegation is both the problem and its solution; that's how important it is for this book. I am not going to provide a general argument for those two claims here because the arguments will be provided in the coming chapters and will be specific to each technological system (or other practice). It is at the end of each of those chapters that readers should evaluate whether the paradox does indeed apply to the system or practice in question, and whether the two claims above apply as well.

Here I just want to very broadly and provisionally elaborate on these two claims before I apply them to the different technologies and practices. The idea that delegating practices generate the paradox is basically built around my distinction between overall control and direct control—and that distinction could also prove to be the solution to the paradox.

Namely, the reason supposedly control-enhancing technologies and practices end up in loss of control (or increased risk of loss of control, or increased fear of loss of control) is that there is a genuine loss when you delegate to control-enhancing technologies and practices, and that's the loss of direct control. So the loss of direct control necessary for successful delegation could also be what produces the paradox in one of its three possible forms, the strong, stronger, and strongest interpretations of the control paradox.

Again, this is just a claim or hypothesis and nothing like an argument— that will come later. And what about the solution? Well, if delegating practices also necessarily involve retaining overall control, so that you have only delegated successfully if you still have overall control, then when you delegate to a control-enhancing technological system or practice, you do not lose overall control and in fact, as I have argued, might enhance control.

And that could be the solution to the paradox: as long as you realize that there is an important difference between overall control and direct control, and additionally see that when you delegate you give up only direct control but not overall control, then there might not actually be a control paradox as such, because what you gain, keep, or improve on is overall control and what you lose or give up is direct control. And even though these two phenomena are both forms of control, as long as they are different there is no incompatibility and therefore no genuine paradox (shit, now I have gone and spoiled the surprise after all).

Think of it this way. If the paradox says that "the more we try to increase control the more we (risk/fear) lose control," then the solution to the paradox is to insert "overall" and "direct" so that it reads "the more we try to increase overall control the more we lose direct control," which already sounds a lot less paradoxical, if at all.

This is the general hypothesis, and after analyzing delegation in this chapter you can now see how the paradox is built on this understanding of control and delegation. In the coming chapters, organized around two distinct parts of the book—part III, "The Technological Paradox," and part IV, "The Political Paradox"—I will apply the work done on control and delegation so far in order to establish which technologies and practices give rise to genuine instances of the control paradox and whether in particular instances there might be a solution to the paradox coming from the very phenomenon that is at its core, namely, delegation.

Part Three

The Technological Paradox

Chapter Six

Control, Drones, and
Autonomous Weapons

The time has now come to apply my conceptual framework of control and delegation, and especially the control paradox, to real-world technologies and practices. In this third part of the book—"The Technological Paradox"— I will especially focus on the growing set of technologies loosely referred to as AI systems, which are increasingly used across sectors, including in defense, transportation, healthcare, the law, and finance.

One of the good things about writing a whole book is that there is space for covering multiple issues; still, choices have to be made, so I will end up discussing only a small, representative selection of technological systems, and then in the next and final part of the book, part IV, "The Political Paradox," I will move on to the political realm.

In this chapter I discuss two different kinds of systems that have been very much in vogue in ethical debates of the last few years,[1] so much so that it almost feels old-fashioned to apply the control paradox to them: drones and so-called autonomous weapons systems or AWSs (emphasis very much on the "so-called" here, given that the question of whether those systems are indeed autonomous can clearly not be assumed at the outset, not in a philosophy book, anyway).

Some ABCs: what is the difference between "autonomous weapons" and "drones"? Quite a bit, actually: a drone is a very specific system, which is traditionally understood as a remotely controlled and unmanned (I know, I know . . . the patriarchy always strikes back I'm afraid) flying system that can but may not be equipped with weapons (together with my colleague Filippo Santoni de Sio, I published a book on the ethics of drones, *Drones and Responsibility* [Di Nucci & Santoni de Sio 2016], which provides a good introduction and overview of the different kinds of systems and the various ethical problems relating to these different drones systems).

Very similar systems to drones are also deployed in the water and for ground operations—both within the military and outside of it, so that in fact small drones have now become widespread gadgets in civilian life as well (even my son got a tiny drone for Christmas last year, I must confess; then again, if what he got counts as a drone, then there really is no chance of conceptual clarity for this chapter).

If you have not been on Alpha Centauri over the last few years, the above is probably familiar, but still it is important to emphasize that the ethical and philosophical discussion does not depend on these systems being flying systems or in fact military systems. Further, it is important to distinguish the relevant features of an unmanned remotely controlled system from the features of a system that might be called "autonomous" or "semiautonomous."

Remotely controlled flying systems are in many ways like planes, only the pilot is not sitting inside them but rather—in some cases—thousands of miles away (on a different continent, in fact—think of Tampa-based drone pilots operating in Pakistan during the Obama administration; other drone pilots operate out of Nevada). These systems raise many important ethical issues but ought not to be confused with systems that are not remotely controlled but rather programmed and automated so as not to need any concurrent piloting.

Finally, commercial airliners are also increasingly automated, including so-called autoland systems, which can land the airplane without the pilots' intervention. At the time of writing this chapter (November 2019), the company Garmin had recently announced an emergency autoland system for small commercial planes (the Safe Return Emergency Autoland System), which could be activated by a passenger by just pressing a single red button in case the pilot was incapacitated (in a simulation reported on by *Wired* [Adams 2019], the pilot has a fictional heart attack and the journalist presses the button and watches the plane land). It is easy to imagine such systems replacing copilots in the future.

This chapter will focus on drones and autonomous weapons, but what is really at stake are the technological systems that operate those vehicles, so that the same analysis can, mutatis mutandis, be applied to both military and nonmilitary systems, whether they are in the air, in water, in space, or on land—one such system, for example, that is very much in vogue right now, both in the media and in academic debates, is that of so-called self-driving cars or autonomous vehicles (again, very much with the emphasis on "so-called").

AUTONOMOUS WEAPONS

To get started, let me pose the following scenario: a remotely controlled military drone is reprogrammed with a new AI system based on machine learning algorithms that allows the drone to fly without being remotely piloted. This refurbished drone now only needs to be given a set of coordinates and it will accordingly calculate the most efficient way to reach the target given weather conditions and the like (just a fancy Google Maps, really).

My refurbished drone can now reach the target without any piloting or "controlling"; it can avoid obstacles and bad weather, take shortcuts, and adapt to unexpected encounters. Maybe on its way it has to take down an enemy drone or even an old-fashioned fighter jet that happens to get in the way. It has been programmed with enough adaptability to deal with these expectable unexpected events.

What else can my drone now do? After all, if it can reach its target on its own, I suppose it can do other stuff on its own too. It can probably take a high-resolution photo or video once it gets there. And if the drone can do that, then it must be able to shoot its target as well.

Also, my new drone could be able to identify targets and their positions without needing any input of coordinates. Maybe the drone is just given the task of surveillance of a certain area, and within that area it is able to identify on its own possible enemy targets. After all, just some basic image recognition plus a sorting task plus mapping software should do the trick.

My drone can now identify targets without concurrent human intervention, and it can fly over to its newly identified targets without concurrent human intervention. The next step is clearly to suppose that the drone can also take any required relevant action toward its target, as above: maybe that's as innocent as filming the target, but if the drone can now also film its target, there is nothing stopping a similarly equipped drone from also shooting the target or eliminating its enemy in a fully automated targeted killing.

Through a couple of reasonable steps, I have now got to the point where a military drone can identify and eliminate a target without human concurrent intervention. The future of war is indeed scary, so why would I even contemplate this madness? Let me take this slowly; for now I just want to clarify why I am saying "concurrent." It makes little sense, independent of how fancy the system in question is, to say with no qualification "without human intervention." As we are always talking of artifacts, there is always some human intervention in the causal chain, as long as we go back far enough.

Clearly the questions about automation, autonomy, intelligence, or AI have to do with how far back we go in order to find human intervention—and some other conditions too. So for now, I just want to emphasize that I am not taking a stand on any of these difficult questions about automation, autonomy, AI, and the rest; that's why I am referring to "concurrent" human intervention. Simply, while the system operates, no human intervenes or needs to intervene.

There might be other actions that relevant humans undertake during the operation (supervision, for example), and there are certainly actions in the lead-up to the operation. *But there is no concurrent agency during the operation*, and that is what makes these systems interesting from the point of view of the philosophy of control, delegation, and ultimately responsibility.

To be clear: I am not suggesting that such systems should be developed or deployed. I am only saying that we already have today the technology to develop and deploy such systems, so it is important to address philosophical and ethical questions relating to such systems, especially in the military but also more generally.

These kinds of systems are sometimes referred to in the ethical, law, and policy literature as "killer robots," and in fact there is a Campaign to Stop Killer Robots and also an International Committee for Robot Arms Control, mimicking campaigns against the proliferation of nuclear weapons (https://www.stopkillerrobots.org/).

Human Rights Watch has also embraced the "killer robots" terminology, and while I don't want to complicate things by adding the term *robot* to my discussion,[2] the way Human Rights Watch describes the systems in question does indeed match the general features that I have been describing:

> Fully autonomous weapons, also known as "killer robots," would be able to select and engage targets without meaningful human control. Precursors to these weapons, such as armed drones, are being developed and deployed by nations including China, Israel, South Korea, Russia, the United Kingdom and the United States. There are serious doubts that fully autonomous weapons would be capable of meeting international humanitarian law standards, including the rules of distinction, proportionality, and military necessity, while they would threaten the fundamental right to life and principle of human dignity. Human Rights Watch calls for a preemptive ban on the development, production, and use of fully autonomous weapons. (Human Rights Watch 2020)

Whether or not these systems are autonomous or indeed "fully" autonomous is at best debatable, but clearly the more important issue is what these systems can achieve. If they can identify, engage, and take down enemy targets without human intervention, that is a capability that must be taken very seriously, independent of any philosophical quibbles about "autonomy."

For the purposes of this book, I am not interested in whether these systems deserve the "autonomy" label; I want to know what consequences for control they have. But those using the "autonomy" label have made assumptions about control. I want to find out what kinds of questions of control these systems throw up, and having done that I could generate some consequences for the labels "autonomous" and even "robot"—but that's not my focus here.

Before I talk about the control of autonomous weapons, let me take a step back to wonder why anybody in their right mind would want to combine AI technology with deadly force. You would think we would want to reduce the quantity of weapons circulating rather than produce new ones. But the story is not quite so simple, especially if we think of military innovation in terms of the quality of weapons and how that might actually affect their quantity.

When evaluating a military operation from an ethical (and then also legal) point of view, there are normally three different parties to consider: your own personnel, enemy personnel, and civilians (the actual story is a bit more complicated—because these distinctions are not so clear-cut; think, for example, of civilians who work in sectors that might be strategic for the war effort [see Fabre 2009]—but for my purposes this should be good enough for now).

When thinking of the three traditional parties affected by war, the interesting thing is that developing drone and autonomous weapons might benefit each of these three parties. The case for your own personnel is easy: if you send in a drone—to say Pakistan—and its pilot is sitting in Tampa, Florida, then it looks as though the drone's pilot is less likely to die as a result of the mission than if you send in a traditional fighter jet, which might be shot down, resulting in the killing, injuring, or capture of its pilots.

The point is so obvious that I will not labor it further, if you don't mind.[3] Basically, innovation in military technology that allows fewer "boots on the ground" is a way of making war safer for our own troops. You might think that, in the longer term, having such efficient war machines could make the whole world more dangerous and so ultimately result in more dangerous situations for our own troops than if we didn't develop such systems (a kind of nuclear-war-like scenario), but given a single mission in Pakistan it seems obvious that it is safer to conduct it from Florida or Nevada than if you were actually parachuting into Pakistani territory.[4]

From the point of view of one's own troops, then, drones and autonomous weapons could be argued to result in increased security. What about the other two parties, enemy personnel and civilians? If you take these machines to be more precise than humans or than other machines concurrently piloted or controlled by humans, then you could also argue that AWSs might be beneficial from the point of view of reducing collateral damages and civilian casualties, just in virtue of enhanced precision.

Enhanced precision, by the way, isn't something that we are just assuming in virtue of these systems being newer, by definition, than the systems we already have such as fighter jets, because clearly as innovation and product development continue, we will have fighter jets that are newer than drones; it's not like we have stopped developing more old-fashioned weapons. The point is rather that a system that does not expose its pilot as much as a fighter jet might also afford more precision independent of the technological specs of its cameras, say. Because the system might fly for longer than if a pilot was sitting inside it, or it might come closer to the target than if a pilot was sitting inside it, or it might fly more quickly than if a pilot was sitting inside it—there might be speeds that would be damaging for the health of human pilots, and also computers might fly quicker than human pilots.

All these features can be thought to make the AWS in question more precise and therefore reduce the likelihood of civilian casualties. Clearly—and unfortunately—enhanced precision will also mean that if the AWS in question was to target civilians, it could cause more damage and kill more than a less effective system. So it does go both ways, but here I am thinking of civilian casualties in terms of the "collateral damages" framework, where civilian casualties are, by definition, unintended (Di Nucci 2014b).

What I have said so far about civilian casualties and enhanced precision clearly applies to enemy personnel too. If I am thinking of a military mission in terms of trying to keep the number of enemy fatalities to a minimum given some strategic goal, then enhanced precision and efficacy can be a positive development to achieve that aim. If, on the other hand, the aim of the mission is to eliminate as many enemy combatants as possible, then enhanced precision and efficacy can still be a positive development.

In short, if AWSs are thought of as more precise and efficient than traditional weapons, then AWSs promise better outcomes on all three fronts: our own military, enemy combatants, and collateral civilian casualties.[5]

That is, if you like, the main ethical argument for AWSs, that they can make war more precise and therefore, if this does not sound too ironic to you, safer. A safer war through killer robots: sounds more like a joke, but it is an actual argument. Does the argument work? Let's look at a couple of objections:

1. The first objection to the argument that AWSs can make war safer is that their enhanced precision also makes them more dangerous and that, others things being equal, it is better to have less dangerous weapons in circulation than more dangerous weapons.
2. The second objection is that AWSs are not actually safer or more precise—this is an empirical objection, so I will not deal with it here.
3. Finally, there are objections that accept that AWSs are potentially safer and more precise and are even willing to go along with their potential exploitation (as in, a more precise weapon is more dangerous when in the wrong hands) but raise independent difficulties for AWSs, like, for example, the so-called responsibility gap (see Matthias [2004] and Sparrow [2007] for two of the original formulations of the responsibility gap).

It's tempting to engage with these ethical arguments here, but do not forget that the aim of this chapter and of the overall book is not a general ethical analysis of the different technologies and practices that I discuss but rather more specific: presenting, applying, and ultimately dissolving the control paradox. So AWSs are only relevant here in so far as they represent a possible application of the control paradox; in that respect, ethical arguments for and against AWSs are important, but only insofar as they are functional to the paradox.

Does the control paradox apply to AWSs? The crucial questions I need to address in order to find out are the following:

1. Do AWSs constitute a control-enhancing technological innovation?
2. Do you end up with a loss of control as a result of AWSs? Or, according to the other two interpretations, do you end up with an increased risk of loss of control, or an increased fear of loss of control?

Let me start with the control-enhancing aspect—and remember that, since I am running this methodology for the first time, what I do in this chapter is a pilot for the analyses in the coming chapters.

It could be argued that AWSs are control-enhancing technologies on the grounds that they are more precise than less autonomous or automatic technologies like old-fashioned fighter jets or remotely controlled drones. If the AI system tasked with guiding an AWS to a certain target or location can, for example, get there quicker than a human fighter jet pilot or a human drone pilot without thereby sacrificing the reliability of the flight, then it could well be argued that AWS technologies are more precise and that, through the AI system guiding the AWS, the commanding officer has more control over the flight of the AWS than the human pilot, whether it's a plane or a drone.

Just to be precise and not to compromise the analogy, what I have to say is that the same commanding officer has more or better control over the flight of the AWS flown by the AI system than she has over the flight of the drone or plane flown by a human pilot. The idea would then be that by deploying an AWS flown by an AI system much like Garmin's emergency autoland in order to, say, run some surveillance on ISIS fighters in northern Syria— instead of deploying fighter jets or remotely controlled drones—mission command has enhanced its control over the operation. If the above condition is met, then I could argue that AWSs, at least in this particular instance, constitute a control-enhancing technology.

What conditions would have to apply, though, for me to argue that by using an AWS instead of a remotely controlled drone, mission command has enhanced its control over the operation? This seems to be the crucial question. And the answer is relatively easy: Imagine that the AWS in question has higher-resolution cameras and, at the same time—because of its increased speed and also the fact that no human is sitting in it—the AWS is able to fly closer to the ground than both a plane or a remotely controlled drone. In this case, mission command would have a better picture of what was happening on the ground, and, crucially, it would have a better picture as a direct result of using the more autonomous/automatic technology instead of the less autonomous/automatic technology for this particular mission.

Having a better picture of what is happening on the ground would, in turn, counts as being in a better position to control the movements, habits, routines, and practices of the ISIS fighters who are the object of this particular fictional mission. With all these conditions in place, I think I can argue that this AWS deployment does constitute control enhancement.

I have chosen this particular scenario to highlight the ambiguous ways the concept of control can be used. Above, for example, I have just argued that through the deployment of an AWS mission command is in a better position to control the movements of the ISIS fighters. But is that the same sense of control that I have been using throughout? Shouldn't I rather focus on the more narrow idea of control over the system itself? Am I, in short, talking about the same thing when I talk about broadly controlling the enemy's movements and more narrowly controlling the AWS or drone?

There seems to be an obvious difference between the two ways I am using the notion of control: one is control as surveillance (over the ISIS fighters), while the other is a more agential sense of control in which I am talking of the "guiding" or "piloting" of the AWS itself rather than what can be done through the AWS. But given what I have said in part II about the concept of control, I don't think I should be too quick to make these kinds of distinctions, especially given the previous distinction between overall control and direct control. Once I accept—as the result of my arguments especially in chapters 3 and 4—that control does not need to be "direct" and that overall control is a different form of control that is just as genuine if not "better," then I can now see that surveillance is a legitimate form of control among others.

Specifically, it might well be that all I need to do when an AI system is guiding the AWS is in fact surveillance, or call it *supervision* or *oversight*. Whether I use the concept of surveillance or the concept of supervision or oversight or, indeed, just the concept of control, the crucial theoretical issue is that these phenomena need not be understood as *occurrent* phenomena but can also be understood *dispositionally*. If you are a philosopher, dear reader, you might need no explanation here, but for the nonphilosophers and also just in case: the idea that control can be understood dispositionally means, basically, that I might be in control without doing any controlling or, in fact, without doing anything.

EMERGENCY AUTOLAND SYSTEMS AND AWSS

The details are important here, so let's look at some scenarios. First, consider the emergency autoland system already introduced. Imagine you are a passenger on a small commercial plane with just one pilot. There are five other passengers on the plane and no flight attendants. None of the six total passengers—we will suppose—has any experience flying a plane, beyond being a passenger in commercial flights; no particular passion, no flight simulator, let alone any flying lesson or license. As the plane goes through its takeoff preparations, a recorded message delivers the usual emergency information, with the added twist that, at the end of the message, you hear that this particular plane is equipped with an emergency autoland, which is a computer system able to safely land the plane should anything happen to the pilot. In that unlikely event, all you need to do is press the big red button above the pilot's seat and then go back to your own seat, relax (yeah, right?), and enjoy the view. As this is one of the first times that the emergency autoland system has been deployed, the pilot takes the opportunity actually to show you the big red button while the message is being played, so that all six passengers know what to do and where the button is. The pilot jokes about her health as she shows you the button. In retrospect, she should not have done that. Half an hour into the flight, she has a heart attack that incapacitates her (for simplicity's sake, let's just suppose that the pilot dies instantly, I'm afraid). As instructed, you take it upon yourself to go up front to press the big red button for the emergency autoland. The same voice from the earlier message now runs you through what is going to happen, but there really isn't anything else that you need to do apart from going back to your seat, putting your seatbelt on, and "enjoying" your first and hopefully last emergency autoland. The computer system does indeed land the plane safely at a nearby airport.

Who had what kind of control in this scenario? There are three relevant parties: the pilot, the AI system, and the six passengers (but I will just stick to you, the one who pressed the red button, for simplicity's sake). Who is in control when? The following seems true: up until the pilot's incapacitation, the pilot was in control. And that was the case whether or not the pilot was using any so-called autopilot systems on the plane at the moment of her incapacitation. Whether the pilot was manually piloting the plane at the moment when she was incapacitated or whether she had already—as it is likely—activated an autopilot computer system like most commercial planes use most of the time, the human pilot was in control all the way up to when she became incapacitated and then died as a result of her heart attack.

Was there any time when you, the passenger with zero flight experience who pushed the big red button, were in control? I would argue that, in fact, you were in control the whole time and that, for most of the time, you had overall control while, for a few seconds, you had some direct control. The few seconds in questions are the ones between the moment when the pilot was incapacitated up to the moment when the emergency autoland system was manually activated by your pressing the big red button.

As it happens, we can suppose that this took just under two minutes: the time it took you to realize that the pilot was having a heart attack, plus the time it took to decide, together with your fellow passengers, that it was serious enough to have to intervene, plus finally the time it took you to actually go up front and press the button, thereby activating the emergency autoland system. In these two minutes, I argue you were directly controlling the plane.

Obviously, someone might object that you were not directly controlling the plane but rather that for these two minutes the plane was out of control—namely, nobody was controlling the plane in the two minutes between when the pilot was incapacitated and when the autoland emergency system kicked in. But I don't think that's good enough, because it fails to explain why—miraculously—the autoland system kicks in and lands the plane. Because clearly it was not a miracle: you had the relevant knowledge (including about the condition of the pilot) and the relevant abilities to activate the autoland emergency system, and you did so successfully.

Now compare the two minutes above in which there are six passengers, at least one of whom is in the right epistemic position to intervene, with another two minutes on a parallel flight with the same system (and also everything else is the same) in which the only difference is that the six passengers did not understand the security instructions at the beginning; maybe the message was in Chinese, or maybe the passengers are kids or whatever. Missing that crucial bit of information, it is difficult to imagine that these alternative six passengers would know what to do; after all, the emergency autoland system has just been introduced, so they might not even know that it exists, and even if they have heard about it, they might not imagine that it is installed on their particular plane, and even if they might imagine the possibility of there being such a system on their plane, they might not know which button to push.

In this alternative two minutes—and in fact independent of what happens after the two minutes—the passengers are not in control and nobody is in control of the plane. It might still be that, in this alternative scenario, things work out for the best. Maybe the passengers manage to contact air traffic control, thereby finding out that they are lucky enough to be in a plane with an emergency autoland system. Air traffic control tells them what to do, and everything happens afterward as in the original scenario. Or maybe not. But the point of this alternative scenario is to emphasize that in our original scenario at least one of the passengers was in control even in the two-minute interval.

In fact, I would describe the original scenario as follows: The passengers delegate flying of the plane to the pilot, who is appropriately qualified. Up to the moment when the pilot is incapacitated, the pilot is directly controlling the plane (or also delegating to some autopilot system, but let's not complicate things here) and the passengers are in overall control. In the two-minute interval the passengers take direct control of the plane, and afterward they are again delegating but this time to the emergency autoland system. The passengers, given that some epistemic conditions are met (which distinguish this scenario from the other one above), are all the time in control of the situation, either directly or through successful delegation. The interesting thing about this scenario is that you can argue the passengers delegated successfully even though something as unlikely and unfortunate as the pilot's heart attack happened.

DESIGNING DIRECT CONTROL

Something interesting about this scenario distinguishes it from a classic AWS scenario: once the emergency autoland system has been activated by the passengers manually, there is nothing else that the passengers need to do, but there is also nothing else that the passengers can in fact do. As in, the passengers do not need to supervise the emergency autoland system that is going to land the plane. And in fact, this is an important feature of the system: given that the average passenger is not an expert, you don't want to develop and implement a system that needs supervision, because passengers wouldn't be in a position to supervise the system successfully.

There is, though, another side to the fact that the emergency autoland system does not need supervision: there is literally nothing that the passengers can do once it has been activated. And that's good and bad. What happens in the extremely unlikely scenario in which, after the human pilot is incapacitated and the system has been activated, the autoland system malfunctions? The passengers are powerless to react to a system malfunction. That's part of the design because of their missing expertise. But doesn't that mean that the passengers are not, after all, in control after the system has been activated?

Before trying to answer this question, I should compare my emergency autoland scenario to an AWS scenario. It seems crazy to even contemplate the idea that an AWS would be deployed the way the emergency autoland is deployed, so that once it has been activated/deployed there is nothing humans can do to stop it. Generally, everybody would agree that some ultimate human control—maybe as general as turning off the machine or as specific as the power to veto particular steps—is necessary for AWSs; the literature talks in this context of so-called *meaningful human control*, as I mentioned in chapter 3.

There is, then, an important and interesting difference between the emergency autoland system and the autonomous weapon system (I find that after enough pages, acronyms should be written in full again, just to keep everybody awake): in one case you want to explicitly rule out, already at the design stage, the possibility of human intervention or interference (emergency autoland), while in the other case you want to explicitly rule in at the same design stage the possibility of human intervention or interference (AWS).

This difference does not actually have much to do with the technologies in place, which could easily be very similar. The difference mostly has to do with two features of the situations that I am comparing: the emergency character of the first situation, combined with the lack of relevant expertise among the passengers, and the lethal nature of AWSs.

The difference I have identified does not need to actually occur, going back to the distinction between occurrent and dispositional that got me started on these scenarios. In fact, hopefully in most cases of both systems, there is no human intervention because things are going according to plan. But still, for the emergency autoland system, once the red button has been pushed, there is no chance of human intervention, while with AWSs, oversight doesn't intervene if the system does what it is supposed to do.

On a side note, I could also imagine regulating AWSs so that there are some activities that could not be carried out with only human oversight but where there is some occurrent action that is needed, so that, for example, one might require that targeting be actively confirmed by some human action, because maybe everybody fell asleep or the whole base has been poisoned so that there is nobody to confirm—compare this to Stanislav Petrov in chapter 4. But—at least in principle—there is no need to stipulate that every step be confirmed by active human intervention. Because if we did, then there would be no point in delegating anymore—and, in fact, no point in using the technological system in the first place.

How can I claim that humans are in control in both cases if the two scenarios are so different such that only in one of them can humans actually intervene? This is, really, another version of the previous question of whether the passengers are really in control after the emergency autoland has been activated, given that there is nothing else they can do. The reason I think I can speak of overall control in such cases, even though the passengers can't intervene anymore, is that the system has been designed to make the passenger's intervention unnecessary based on a reasonable assumption about their lack of experience. Basically, the average passenger's intervention was likely to reduce overall control instead of increase it. And that assessment stands even if I include the very unlikely cases in which the emergency system malfunctions—if the system has been designed well, that is.

Let me explain: given the likelihood of a passenger being able to manually land the plane in such an emergency, and given the likelihood of the emergency autoland system malfunctioning, it is actually beneficial from a control-design point of view to rule out the possibility of passenger intervention after the system has been activated. Maybe those probability values could be different, like in a future world in which the average person is as knowledgeable about flying as they are now about driving, or maybe in a parallel world in which the designer of the emergency autoland system has developed a technology that is not very reliable.

Combine those two possibilities and you might get a different outcome, where it is actually beneficial for the system to be vulnerable to human intervention. But given reasonable expectations about the flying abilities of passengers plus reasonable expectations about the safety of a system that the authorities would authorize (or maybe this one is in fact less reasonable; ask Boeing), then designers are, from the point of view of overall control, well advised to rule out passengers' intervention, because they might just get in the way of the safe landing of the plane by the emergency autoland system.

This is why I think that, in the particular scenario of the emergency autoland system, the fact that the passengers can no longer intervene after the system has been activated does not actually rule out their overall control. But I would want to resist this conclusion in a parallel AWS case, even if I keep steady the reliability of the computer system and the fallibility of the human chain of command. So that, when it comes to AWSs, there should be active human confirmation before the system can take particularly significant steps such as lethal ones.

Was this discussion not a great illustration of the control paradox? A certain technological system—the emergency autoland—is developed in order to enhance control, to make sure, specifically, that the pilot's incapacitation does not result in loss of control over the plane. At the same time, the very introduction of this supposedly control-enhancing system raises serious questions about whether there isn't, as a result of the system, loss of control, because the passengers cannot directly control the plane or in fact do anything once the system has kicked in.

What I appear to have is indeed a trade-off between overall control and direct control: in order for overall control to be maintained and enhanced, you need an automatic system that lands the plane while ruling out possible human interventions, namely, direct control. In the particular case of the emergency autoland system, you might argue that there is no real loss of control because, clearly, for passengers with no flying experience, the ability to manually intervene once the system has kicked in is no real advantage. So that you only have something to gain from having the automatic system kick in and land the plane, and you also gain from not designing into the system any further human intervention after the system has been activated.

So, for the particular case of the emergency autoland system, it might be argued that I have no control paradox because there is neither genuine loss of control, nor is there any increased risk—in fact, risks should be decreasing as the result of introducing such systems—nor, finally, is there any reasonable fear of loss of control that should result from the introduction of such systems.

Here, importantly, I must distinguish between a normative and a descriptive version of the "fear" interpretation of the control paradox.

Descriptive Fear of Control Loss

Here the idea is simply that control-enhancing technologies increase fear of loss of control, whether or not these fears are reasonable. Again taking the emergency autoland case, one could imagine a group of passengers that— even though they have been informed regarding the functioning of the system—are still afraid of the prospect of the automatic autoland system landing the plane without human intervention or assistance. Even if this fear turns out to be unreasonable, if the third interpretation of the control paradox is understood in purely descriptive terms, just the psychological or statistical reality of such fears connected to technology will be enough.

Normative Fear of Control Loss

Here the idea is that there is only a paradox when control-enhancing technologies give rise to reasonable fears about losing control. Who is going to decide which kind of technophobia is reasonable and which is not? This question is why it is often advisable to stay clear of normative characterizations, but I still think that there is quite a bit I can say in trying to give some answer to the question. How reasonable is it, for example, to be afraid that the emergency autoland system will malfunction? After all, using statistics to calm down a passenger whose pilot has just had an incapacitating heart attack will clearly not do, given the minimal statistical chances that a pilot has a heart attack in flight in the first place.

These are difficult questions, but again that does not mean that the questions cannot be answered at all. Take the following case: even though none of the passengers has any experience of landing a plane, your technophobia is such that you prefer taking a huge risk—having a complete amateur try to land a plane for the first time in an emergency situation—to activating the emergency autoland by pressing the red button, even though you have been fully briefed about the way the system functions and the way it has been tested and how it came to get FAA approval (you are a technophobic geek, so you researched all these questions in advance of your first flight on a plane equipped with emergency autoland).

I am not going to labor this point any further; it was just meant as a representative example of the ways we can try to make some sense of what it means to distinguish between reasonable and unreasonable technophobia.

THE AWS CONTROL PARADOX

There is one final question I must answer and then I can move on: the control paradox, I have shown, does not apply to emergency autoland. But does it apply to my original example for this chapter, AWSs? Now I have many more tools to try to answer this question, because I have discussed at some length the way AWSs might constitute control-enhancing technologies—more precision and efficiency, more overall control. And I have also shown in some detail the way AWSs could be argued to challenge control, for example, with systems in which human intervention has been designed away.

One possible way out of the paradox for AWSs could be to argue, along the lines sketched in this chapter, that some steps should still be subject to

active human authorization, while other steps might only need

passive human supervision, and maybe there are even further steps that can be

fully automated; what that will mean in practice is obviously a crucial further question, because lots of safety mechanisms and feedback loops relating back to both human authorization and human supervision would have to be designed into a "fully automated" system; still, I believe the language of automation and even full automation is much more helpful than the language of autonomy, when it comes to these AI systems and machine learning algorithms.

And exactly which tasks should belong to which category does not need to be decided here in any detail and could in fact depend on the particular technology and the specifics of the mission, so that a surveillance operation might distribute tasks differently from a lethal targeting operation.

Where does this leave the AWS control paradox? I can now answer: is it reasonable to be worried about the prospect of lethal targeting or killing decisions being fully automated? On the evidence of this book so far, it is certainly not completely unreasonable to be preoccupied. And that's not because of some slippery-slope argument about increasing automation or the possibility of AWSs coming into the hands of some evil power. Rather, I just need to think about this book's hero, Stanislav Petrov. When it comes to defense mechanisms, effective prevention might have everything to do with time, so that the reason to automate a defensive reaction—which might be a killing decision—could well end up being that only a fully automated defensive reaction would be, in some particular set of circumstances, effective. Just because human authorization might be too slow, and come too late.

Paradoxically enough, these reasonable worries about loss of control come from a system that is designed for the very purpose of increasing control over tasks such as military surveillance or lethal targeting. So a technological system designed to improve control ends up giving rise to reasonable fears of losing control. That's the control paradox for you, at least in its normative *strong* interpretation. And if we do end up in a world with fully automated lethal targeting, maybe the stronger and strongest interpretations of the control paradox will also have been vindicated. Hopefully not.

Chapter Seven

VAR, Authority, and Loss of Control

Philosophy is fun, but it is still work. Not just in the sense that it is difficult and that you need to work at it; it is work also in the sense that it is what I do for a living. That is why it is with a funny feeling that I approach this next chapter, because I never expected I would write about football on the job. But here we go. If I get carried away—and I already know that I will—you have at least been warned.

If you are interested in control and technology, and you also happen to follow football, then you must have given some thought to one of the few technological innovations that football has been going through over the last couple of years: the video assistant referee or VAR. I think we can learn quite a lot about control and technology from the debates on VAR that have been raging recently, even just in the media or in the stands, and that's what this chapter will try to do, ultimately applying my control paradox to VAR.

VAR, as you will find out in this chapter, happens to be quite a complex phenomenon, but in its most simple instantiation it is just the possibility for referees (which have been complemented by extra VAR specialist referees) of reviewing something that has happened on the pitch through video—think offside, handball, penalties, red cards, whether the ball has crossed the line, and the like.

Before I start, I must tell you the story of my own little football trauma as a kid. It was the Year of the Lord 1998—and in some communities I would not have to mention anything other than that year and everybody would immediately know. But if you don't happen to belong to any such football community, just Google a combination of the following terms: *Ronaldo, Iuliano, 1998*. That's enough to get the evidence you need; don't worry about the name of the referee—spare me the pain of writing down his name!

Have you seen it? Okay, now I can give you some context. Like most Italian boys growing up in the 1980s and 1990s, football was my social life. That wasn't so bad if you were a supporter of, say, Juve or Milan—less so if you happened to be, like myself, an Inter supporter. Because we lost, and then we lost again, and then we lost some more, and finally, we lost one more time. In fact, the losing did not stop on that infamous day in 1998; the losing went on, long enough for there to be another infamous day, the 5th of May 2002, even though that one is less relevant as background for VAR, so I can thankfully spare you (and me) one more losing story.

Anyway, in the spring of 1998, I was a sixteen-year-old Inter supporter who, for the first time, dared to consider the possibility that maybe, one day, the losing would stop. And the reason for that was simple enough: Inter had acquired a literally unstoppable striker by the name of Ronaldo who had already won a World Cup and would go on to win a second one before leaving Inter, in between overshadowing the final of a third World Cup because of his conspicuous struggles on the pitch.

So anyway, this Ronaldo fellow could not be stopped, and the video that you will have seen by now shows you the lengths to which Italian defenders would go to take him down. Now the surprising thing about that video—and let me reassure you, I really don't need to watch it again—is that no penalty was given. In fact, in a particularly cruel twist of events, they kept playing and—at the other end of the pitch—it is Juve that got a penalty (but they missed). That Ronaldo–Iuliano penalty that never was decided not just that match or that whole season; it became the paradigmatic example of a whole era of Italian football that would end, in 2006, with Juve being stripped of titles and relegated to a lower league.

So it was a pretty big deal, that penalty—and you won't find many Italians or indeed many football fans of a certain age who don't know about the episode. Basically, Ronaldo with a single touch had already moved the ball past Iuliano, going around the defender's left side, when Iuliano completely ignored where the ball was to just bodycheck Ronaldo and take him down in the middle of the penalty area. Clear as day, but the penalty was not given.

RONALDO, IULIANO, AND VAR

Let's see what would happen today in such a situation now that we have VAR. Basically, there are three possibilities:

- The referee herself could ask for advice from the video referee.
- The referee could ask to watch video footage of the episode herself by interrupting play and going to a dedicated screen on the side of the pitch.
- The video referee could call the referee to point out the mistake.

As you might anticipate, the technology itself is pretty basic, just screens and video footage—if necessary in slow motion. Sure, there are multiple cameras, and these days, for big matches, there might be quite a lot of cameras and quite a lot of different perspectives that the cameras give you on any single event on the pitch. And finally there are those additional referees, who now spend the game behind the screen (and in fact the term *VAR* itself does not refer to the technology but to the human person who watches those screens). But still we are not speaking of intelligent technologies like in other chapters in this book; not much is automated with VAR, and there still is a lot of human judgment involved. In fact, you will see that, according to some, there is still too much human judgment involved.

The Iuliano–Ronaldo episode was so clear-cut that you can imagine the following: if the referee had not herself asked for advice from the video referee, then the video referee would have surely called upon the attention of the referee, and it is easy to imagine that the video referee would have pointed to the "possible" penalty, and that the referee would have interrupted the match to go check for herself, at the end of which (it can take some time) the referee would have surely concluded from the video footage that it was a clear penalty. Would Inter then have gone on to win that game and the title? Surely!

What is the point of VAR technology? Briefly, it is a technological system that assists referees to reduce the number of mistaken decisions they make. So VAR is a decision-support system, like the Soviet system in chapter 4 and like the healthcare systems you will learn about in later chapters. Whether such systems are intelligent or not, what they have in common is that they assist human judgment; at least in theory, they are not supposed to replace or automate human judgment.

It is still the human referee who makes the decision, but the evidence upon which the decision is based is now supplemented through VAR. You can think of it in terms of how, in the old days, referees might sometimes consult their linesmen before making some decisions. It was still always the referee making the final call; all the linesman could provide was a piece of additional evidence. The same is—at least in theory—true of technological decision-support systems, and the same should be true of VAR.

This also tells you the real reason a philosophy book contains a chapter about VAR: namely, VAR provides a good case study in decision-support systems, and given that a lot of the AI systems that we are currently delegating control to are decision-support systems (for example, IBM Watson for Oncology), it is important to get an understanding of what happens to control when we deploy decision-support systems as our trusted advisers.

Small aside: given that in the last part of this book I will apply this discussion to political power, it is useful here to stress the similarity between decision-support systems and politicians' special advisers. The structure appears to be the same, where the person who carries the political responsibility (say, the minister or secretary of state) will ultimately have to make the decision and pass judgment, but that decision and judgment are made on the basis of (expert) advice. In reality, only the most momentous decisions are made by those carrying political responsibility, while all other decisions are ultimately delegated to advisers and subordinates.

Why is that important? Because it allows me to distinguish between two different roles for decision-support systems, whether they are human or technological ones:

- Decision-support systems might have the role of providing advice and evidence—whether automated or not—to the decision-maker.
- Decision-support systems might alternatively be delegated to in order to make decisions themselves.

Take the simple case of VAR. It's one thing for the referee on the pitch to ask a second opinion from the referee behind the screen, but it's a different thing if the referee on the pitch admits to the one behind the screen to not having seen what happened and asks them what happened, thereby asking them to make the decision on her behalf, even though the decision-making authority has not left—at least in principle—the decision-maker on the pitch. This last point will be crucial beyond this one chapter, so keep it in mind. Who is the real decision-maker in these latter kinds of cases? And what happens to control and authority as a result of it?

VAR RULES

Before I continue, here is a summary of the official VAR rules from the International Football Association Board's Laws of the Game (IFAB 2018):

> The VAR protocol, as far as possible, conforms to the principles and philosophy of the Laws of the Game. The use of video assistant referees (VARs) is only permitted where the match/competition organiser has fulfilled all the VAR protocol and implementation requirements (as set out in the VAR Handbook) and has received written permission from The IFAB and FIFA.
>
> Principles: The use of VARs in football matches is based on a number of principles, all of which must apply in every match using VARs.
>
> 1. *A video assistant referee (VAR) is a match official,* with independent access to match footage, who may assist the referee only in the event of a "clear and obvious error" or "serious missed incident" in relation to:
> a. Goal/no goal
> b. Penalty/no penalty
> c. Direct red card (not second yellow card/caution)

d. Mistaken identity (when the referee cautions or sends off the wrong player of the offending team)

2. *The referee must always make a decision,* i.e. the referee is not permitted to give "no decision" and then use the VAR to make the decision; a decision to allow play to continue after an alleged offence can be reviewed.

3. The original decision given by the referee will not be changed unless the video review clearly shows that the decision was a *"clear and obvious error".*

4. *Only the referee can initiate a "review"*; the VAR (and other match officials) can only recommend a "review" to the referee.

5. *The final decision is always taken by the referee,* either based on information from the VAR or after the referee has undertaken an "on-field review" (OFR).

6. There is no time limit for the review process as accuracy is more important than speed.

7. The players and team officials must not surround the referee or attempt to influence if a decision is reviewed, the review process or the final decision.

8. The referee must remain "visible" during the review process to ensure transparency.

9. If play continues after an incident which is then reviewed, any disciplinary action taken/required during the post-incident period is not cancelled, even if the original decision is changed (except a caution/sendoff for stopping a promising attack or DOGSO).

10. If play has stopped and been restarted, the referee may not undertake a "review" except for a case of mistaken identity or for a potential sending-off offence relating to violent conduct, spitting, biting or extremely offensive, insulting and/or abusive gesture(s).

11. The period of play before and after an incident that can be reviewed is determined by the Laws of the Game and VAR protocol.

12. As the VAR will automatically "check" every situation/decision, there is no need for coaches or players to request a "review."[1]

I have taken the liberty to emphasize what I take to be crucial aspects of the VAR rules. First of all, these rules make an important clarification about the metaphysics of VAR, if you will. Namely, as you can clearly read under point 1, VAR is not a technological system; VAR is a person, the human referee who sits in front of the screens. It is interesting to note how already in these first few years, though, the terminology of VAR has developed to refer to the whole system, which includes the rule changes and the technology, while it was clearly originally intended as referring only to a person.

And this is no small matter, whether you have complicated the decision-making process by delegating part of it to a further human referee without any decisional authority or you are delegating to a complex technological system, with or without decisional authority. At least the intention, you might gather from point 1, was to keep things simple, but the simple historical fact that we now use the term *VAR* to refer to the technology rather than the additional referee shows that the change was underestimated or, at least, that the choice of terminology was meant to present the change as less disruptive than it turned out to be.

Yes, let me say it in such simple terms because it is helpful: *VAR has disrupted football*, which does not yet mean that it has *destroyed* it, obviously. Was the disruption worth it? Before I turn to that question, a few more comments on the VAR rules I have emphasized above. If you look under points 2, 3, 4, and 5, it is interesting to note that all of them seem aimed at limiting the disruption and also at doing damage control in terms of the referee's empowerment. It looks as though the rule makers understood that VAR was going to represent a threat to the referee's authority and took some steps to limit the damage and contain the threat, such as with the idea that the referee must still always make a decision.

Apparently, according to point 2 of the VAR rules, VAR can also be deployed to assess a decision made by the referee but not to make itself a decision where the referee made no decision. But this point rings hollow, and in fact the rule goes on to say that *a decision to allow play to continue after an alleged offence can be reviewed*, which pretty much contradicts the previous point, as now suddenly you also have the possible decision to allow play to continue, which is not a decision. Or, at least, if allowing play to continue also counts as a decision, then is there anything that will not count as the referee making a decision? Namely, is it even possible to violate VAR rule number 2?

Two points here: First, these rules can be understood as guidelines, so maybe even if it is not possible to actually violate rule number 2 because the referee is always deciding even when they are not actually making any decision or intervention but rather allowing play to continue, the VAR rules understood as guidelines are helpful in emphasizing that the referee should not become more passive as a result of the introduction of VAR. So really what point 2 represents is a reminder to the referee not to become too passive, instead of an actual rule that the referee ought not to violate, given that it might actually be impossible to violate the rule, because allowing play to continue also counts as a decision.

Second, maybe there still is a difference—at least philosophically—between allowing play to continue as a decision on the part of the referee and not making a decision. You could appeal to the difference between omissions and not-doings (Sartorio 2005, 2009; Clarke 2014). To see this difference, imagine the distinction between a version of Ronaldo–Iuliano 1998—call it RI98A—in which the referee (no, don't ask me his name . . . I remember it too well but won't write it here!) sees the foul but decides that it is not a foul and therefore allows play to continue, and another version of Ronaldo–Iuliano 1998—call it RI98B—in which the referee does not see the foul; in fact, you can also imagine a third version of Ronaldo–Iuliano 1998—which is the one endorsed by Inter fans—RI98C, in which the ref sees the foul, recognizes it as such, but still does not give the penalty (because the ref is supposedly in Juve's pocket, as Inter fans have been arguing for the last twenty years).

Those three versions of events are importantly different, first of all from an ethical point of view. But what those three versions have in common is that in all of them referees allow play to continue. But in which of these three versions do referees make a decision? It seems to me that referees only makes a decision in RI98A and RI98C, while referees do not make any decision in RI98B, simply because they didn't see anything on which to make a decision. Things could easily get more complicated here if I added the intentions of referees to the equation, but for now it is enough to have shown that it is in fact possible to distinguish between referees making the decision of allowing play to continue and referees making no decision, with the result that play continues.

I have a similar problem when I look at point 4 of the VAR rules, where you read that only referees can *initiate* a review but that VAR referees can *recommend* a review. What's the difference here? Again it sounds like what the rule makers had in mind was protecting referees from disempowerment. Only referees have the authority to decide whether to involve VAR, according to rule 4. This is important because it means that at least in principle referees could run a game like in the old days and never rely on VAR or call on its assistance. And it is indeed easy to see the difference between self-confident authoritative refereeing, on the one hand, and relying on VAR too much and thereby losing authority, on the other.

What I want to focus on for point 4, though, is this supposed distinction between the referee's decisional authority over initiating a VAR review and the VAR referee's role being limited to recommending a VAR review. There are different ways of understanding this. For example, one could imagine a system in which it is only if the referee actually makes contact with her colleagues behind the TV screens that a review can be initiated. That way, you could imagine a case in which the referee makes contact and asks the VAR referee whether there are any grounds for initiating a review. That gives substantial authority to the referee, who cannot even be disturbed by her colleagues behind the TV screens. She can call them, but they are not allowed to call her. That would be a simple structure to preserve referee authority on the pitch, but as you will see that's not the model currently being used.

In fact, what the possibility of the VAR referee recommending a review to the on-pitch referee points to and the way the rules have been applied in different leagues is that the two referees are in constant contact with each other, and if the VAR referee sees on the screen something that she believes deserves the attention of the on-pitch referee, then she just tells the referee that something is wrong. It is, in short, a proper collaboration—it is not even clear whether it is a form of delegation; the on-pitch referee might not even have the kind of power, authority, and control that comes with delegation. It is to this question that I now turn: is VAR a form of delegation?

VAR AS DELEGATION

Is the on-pitch referee delegating any task to the VAR system? On the face of it, the referee is not delegating anything, at least in the sense that there does not seem to be any task that the referee used to fulfill herself and that now has been delegated to the VAR. But surely one could imagine a psychologically plausible scenario in which, say, a referee does not need to pay as much attention to what happens on the pitch (which is an awful lot, I don't know how they do it, and, apart from that particular 1998 referee, they have my utmost respect).

Now I am slowly approaching the paradox: should we be worried that VAR is making referees both less authoritative on the pitch but also less attentive? After all, they now have backup; they can afford to make mistakes in a way that they could not have afforded in the old days. So here is a paradox of sorts: You provide on-pitch referees with backup in the form of many cameras covering (almost) every corner of the pitch; they should, equipped with all these fancy high-resolution cameras, have a much better idea of what happens on the pitch. And in fact error rates have been substantially reduced. VAR has been found to reduce errors by about 80 percent, even though there are genuine questions—given the nature of the relevant decision-making[2] —about how to measure error reduction through VAR (see *Economist* 2018).

Given these numbers,[3] it would not be out of the question to argue that referees have been empowered and that they have more and better control over what happens on the pitch. But I think that this characterization would be premature: first of all, an error rate reduction of 80 percent—even if we take it at face value—cannot be attributed to the on-pitch referee alone but must be attributed to the on-pitch referee plus VAR.

Here a couple of boring distinctions must be made. First, there could be ways of measuring the performance of referees now that there is VAR without accounting for VAR corrections. I am not familiar with any such study, but the idea would be that we check for whether referees, on their own, are making more or fewer mistakes than before. After all, the video footage that we now have with VAR we had before; it's just that it can now play a role during the game. So it should in principle be possible to test the current performance of referees on their own, now that VAR is there as backup.

As I said, there are plausible psychological hypotheses going both ways. It could be that that referees now know that they have backup, pay less attention, relax too much, and make more mistakes. Or it could be that referees now know they can be instantly corrected all the time, are much more focused, and make fewer mistakes. Again, the point here is not which way the evidence points; the point is more simply that the very possibility of such an experiment shows that there are at least two different ways of measuring error rates, and that the 80 percent reduction referenced above refers to error rates for referees plus VAR and not to error rates for referees on their own.

The other boring point is related: are we really allowed to say, conceptually, that those error rates refer to referees plus VAR rather than to referees alone, given that the decisional authority—as you saw in the VAR rules—lies with the on-pitch referee alone? So it is, after all, the on-pitch referee that is now making fewer mistakes, because only they make decisions.

Is this conceptual cherry-picking? I am not so sure. After all, if you can make sure that the on-pitch referee really has decisional authority and that such authority is not undermined by the VAR, then you might be able to conclude—meaningfully—that it is the decision-maker who has gotten better, because they have better advice, or better evidence. That is, in itself, an interesting question, whether to characterize the VAR as advice, evidence, or even shared decision-making, a technical term from healthcare (see McDougall [2019a, 2019b] and Di Nucci [2019] for a debate about shared decision-making and AI decision-support systems within healthcare).

This methodological discussion about error rate reduction was meant to address the hypothesis according to which, given that now fewer mistakes are being made, you can argue that the referee has more or better control of the pitch, and given the point about the ultimate decisional authority being in the hands of the ref, you can make that hypothesis specific to the human referee on the pitch rather than together with VAR or some such aggregate.

Let me then suppose that, indeed, through VAR, the human referee on the pitch has been empowered, at least in terms of control; she does not miss as much of what goes on as she did before. What consequence does that have for my control paradox? More importantly, what consequence does that have for the ethics of VAR and of football in general? The rest of this chapter will to try to establish this.

Having taken error rate reduction as evidence of control enhancing, the obvious next question is whether there is any control loss associated with VAR. I have already covered the issue of loss of authority for on-pitch referees: as you have seen, that issue is so serious that the VAR rules take some pains to protect the referee's authority. But there is another passage in the rules that might point in the opposite direction, point 12, according to which, "As the VAR will automatically 'check' every situation/decision, there is no need for coaches or players to request a 'review.'"

What is relevant for my argument here is this idea that VAR automatically checks every situation/decision. You might be tempted to say that even though I did not find any evidence of the on-pitch referee delegating to the VAR, ultimately it is the VAR that delegates to the on-pitch referee. That is, if the VAR checks *automatically* (whatever that means, but obviously this choice of terminology is a big deal in this book) every situation/decision, and if at the same time the VAR is allowed to recommend reviews, what is actually left for the on-pitch referee to do? They are supposed to be the decision-maker, but are they really, given that there is a complex human-technology system in the background (in the referee's ear, in fact) that checks everything and gets in touch when something is not right?

That's like the supervisor from hell, leaving hardly any flexibility to the supposed decision-maker. What rule number 12 points to—though whether it is being applied in reality is a different question—is the idea that the referee gets to decide only if they decide the way the VAR would have decided. But is that in any way an autonomous decision?

Imagine the following boss from hell, who delegates some task to you but is always checking you on both video and audio and corrects every tiny mistake you make. The first question you would have to ask is what the point of this supposed delegation is in the first place? The boss is doing live quality control, thereby not really sparing any resources. And given that he will always intervene if something does not go according to what he takes to be "right," there cannot be any strategic delegation either. So no economizing of resources—and therefore no economic delegation—and no improvement of performance—so no strategic delegation. What's the point of it all? In fact, does it even qualify as delegation according to my definition?

The boss from hell does not give up any direct control to you, given that he constantly surveils and corrects you at very misstep. And at the same time, the boss from hell not only has overall control; he actually has direct control. So it does not count as successful delegation according to my account from chapter 5, whatever the intentions of the boss from hell are. In fact, the only case in which you might imagine this to be a reasonable strategy would be for training purposes.

Is VAR the boss from hell? On the one hand, VAR, like the boss from hell, is always watching over the referee. On the other hand—as the referee has the decisional authority—one could argue, as I did earlier, that a referee could, at least in principle, run a whole game with no VAR involvement, no matter what came through the earpiece, which the referee has the authority to just ignore. So the referee is her own boss, and therefore, it could be argued, the VAR cannot be compared to the boss from hell. But this story is only true in principle, because the worry is that even if in principle the referee on the pitch has full decisional authority, by having the VAR always watching over the referee, that authority will inevitably be eroded. After all, anyone would lose her self-confidence if Big Brother was checking her every move and every decision.

I need to distinguish between the principled point recognized by the VAR rules that the referee has ultimate decisional authority (point 5, "The final decision is always taken by the referee") and the possible erosion of such authority through this idea that the VAR checks automatically every decision/situation (point 12, "the VAR will automatically 'check' every situation/decision").

One small caveat: you should not read too much into this idea that the VAR "automatically" checks every decision/situation. Even though this could erode authority, it is also plausible that the reason the Laws of the Game emphasize the "automatic" nature of these VAR checks is again to stress that the referee behind the screens has no discretion (because they cannot decide what to check and what not to check but must rather check everything *automatically*), because all the discretion resides with the referee on the pitch.

Here I could have again an instantiation of the paradox, where the rule makers stressed the "automatic" nature of the checks in order not to give any discretion and authority to the VAR, but ended up creating a monster that watches over the referee all the time, ultimately eroding the authority of the referee—exactly what the rules are trying hard to avoid.

So I have my paradox in the end, in some form or another. It might end up being a paradox of authority instead of one of control, or it might be that it is no paradox at all because it is a trade-off between two different things—say, more control of what happens on the pitch, the price of which ends up being authority erosion.

To conclude, I just want to stress the obvious in saying that this was not a full-blown evaluation of VAR, and it wasn't even a full ethical evaluation of VAR. I was just interested in stressing the control and authority aspects of the implementation of VAR. Two obvious points that have therefore been left out of my analysis are, first, the idea that some decisions in football are intrinsically discretional and therefore cannot be fully automated, and, second and arguably more important, the idea that, independent of error rate reduction or authority erosion, VAR might not be worth it because it spoils the excitement of football, which exists very much in the moment. On that 26th of April 1998, that moment was the seventieth minute.[4]

Chapter Eight

Self-Driving Cars and Meaningful Human Control

Having already analyzed drones, AWSs, and emergency autoland systems, I feel like there is hardly any need left to look into so-called self-driving cars.[1] Also, I must admit some basic skepticism of the hype surrounding self-driving cars. Does innovation in the twenty-first century really still have to go through the automobile? Shouldn't the future rather be car-free? Think of the environment, and don't mistake self-driving cars with electric ones. Basically, it seems to me that too much emphasis on self-driving developments within the automobile industry is just another way of supporting that—dying?—sector. That's why, together with the similarity between self-driving cars and the systems I have already analyzed in previous chapters (see especially chapter 6), I was very tempted to just skip the topic.

But the self-driving car is undeniably one of the most discussed applications of AI systems within the philosophical and ethical literature,[2] so before declaring it defunct and skipping it altogether, I had better make sure that there are no unique features of self-driving cars that transcend what I have discussed so far and that might indeed be relevant to the control paradox (also, given how prominent the old-fashioned Sally and Lola dual-control car scenario has been in previous chapters—see chapters 3 and 4—it seems only appropriate to cover my bases when it comes to cars). So that's what this chapter aims to do, but don't be too surprised if it ends up being short, the chapter. I for one would be delighted with that outcome.

A self-driving car is an automobile that is not manually driven by a human driver but rather by software that, through sensors and GPS, controls the car's direction, speed, and the like.[3] A self-driving car is, in this respect, more like an AWS than a drone, because there is no remote controlling. On the other hand, self-driving cars are meant to carry people from one place to another, so they are not—that ugly word again—unmanned. There is at least one person sitting inside the self-driving car. In fact, so far, that person is also in a position to take over direct control of the car from the software, but that might just be a transitional feature of this technology. One can easily, at least in principle, imagine a self-driving car carrying a child, a sleeping adult, or someone suffering from dementia—in fact, self-driving ambulances should be all the rage now that I think of it.

Here it already gets complicated—think of the emergency autoland discussion—but let's not get bogged down just yet, because obviously a self-driving car carrying a person with dementia or a child would have to have been programmed differently from one carrying a competent adult with a driver's license who could in theory intervene and take over direct control. So, for example, meaningful human control (see chapter 3 if you have forgotten about this concept) in the two different cases of the competent adult with a driver's license and the child or person with dementia ought to be different, as more intervention possibilities will only be meaningful for the competent adult while, in fact, the possibility of intervention might be detrimental for the child or otherwise impaired person, as you saw in chapter 6 with the emergency autoland system.

As in chapter 6, this point is crucial to my overall argument in this book, so I want to be very clear here: if the vehicle is transporting a child or a person with dementia, just about any access to the vehicle control mechanisms would amount to less control rather than more control. Still, I should be careful with exceptions here, because given the child's age or the stage of the dementia, it might still make sense to give whoever is inside access to some nondriving controls, such as the ability to open the doors in case of an accident or if the car hasn't moved for a certain amount of time. But that would be very different from, say, giving access to breaking controls.

And obviously the same applies even when I come away from these kinds of extreme cases, so that whether or not the person has a driver's license should also make a difference to access to controls. You could, for example, imagine self-driving cars in which the person instead of having to use a key to turn the ignition would have to insert a digital driver's license or code so that the system can reconfigure accordingly to whether it is driving around a competent person or not—whether competent can be defined cognitively, like in the former case, or just in terms of driving capacities, like in the latter case. It is very plausible to think that the amount of access and control that the self-driving system should give to those sitting inside the car will depend on the following:

- Cognitive capacities, to give protection to children, elderly people, or persons with disabilities

- Driving capacities, to run a different algorithm when the person inside the car has a driver's license as opposed to not having one—yes, there is an increasing number of adults without licenses . . . young people these days, eh?
- The system's programming, which should be flexible for different wishes of the customer, the way traditional cars have already for a while had the option of activating or deactivating some kind of speed control

The details of the above alternatives are well beyond the scope of a philosophy book: the point is just that more access does not mean more control given a set of background capacities, and in fact given those capacities less access might mean more control, like with the emergency autoland system. There is therefore no need to go into further details about these different possibilities, but it was important to set out from the beginning of this chapter ways control can be more or less meaningful, which is actually another way of saying that control can be more or less control—the usefulness of talking of "meaningful" in the context of an already normatively loaded concept such as control being one of the questions I should answer by the end of this chapter.

Basically, my starting point is that control can only be meaningful because meaningless control is no control at all. But things are not that simple because, within the "meaningful human control" concept, it might well turn out that "meaningful" does not refer to the "control" element—which is obvious, as you have seen—but to the human element, the basic claim being that humans must be meaningfully involved in control processes. Having anticipated this complication, I can now proceed with my analysis of self-driving cars.

SELF-DRIVING CARS AND DIFFERENT FORMS OF DELEGATION (INCLUDING SOME NEW ONES)

A self-driving car is controlled through software, like AWSs, but, different from AWSs, is not unmanned. Why, you might wonder, would anybody be interested in self-driving cars? Driving is, after all, fun, right? Well, first of all, driving is not fun for everybody, and certainly it is not fun all of the time—think of traffic, or if German motorways were tempo-limited to 120 kilometers per hour. Not that much fun anymore, I bet. In fact, in that case, probably automakers would finally go bankrupt and nobody would be pushing self-driving cars anymore, and I could spare myself this chapter. But that won't happen anytime soon, I don't think. Anyway, so driving is not always fun and it is not fun for everybody, and for the times when driving is not fun—and for those people for whom driving is no fun—there's software for that.

It is, obviously, not just a question of fun. Driving is time and energy consuming, especially in terms of attention resources (look back to chapter 3 if you have already forgotten about attention resources). Think of everything you could get done if you didn't have to drive your car: work, play with your kids, read, or finally finish that never-ending TV series before winter comes.[4] All those things and many more you could do while software drives your car.

Already, I can see some basic problems with this motivation for self-driving cars: first of all, some folk drive for a living, as in, their work *is* driving, so it's going to be difficult for them to find more time for work while someone or something else does the driving. In fact these people, like lorry drivers, have the opposite problem of freeing up more time for work; their problem is that self-driving cars might actually take work away from them. Their jobs will be, as people say these days, automated away (Susskind & Susskind 2015).[5] The economic consequences of automation have recently been promoted from geeky academia to geeky current affairs and politics through the surprisingly prominent if ultimately unsuccessful (dropped out after New Hampshire) primary campaign of Andrew Yang, but it is a complex topic that is all but new; employment increases and decreases but, most of all, changes its nature, location, and skill sets. So while it is probably not much more than an empty slogan to speak generally of jobs being automated away, specific jobs for particular workers in given locations are being automated away all the time and have been ever since at least the Industrial Revolution but probably even earlier.

There is also another problem with this basic application of my economic delegation framework to self-driving cars (I will look at the other framework, strategic delegation, in a minute, don't you worry): if you want more time for work, kids, Jon Snow (or reading a book!), then there is no need for such fancy new technologies such as self-driving cars. Trains have been providing that kind of attention resource efficiency for almost two hundred years now.

Economic delegation alone, then, can hardly provide a conclusive argument in favor of self-driving cars.[6] But what about strategic delegation? If on top of freeing up resources, having your car driven by software would make it—say—safer and quicker, then the argument starts to look much stronger. And it is in fact plausible that self-driving cars could prove both safer and quicker than cars driven by humans.

Just imagine that the relevant software can be taught, at the same time, how to drive safely and how to do things that human drivers cannot achieve—say, keep a minimal distance from the car in front, because break reaction times have been reduced and because the car in front is also driven by the same software, making it more predictable. This would allow for greater coordination in traffic.

So there could indeed be less traffic, and fewer accidents—which would cut transport times. That means that the benefit in terms of resource economizing would be double: you could get stuff done while the car drives itself, so that time spent in the car would not be wasted, and at the same time, you would end up spending less time in the car overall. Traditional cars are—it turns out—very inefficient, and that does not even have anything to do with climate.

Here I find an element that I have indeed not seen before, maybe making this chapter worthwhile after all. It's not just economic delegation and strategic delegation and delegation practices that are both economic and strategic (a washing machine, after all, can spare resources that you can reinvest elsewhere and also does a better job of washing your clothes than you would). Here I find a further link between economic delegation and strategic delegation: namely, strategic delegation can lead to economic delegation, because improved performance is not only an advantage in itself but also can result in resource economizing. So there are the following possibilities:

1. Economic delegation
2. Strategic delegation
3. Delegation that is both strategic and economic (self-driving cars might be such a case)
4. Strategic delegation leading to (further) economic delegation (is this the case for self-driving cars?), but there might be cases in which the only economizing is the result of improved performance

What about the reverse, economic delegation leading to strategic delegation? In a certain respect, most cases are supposed to show economic delegation leading to strategic delegation.

Take so-called medical AI, which uses machine learning algorithms within healthcare (chapter 10 covers medical AI in some detail, so I will be brief here). The idea is that delegating some of the human doctors' tasks to AI systems frees up resources for human doctors, already overworked, to provide better care to patients (I have recently written on this elsewhere; see, for example, Di Nucci 2019, Di Nucci et al. 2020; Grote & Di Nucci 2020; Tupasela & Di Nucci 2020).

Here, importantly, it doesn't in the first instance matter whether the medical AI provides better performance or enhanced control over the performance of human doctors. Because what I am looking for is a case of economic delegation leading to strategic delegation, it is enough to have equal performance from the AI system that frees up resources for the human doctors to provide better care—which would be the strategic bit. The only problem, and the reason I have not included this in the taxonomy, is this might in fact be a case of economic delegation providing better performance and therefore leading to strategic gains in terms of improved care, but that's not the same as saying that it leads to strategic delegation, because human doctors providing better care to patients is not be a case of delegation that would fulfill the criteria I set out in chapter 5.

Still, the important message is that economic delegation and strategic delegation can interact, and that economic delegation can lead to strategic gains and strategic delegation can lead to economic gains (remember how I defined this in chapter 5: "economic" does not mean "financial" in my framework; in fact, "economic" delegation can and often does cost money).

CONTROLLING SELF-DRIVING CARS

Let me go back to self-driving cars now, lest you, dear reader, should start believing I can't be bothered to discuss them. How does delegation work with self-driving cars? Straightforwardly, I appear to have a case in which you—the old-fashioned human driver—delegate the driving task to software; you give direct control of the car to the software in the same way Lola gives it to Sally, but you—in principle—keep overall control of the car the same way Lola does, ready to intervene if necessary.

This delegation has both strategic promise (less traffic, fewer accidents) and economic promise (sparing attention resources to be reinvested somewhere else: working, reading, kids, streaming, etc.). Put this way, it sounds like a paradigmatic case for my delegation framework: what could possibly go wrong?

At the time of this writing, there are six documented fatalities (over a period of just under four years) that can be attributed to self-driving cars, the most prominent being a pedestrian killed by a level 3 self-driving system (Lubben 2018), while all the other fatalities are drivers killed while on autopilot (level 2).[7] For context, within the same period in the United States alone, there have been around 140,000 deaths related to car accidents.[8] Obviously, the comparison is premature; if at all, what the numbers show is that there is a lot of potential for saving lives through self-driving cars.

Oh, right, not everyone is a self-driving car geek—fortunately—so I'd better explain level 2 and level 3 here. There are more, in fact: six automation levels are recognized by SAE, the Society for Automotive Engineers.[9] The levels go from 0—no automation—to 5—full automation. Figure 8.1 gives some further insight into how these classifications have been made. If you take a few seconds to study this figure, you will soon notice that, like any taxonomy, it's a guilty pleasure for a certain kind of philosopher, but I will try to indulge as little as possible, while at the same time reminding you that this book is not about the ethics of self-driving cars, so we only care about the relevance of these technologies for the control paradox. And even within the scope of just this chapter, my focus is on the paradox and the idea of meaningful human control and not on self-driving cars per se.

In trying to keep to that focus, allow me to make some very targeted comments on the taxonomy, the first being that levels 0, 1, and 2 are not normally considered self-driving systems in any sense of the word; they are just traditional cars equipped with the kind of assistance systems that we have been familiar with already for a while and that have been on the road for decades—so it is fitting that these levels are set off from the others. For my oversimplifying philosophical purposes, I can just say that levels 0 to 2 are not self-driving cars, even before offering a proper definition of self-driving cars. And the fact that most of the very few fatalities relating to self-driving cars are actually level 2 fatalities really means that these are not self-driving car fatalities. That is why—for once, appropriately—the only level 3 fatality has received so much media attention. It is only from level 3 upward that we should be talking of self-driving cars. Also, in another note of appreciation for this taxonomy, let me say that nowhere can you find talk of "autonomous" driving; the concept used is, rather, automation—and rightly so.

In addition on the taxonomy: it is difficult to see what the difference between level 4 and level 5 is supposed to be, from a system point of view.[10] So from a control perspective, the most important distinctions within this taxonomy seems to be between levels 0–2 on the one hand (manual control, if you like), level 3 (system control), and then levels 4 and 5 (full automation).

Levels 0–2 are pretty much a human driver, with more or less assistance, up to a human driver who has pressed autopilot and is only monitoring, the way pilots have been doing on commercial flights for a very long time—that's, I suppose, the standard model for level 2: autopilot. Importantly, level 2 autopilot needs to be manually activated and deactivated and needs constant monitoring.

The figure is useful in identifying three different tasks and assigning them to either the human driver or the system:

• Execution
• Monitoring
• Fallback performance

Execution is what distinguishes levels 0–1 from level 2, where in level 2 the human driver is no longer pressing pedals or steering the wheel, even though her feet will be near the pedals and her hands on the wheel.

Monitoring is what distinguishes level 2 from level 3, because in level 2 there is no intelligent system that reacts automatically to the road apart from

SAE level	Name	Narrative Definition	Execution of Steering and Acceleration/ Deceleration	*Monitoring of Driving Environment*	Fallback Performance of *Dynamic Driving Task*	Sy Cap (D Mo
Human driver monitors the driving environment						
0	No Automation	the full-time performance by the *human driver* of all aspects of the *dynamic driving task*, even when enhanced by warning or intervention systems	Human driver	Human driver	Human driver	
1	Driver Assistance	the *driving mode-*specific execution by a driver assistance system of either steering or acceleration/deceleration using information about the driving environment and with the expectation that the *human driver* perform all remaining aspects of the *dynamic driving task*	Human driver and system	Human driver	Human driver	Some m
2	Partial Automation	the *driving mode-*specific execution by one or more driver assistance systems of both steering and acceleration/ deceleration using information about the driving environment and with the expectation that the *human driver* perform all remaining aspects of the *dynamic driving task*	System	Human driver	Human driver	Some m
Automated driving system ("system") monitors the driving environment						
3	Conditional Automation	the *driving mode-*specific performance by an *automated driving system* of all aspects of the dynamic driving task with the expectation that the *human driver* will respond appropriately to a request to intervene	System	System	Human driver	Some m
4	High Automation	the *driving mode-*specific performance by an automated driving system of all aspects of the *dynamic driving task*, even if a *human driver* does not respond appropriately to a request to intervene	System	System	System	Some m
5	Full Automation	the full-time performance by an *automated driving system* of all aspects of the *dynamic driving task* under all roadway and environmental conditions that can be managed by a *human driver*	System	System	System	All me

ix SAE levels of automation for self-driving cars.

the human driver, while in level 3 there are at least two intelligent systems enabled to react to the road, both the human driver and the software, either of which can, say, take a left turn. And given that the software can do that, the human driver does not need to, within normal function.

That's the difference between level 3 and levels 4 and 5, finally—namely, what happens outside of normal function, for example, if the system requests human intervention. In level 3, you need a competent driver who can be expected to intervene if necessary—while levels 4 and 5 have also automated that fallback function and have been trained to no longer expect the assistance of a competent driver. That's—from level 4—where my earlier distinctions between competent and incompetent drivers come in; that is where the distinction between a human inside the car and no human in the car comes in as well.

This latter point should not be overemphasized: there could be human intervention from outside the vehicle, so one could imagine a level 3 system that requires human intervention as fallback, but where that human assistance is not provided by a competent human driver inside the car but rather by someone far away in a control room, for example—the way U.S. drones operating over Pakistan are remotely controlled from Tampa, Florida. The SAE taxonomy presupposes then the possibility of human intervention for some of its steps, but that is importantly not the same thing as presupposing a competent human driver inside the vehicle. And this in turn allows for the possibility of level 3 systems carrying incompetent people—so, for example, the ambulance of the future does not need to be a level 4 or level 5 system; it could be a level 3 system where human intervention if and when necessary would be provided from far away.

Another way to show that the taxonomy works independent of having a competent human driver inside the vehicle is to use it to draw the kinds of distinctions I made in previous chapters, for example, the distinction between drones and AWSs. It seems to me that a traditional drone—if evaluated on the SAE taxonomy—would hardly make it past level 2 and might even have to be classified as a level 1 system, as remote control is less automated than autopilot, I would argue. AWSs, on the other hand, are probably further up the automation scale, so that it would be difficult to argue for less than level 3, and in fact, depending on precisely which tasks have been automated, the kinds of AWSs I discussed in chapter 6 would probably qualify as level 4— and again, here I am not sure how to draw the distinction between level 4 and level 5.

This book has been trying throughout to avoid unnecessary complexities, so here you could reasonably expect me to draw some conclusions about, for example, which of the above levels qualifies as meaningful human control. Further, you might reasonably expect to find here some discussion of how the control concepts in this book—overall control, direct control, control delegation, and so on—can be mapped onto the SAE taxonomy. But I'm afraid there is only so much oversimplifying a philosopher can get away with. Still, I won't be criticized for lack of trying, so here are some preliminary conclusions.

Meaningful human control of complex automated technological systems such as the ones discussed in this book is, at a first superficial glance, to be located somewhere around levels 3 and 4; namely, below level 3 the systems are not complex or automated enough to warrant the concept of meaningful human control—even though there will still be plenty of control and responsibility questions. The question, then, is how to develop systems at level 3 and level 4 (again, let's just ignore the difference between level 4 and level 5 for now) that still respect the criteria of meaningful human control. And as you have seen in this chapter, more human intervention does not necessarily result in meaningful human control. Indeed, it is by denying access or intervention to noncompetent humans that, in many of these systems, constitutes protecting and respecting meaningful human control criteria, like with the average passengers in the emergency autoland system of chapter 6.

The other relevant question, for us, would be where to locate specifically control delegation and direct control in the SAE taxonomy. Two obvious places where I can see direct control being abdicated are

1. Once we move from the driver steering the wheel in levels 0 and 1 to the software steering it from level 2 upward
2. Once the possibility for human intervention and fallback on the human driver has been removed at level 4

Those two "moments" can both be considered, for different reasons, an abdication of direct control and, therefore, when successful, also instances of control delegation, in which first the human driver delegates control of specific driving tasks to the systems, such as steering or breaking, and, second, the human driver abdicates monitoring and ultimately fallback and her capacity for intervention to the system.

Here is as good a place as any to emphasize what's hidden behind the talk of "abdicating" as opposed to "losing" or "giving up" direct control, in the sense that this could be a choice at the system level before the human even starts using the vehicle, but it could also be a choice at the user level, where the human can, for example, set up her car every time with or without human fallback.

If you want to sleep, for example, you might want to delegate not only execution and monitoring to software but also fallback, because by the time the software wakes you up it might be too late to intervene. But if you only want to read, watch telly, or play with your kids (reminder to self: play more with my kids), you might set it up differently and only delegate execution and monitoring but not fallback—especially if your kids are in the car, you might not want to give up your intervention capacity. Or your kids might be the very reason to delegate fallback, in order to make sure they don't press the wrong button. And in fact—as you have often seen in my analysis in this chapter—the same applies to traditional cars, where you, for example, have the alternative to lock the back doors or back windows when your kids are in the car and then unlock them if you are driving around grown-ups (maybe you are an Uber driver at night to make ends meet; kids are expensive).

So my talk of losing or giving up direct control should actually, for once, be taken literally: system design choices might result in *losing* direct control, while user setup choices might result in *giving up* direct control, where the difference can be interpreted in at least two ways:

1. Giving up direct control is a voluntary activity, while losing direct control is involuntary.
2. Giving up direct control is active, while losing direct control is passive.

In this particular dichotomy, the other expression I have used throughout—"abdicating" direct control—would fall under "giving up" direct control, the voluntary or active interpretation. It is important to stress at least one difference between 1 and 2, namely, that talking of voluntary and involuntary in interpretation 1 means that the loss of direct control would itself not be under our control, supposedly. Talking of active and passive—on the other hand—has no obvious consequences for whether loss of control would be under our control or not.

THE ETHICS (AND HISTORY) OF TRANSPORT

Remember: I am not here to offer an ethical evaluation of particular technological innovations—in this case, self-driving cars. I am only offering an analysis of particular technological systems from the point of view of my control and delegation framework, in order to establish whether the control paradox applies to the system in question. So this is, again, what I am going to do with self-driving cars, and while the number of fatalities on either side (manual/automatic ["driven"] vs. self-driving) might be relevant to the control paradox, it is so only insofar as I am interested in the question of the relative benefits and risks of self-driving cars as compared to "driven" cars.

Come to think of it, the self-driving-cars case gives me an analytical opportunity that has not been available before: namely, to ask whether and how the control paradox could possibly apply to the technology that self-driving cars are supposed to replace—old-fashioned "driven" cars. After all, "driven" cars are also complex technological systems, and therefore "driven" cars are also plausible candidates for the control paradox. We will, I believe, learn quite a bit about the control paradox by trying to apply it to "driven" cars, so let me try to do just that.

Historically, the first thing to notice is that transportation has been developing in terms of more individual control; think again of the train/car comparison. If you take the train to your destination, you are delegating to the train driver in the same way you would to the taxi driver if you took a taxi—in both cases, you can sit back and relax—as opposed to driving yourself to the destination. Arguably, if you drive yourself, you can decide the exact route and speed of your journey in a way you cannot with a train. And on these grounds, you could be argued to have more control, at least more direct control anyhow.

The taxi case is perhaps somewhere in between: you can ask the taxi driver to speed up or slow down, and you can even try to exercise some influence on the precise route in ways that are unthinkable on a train; still, the average taxi driver will probably have none of it, so your influence will indeed be more limited than if you drove yourself.

Before proceeding with this exercise, let me remind you why I believe it to be useful: like with any analytical tool, I need to make sure that the control paradox cannot be applied to just any technology and system. Because that might make the book a bestseller (dream on), but only at the cost of making the analytical tool not very useful and ultimately meaningless, simply because then I would lack criteria for the application of the control paradox.

What I want, then, are cases of complex technological systems to which the control paradox does not apply, so that I can then compare them with cases of complex technological systems to which the control paradox does apply, thereby finding the criteria for application of the control paradox. And this is exactly what the comparison between the "driven" car and the "driverless" car can possibly provide.

After all, driven cars—which are still the overwhelming majority of cars—are already very complex systems, and their complexity is also increasing with time. And in fact, a lot of the systems that are contributing to such increasing complexity for driven cars are also the very systems that then, taken all together, make up a self-driving car. So that, for example, a lot of the breaking functions of today's new driven cars are automated to compensate for a driver's possible delayed response.

When evaluating whether driven cars might count as examples of the control paradox, what's crucial is whether there is any loss of control involved in these systems directly related to how they are designed to give the driver more control. Again—as a reminder—any loss of control will not do; the control paradox only applies to losses of control directly related to control-enhancing innovations or developments.

The other thing to be said about traditional cars—and you will see more of this in the next chapter as well—is that they have had a history of empowerment and emancipation, so that in a lot of industrial societies, especially after World War II, getting your own car was one of the traditionally most common and important ways of becoming independent and emancipated, from your employer, parents, partner, and more.

In this particular historical context, it is difficult to deny that cars—as opposed to public transportation, say—have always raised questions of control. And on the other hand, it can be argued that as cars became widespread and drivers were no longer only professional ones, accidents became a major cause of death across the world—as they still are.

The very thing, then, that is supposed to have been empowering and emancipating—getting your own private vehicle—was also the cause of a lot of accidents. Trains and planes, for example, crash a lot less than cars, in part because there are almost exclusively professionals involved. Buses and trucks are somewhat in between in this analysis, because buses and trucks are themselves driven by professionals, who on the other hand have to cope and interact with all those amateurs on the road (and the same could be said of police cars, ambulances, taxis, etc.).

Can I argue that this dialectic of emancipation, on the one hand, and more accidents, on the other hand, is an instance of the control paradox? As I said, there will be more to come on this particular question and more generally on the ways emancipation and empowerment relate to control in the next chapter. For now, I am skeptical of the application of the control paradox to traditional cars, and this is better explained by contrasting the control paradox's possible application to traditional cars with its application to self-driving cars.

With self-driving cars, if you delegate execution (say pushing pedals) to software, you voluntarily give up direct control to software; this is supposed to both free resource and enhance performance, thereby giving us more overall control. And the same goes for our delegating of monitoring and, ultimately, fallback to software.

What is particularly interesting in terms of whether the control paradox applies to self-driving cars is the possibility that only one of these three functions gives rise to the paradox. Whether or not I have a control paradox will depend—if I take the execution function alone, as above—on whether delegating the pedals to software in order to free resources and enhance performance will actually result in

- loss of direct control and overall control
- enhanced performance or at least attention resource economizing

Those, as you know well by now, are the two crucial conditions. If you only lose direct control, then there is no genuine paradox because direct control is supposed to be given up through delegation—that's the point of delegation, to spare the burden of direct control. And if you don't get improved performance or at least resource economy—in ways that are beneficial to overall control—you again don't qualify for the paradox, even if you had genuine control losses and not just direct control losses.

Wait. Something was too quick above. Did you notice? You can't have both genuine loss of control (and not just direct control) and genuine gain of control at the same time; that's just not logically possible if you are using the same concept of control both in the loss part and the gain part. So what was too quick above is that, as I explained at length in the early chapters, the "enhancement" condition doesn't need to be understood extensionally, and for an intentional understanding of the "enhancement" condition, genuine promise or potential will do (as in, a genuine intention and not just a desire to enhance control—see Grice [1971], Bratman [1984, 1987], and also my own work on this [Di Nucci 2008]).

At the same time, you will remember that the loss-of-control condition can also be fulfilled by increased risks or even reasonable fears of loss of control. But even once I add these clarifications, I might still end up with an analysis in which I don't have a genuine paradox for the execution function of self-driving cars nor for the monitoring function of self-driving cars, but I finally do have a genuine paradox if I also delegate the fallback function to software. And in fact many in the debate on self-driving cars and meaningful human control suggest that the possibility of intervening for the driver is the crucial element in order to keep meaningful human control (see, for example, the already cited Santoni de Sio and van den Hoven [2018]). [11]

Let me therefore conclude with the following hypothesis: When it comes to so-called self-driving cars and the control paradox, even if you successfully delegate crucial functions such as the triad of execution, monitoring, and fallback to well-programmed and properly firing software, you are inevitably sacrificing direct control over such familiar things as pedals or the wheel. The loss of direct control might be compensated for by enhanced performance or other benefits (fewer accidents, shorter commute), but it is not unreasonable to suppose that giving up direct control over familiar tasks will result in fears of genuine loss of control and also in the risk of increased manipulation and surveillance by those in charge of the software, whether private corporations or public authorities. [12] Therefore, some version of the control paradox does ultimately apply to self-driving cars. And even if it doesn't, we have learned an awful lot more about control by trying—which was the point all along.

Chapter Nine

Smartphones, from Empowerment to Surveillance

Local Control and Global Control

What's the first rule of creative writing? No, this book is not a novel, or a book on how to write, but I am reminded of that rule when it comes to this particular chapter because, as I have mentioned a couple of times already, I don't have a smartphone. Then again, that's the liberating thing about being a philosopher: we don't know anything, and still we write. So here comes a chapter about how smartphones went from the promise of empowerment to a tracking and targeting surveillance tool in the space of a decade, written by someone who doesn't even have one.

Let's get some preliminary stuff out of the way, most of which should be obvious by now since this is chapter 9: the argument in this book is not an ethical one about whether some technology or practice is good or bad or should be banned or publicly funded or whatever; the argument is only about whether some technology or practice is subject to the control paradox. That in turn might have ethical consequences, but those are beyond the scope of my argument here—so the same goes for smartphones; my argument is not whether or not smartphones are good for you, ethically or otherwise.

The fact that I started with a confession of my personal attitude toward smartphones might muddy the waters here—maybe I really am biased about the topic and should shut up—but the theoretical distinction between an ethical assessment of the risks and benefits of some technology or practice on the one hand and on the other hand an action-theoretical analysis of the control paradox applied to specific instances should be clear enough. And if you really believe that someone who is personally invested in a topic to the extent that they don't own a smartphone (in the Year of the Lord 2020!) cannot write about it in a philosophy book, well, then just stop reading or jump to the next chapter or whatever; that would be way too ad hominem a worry to be worth my time or ink.[1]

Back to the argument: do smartphones represent the most widespread application of the technological control paradox? If they do, they probably also represent the most widespread application of the control paradox full stop, given that—notoriously—smartphones are now more widespread than democracy and the gap is only growing. That would be enough reason for a book about the control paradox to tackle smartphones. There is also the added consideration that given widespread familiarity with smartphones, if they do represent a genuine application of the paradox, then they also constitute a really good and accessible illustration of the paradox for the masses, because just about everybody is then a victim of the control paradox.

One more preliminary clarification before I get down to business—and again this should be clear by now. It will not do to end up with a result in which there is this good thing that we get with smartphones—say, we are better at finding the route to a new destination—but there is also on the other hand this bad thing that comes along with it—say, we are manipulated by Facebook's algorithms. That would neither be a paradox nor be about control: it's just life or, another word for "life," compromises and trade-offs—okay, that was two words, but you get the point.

For the purposes of my argument, I am only interested in control-related trade-offs, and more precisely, not all control-related trade-offs will end up qualifying as an instance of the control paradox if they don't fulfill the control-enhancement condition and the control-loss condition in the specific way I have discussed, namely, giving up direct control while retaining overall control.

Okay, you should be up to speed again, and I can finally address the question of whether smartphones qualify for the control paradox. The first thing I need to talk about is whether and how smartphones might be control enhancing. Like in the other chapters, this kind of analysis is not only supposed to answer the headline question but also should allow me to better understand control in its different forms and manifestations: think of the referee's authority in chapter 7 and the question of whether authority is a form of control.

In this particular case, when I look at whether smartphones are control enhancing, the new version of the authority-as-control question is the emancipatory power of smartphones, namely, the idea that, through the technology, you—at least superficially—need to rely less on other people. You can do on your own a lot of stuff that, before, needed the involvement (if not the help) of other people.

I say superficially because, obviously, you are not doing it on our own in at least two important ways:

- First, you are doing it with and through the device.
- Second, and more important, there is a lot of human work and collaboration hidden behind the device, so are you really alone?

This going-it-alone issue is interesting from multiple perspectives, the least of which is the banal truth that hidden behind the device there might also be (and there are, as we have known for a while) both human and nonhuman observers who are tracking you.

From an action-theoretical point of view, what's at stake in the question of going it alone is what counts as individual action and what counts as nonindividual agency (group agency, joint agency, collaboration, delegation, competition, exploitation, etc.) given the social and technological complexities of the contemporary agent.

Do you go it alone when you act through or with the assistance of a smartphone? And if you do, is that emancipatory? And if it is, is that a control-enhancing consequence of using smartphones? Please do not underestimate the middle question squeezed in there, because it is not obvious that going it alone should count as emancipatory. It could be something else that has an even bigger tradition in philosophy—namely, alienating.

EMANCIPATION AND ALIENATION

This is a big question, not just for the control paradox or for smartphones; in fact, it is a big question that goes beyond technological systems and practices: what's the thin red line between emancipation and alienation? Is it even possible to avoid crossing it whenever we scale up? Could it be that, hidden behind this action-theoretical idea of the control paradox, there actually is this big issue of the dialectic between emancipation and alienation and that looking at something as mundane as smartphones can help us there?

Think of the Marxian understanding of waged labor (I am too young to really care about the difference between Marxian and Marxist, but then again I am too old to honestly tell myself that this sentence can be formulated without reference to Marx); the question is really the same. Is the proletariat emancipated through waged labor, or is it alienated? Well, obviously Marx didn't just have a question there—he had a pretty fuckin' big, both historically speaking and theoretically speaking, answer to the question. But here I am actually more interested in the question than the answer because I am interested in the difference between emancipation and alienation, *between the emancipatory promise of work against the alienating reality of waged labor,* if you like.

This is one of these sentences where one really needs to put almost every word in italics, so I'd rather just leave it . . . but to be clear, there are three important differences that generate more variables than a poor philosopher like me can compute: there is the emancipatory/alienating dialectic, obviously, but there is also the promise/reality dialectic, and finally the difference— because not everything is a bloody dialectic—between "work" and "waged labor." So, for example, one could dispute the cheap distinction between promise and reality while still hanging on to the other two important contrasts between emancipation and alienation and between work and waged labor. Oh, yes, and "between . . . against" isn't proper English, I know, but that sentence is so important I just wanted to make sure you didn't fail to see the tension.

Emancipation is empowering; alienation is exploitative. Things are actually not that simple, probably, but that's the tension I want to analyze here, and that is, possibly, also going to turn out to be at the root of the control paradox. So if it wasn't already clear enough how the concepts of both emancipation and alienation are crucial for making determinations about control—who has it, who loses it, and so on—think in terms of empowerment and exploitation, which might just be the more modern versions of those two classic concepts.

Allow me a bit of conceptual landscaping before I proceed: I am not going to argue for the relationship between emancipation and empowerment—I am just going to assume that. Neither am I going to argue for the relationship between alienation and exploitation—I am, again, baldly assuming that one too (I could be convinced to develop some sympathy for the following objection, but I think it's beyond the scope here so I will ignore it: the former relation between emancipation and empowerment is closer and more plausible than the latter relation between alienation and exploitation). All I am interested in arguing for here is the dialectic between emancipation and alienation and how that informs my analysis of the concept of control (well beyond just smartphones, hopefully).

If you don't mind, I will keep up the analogy between jobs and smartphones for a while longer, no disrespect (to jobs, that is—and not Steve, definitely not Steve). Because no one in their right mind should doubt, for example, the emancipatory role that access to employment has had for women (in the West over the last couple of centuries, say—if you want some historical context). And—which is the same—no one in their right mind should doubt that employment discrimination at all levels continues to be a problem for the empowerment of women in the twenty-first century: lower wages, slower career progression, more part-time work, lower employment rates, lower pension contributions—do you want me to continue?

Let me make sure not to confuse the above tension with the other tension between emancipation and alienation. One thing is the issue of employment being a potentially emancipatory vehicle for the empowerment of women. In that context, employment discrimination should not necessarily be considered alienating; rather, it is just a big fat roadblock on the way to emancipation. So the tension between the promise of women's emancipation through employment and the reality of employment discrimination persisting even in the most advanced countries in the twenty-first century (I happen to live in the one that always comes on top in these kinds of nerdy rankings—Denmark) should not be considered an instantiation of the thin red line between emancipation and alienation, but just a further dynamic within the issue of emancipation.

Where does alienation come in, then? Well, did I not mention one Karl Marx? The whole idea of the analogy between smartphones and jobs is that jobs have emancipatory potential (see, as above, the case of women after industrialization) that comes together with alienating reality. And the reality of alienation, according to Marxian historical materialism, transcends employment discrimination; namely, waged labor is alienating whether or not you are discriminated against in the workplace or are the victim of discriminatory hiring practices or harassment on the job and all the rest of the ugliness that women are still subjected to at work. Two distinctions, then:

1. First there is the distinction between *the emancipatory potential of work* on the one hand and *employment discrimination* in its many forms (hiring bias, harassment, etc.) on the other.
2. Second, there is the distinction between the *potential for emancipation* through work and the *reality of alienation* through waged labor.

The latter distinction is, admittedly, dependent on Marxian historical materialism, but, importantly, the former is independent of it and, basically, something that we can, today, still unfortunately take as empirically given.

This chapter is about smartphones and the control paradox, so I don't want to complicate this analogy too much, but I must at least add one further possibility, namely, that emancipation and alienation move on two different levels so that they are actually not incompatible with one another. For example, you can easily imagine that the emancipatory potential of work refers to a woman's emancipation from her family, father, husband, or other oppressor, while on the other hand the alienating reality of waged labor refers to the economic conditions—from one oppressor to another, so to speak.

This further possibility is particularly important because it might end up resembling the control paradox the most, namely, the idea that control enhancement inevitably brings with it control loss as well. Why was it important to keep these two distinctions separate? Because once I move back to smartphones, I will have two different possible analogies for the control paradox instead of just one.

When assessing the emancipatory potential of smartphones, I need a working definition of emancipation that can survive the move from work to smartphones. Minimally, you can think of emancipation as nondependence, so that something is emancipatory or has the potential to emancipate if it can contribute to making a person less dependent on another person or group/institution.

Here is a very basic way smartphones contribute to making their users less dependent on other people: When was the last time you approached someone in the street to ask for directions? Or—which is almost the same—when was the last time someone approached you? I say almost the same because it does depend on whether or not you are a user (of a smartphone, that is). I still approach people to ask them for directions all the time—but nobody ever does that to me. Now, if you saw a picture of me, you might doubt it's got to do with smartphone use, but this is, actually, a serious point in at least three ways:

- Are people being emancipated from their fellow human beings through technology?
- If so, are they really being emancipated, or is it just that they move from being dependent on one person or thing to being dependent on another person or thing?
- Finally, there is the issue of the asymmetry between users and nonusers. Users, the majority, ask as little as they are asked, but nonusers, the minority, ask a lot more than they are asked.

This final point also raises the interesting question of whether the talk of nonusers (of smartphones) as a minority is legitimate and useful for my analysis; is lacking a smartphone increasingly to be understood as a form of disability? The thought is not too wild, especially if you think of these kinds of technology as cognitive extensions—see Andy Clark and Dave Chalmers (1998) on the extended mind hypothesis. You might plausibly think that the lack of this extension is a form of impairment—whether this is voluntary isn't actually crucial, in this respect, to the question of whether it is an impairment.

You might think that defining emancipation in terms of nondependence is so minimal and prudent that it needs no argument at all, but there is at least one aspect of this prudent, minimal definition that calls for further clarification, namely, the difference between emancipation as no longer dependent and emancipation as empowerment, because as I will show below, no longer dependent and empowerment are not necessarily coextensive.

Smartphones themselves, indeed, might be a case in point here: being a competent smartphone user allows for both so many efficiencies in time, attention, money, and other cognitive resources (yes, money is one too), and also novel tasks and possibilities, that it is easy to argue that smartphones, to begin with, are empowering. You can do more with less, basically—and if that's not empowering, I don't know what is.

I know, I know—this is not an argument. So let's say that you grant me the empowering potential of smartphones. Because even once I have assumed that smartphones are empowering, it is easy to see that their empowering potential does not translate into emancipatory potential—for the simple reason that, as my map example already showed, the fact that a user is no longer dependent on other people to find her bearings does not mean that she has emancipated herself. It rather quite obviously just means that she has become dependent on something different: rather than a random human stranger on the street, a nonrandom (and corporate) human collective—or human/nonhuman collaboration, if you believe in so-called AI—named Google, Apple, or whatever your favorite oppressor is.

Seriously, though, you cannot take the oppressive character of the Big Five tech companies for granted—that can only be, at most, the outcome of my argument. But here the point is not whether the Big Five are oppressive. My claim is much more minimal: through smartphones you might be genuinely empowered, but that does not imply genuine emancipation, even in cases in which you are, on the face of it, no longer dependent on X—because you are now dependent on Y. And Y is big, rich, and powerful—infinitely more, in fact, than the random stranger on the street.

It won't do, by the way, to just object that Y is more accurate and reliable than X—Y always knows the way, Y even knows the quickest as opposed to the shortest way, and Y hardly ever tells you to fuck off (which I get all the time—again, do you want to see my picture?). The reason this is not an objection—namely, the fact that depending on Y is more efficient than depending on X—is simply that I am, in this particular argument, not talking about empowerment but about emancipation. And even if you are now dependent on a more accurate source, that does not equal no longer dependent. Though, yes, in order to argue for the empowering nature of smartphones, you can easily appeal to the improved accuracy and reliability of your new "oppressor."

One clarification: when I talk about "smartphones," I am obviously not just talking about hardware; I am talking of all the software, data, and so on that smartphones make available to us. In fact, this is true to such an extent that *smartphones* might no longer be a useful term to identify my subject matter. But the term is widespread and intuitive, so I will keep using it. Still, do not mistake the Trojan horse for the Greeks.

Another clarification: some of my analysis here might appear too quick in order to establish anything, and that, combined with my confession of not having a smartphone, might lead readers to the conclusion that mine is just another technophobic little book trying to ride the apocalyptic wave. I have some sympathy for this objection, especially because it points to something I believe is important in terms of the dialectic of both academic and media analysis of technology, namely, that both the Big Five and the skeptics have the same common goal, talking up the technology to make it look and sound bigger, scarier, and mightier than it actually is. So one must indeed proceed with care here. But, importantly and in my defense, remember that mine is not an ethical argument: I am not trying to establish or clarify the benefits and risks of particular technologies or practices (even though I have done that in the past, admittedly; see, for example, Di Nucci and Santoni de Sio [2016] on drones or Di Nucci [2019] on medical AI). I am only providing an action-theoretical analysis of what such technologies mean in terms of control.

What have I learned so far? I have learned to distinguish between emancipation and alienation in the first instance, and to further distinguish between emancipation as no longer dependent and emancipation as empowerment in the second instance. I have not said it but—clearly—which version of emancipation one endorses might also make a difference to the relationship between emancipation and alienation.

On this understanding, I have concluded that smartphones—and the data and software feeding them—are not emancipatory in the no-longer-dependent sense; in fact, what happens is just that you change the partner on which you are dependent; you exchange less reliable but also less powerful partners (the stranger on the street) for more reliable but also more powerful partners. Again, you might be skeptical of this simplified analysis, but here I am not trying to reach a conclusion on which practice is more responsible, just trying to show that, minimally, if you go from asking a stranger on the street about directions to consulting your Google-powered or Apple-powered gadget, then you are exchanging one relationship of dependence for another relationship of dependence.

To be sure, you will have noticed that some of my analysis here correlates with what I said about delegation in part II, but that should not lead you to misunderstand emancipation as no longer dependent for delegation. It is neither clear that when you ask some stranger on the street for directions you are delegating any task to them (you really are just asking for information, and then you will have to take action yourself, so the interaction is purely epistemic), nor is it clear that you are delegating to your Google-powered or Apple-powered smartphone when you use its mapping functions. Here again, the details are important, but for now it will suffice to say that delegation and emancipation are, in principle, supposed to be different phenomena, whether one thinks of emancipation as no longer dependent or emancipation as empowerment, even though these admittedly have some crucial features in common, such as efficiencies of cognitive resources.

There is an important consequence for the control paradox of my distinction between emancipation as nondependency and emancipation as empowerment. Namely, you can easily grant that all the fancy stuff that can be done with smartphones, and that might result—at the same time—in empowerment and also in dependency on more reliable but at the same time more powerful entities, can, at least sometimes, count as control enhancing. Theoretically, once I have distinguished between these two different understandings of emancipation, and further distinguished between emancipation and alienation, there is hardly any argumentative price to pay in just granting that all the fancy stuff nerdy twelve-year-olds can do with their gadgets can, in some circumstances, be genuinely control enhancing and therefore fulfill the first condition for the control paradox.

What kinds of examples am I thinking of here? Remember that in order for the control-enhancing condition to be fulfilled, it is not enough that I have enhanced performance or, indeed, that I can do some fancy new thing or perform a new task. It has to be *control* enhancing, so not every improvement will do. But it is indeed easy and banal to show that smartphones can uncontroversially fulfill the control-enhancing condition.

Just think of your banking app—and I do mean yours, because I haven't had one in years—and I don't think my wife has one either right now.[2] Any standard banking app, these days, gives you enhanced control over your finances. In a way, through a banking app you have the benefits of cash—always knowing how much you have of it, literally at your fingertips—while at the same time also preserving the advantages of a bank account—security, for example. The claim that banking apps enhance your control over your finances does not depend on empirical issues such as whether you will end up spending more responsibly as a result of being able to find out instantly and constantly how much money you have left. But what about security? Suppose having a banking app made your bank account more vulnerable to hacks than not having a banking app—wouldn't that be a challenge to the notion that banking apps are control enhancing?

This question really points to the following issue: what kind of control am I appealing to when I say that a banking app enhances control over finances? If it's a purely epistemic consideration of always being able to know in an instant precisely how much money you have in your account, is that really a form of control? First of all, that purely epistemic notion might already count as a form of control itself, but obviously there is much more to a banking app than just the ability to instantly check your balance—you can, for instance, move money, make investments, and pay bills.

Obviously there are other ways of spending money through your smart-phone—increasingly, for example, by using the smartphone itself as the pay-ment method, but also by just spending money while you are using an app or browsing the internet. This is important for my example for two reasons. First, there would be no point in challenging the banking app itself as limited, as really the question is whether whatever it is that you can do with a smart-phone might enhance your control of your money. So it's not just its banking app but the whole thing. But the second consideration goes in the other direction: it might be that there is a tension between different functions of your smartphones when it comes to your supposedly "enhanced" control over your finances. So having your bank account available while mobile might indeed give you enhanced control, but then that enhanced control has to be balanced against the fact that spending money is much easier through mobile technology, both online and off.

This issue points to a problem about what counts as enhanced control that I have not yet encountered in this book, I don't think, but that was always going to come up, namely, whether to endorse an all-things-considered no-tion of enhanced control or not. For the nonphilosophers, cutting the jargon, that just means I need to decide between two alternative definitions of en-hanced control:

1. Tech or practice X enhances S's control if and only if S has more/better control overall as a result of X.
2. Tech or practice X enhances S's control if and only if S has more/better control over some relevant task as a result of X.

This is a really simple distinction, but it matters, as you just saw with the example above of the way your banking app might give you more/better control over your finances, while at the same time Apple Pay might compro-mise or even offset that local enhanced control by making it so much easier to spend money. In fact, now that I think of it, that's why I don't want my kids to have smartphones—it must have been the money all along.

LOCAL CONTROL AND GLOBAL CONTROL

This distinction between overall control enhancement and task-based control enhancement brings to the fore a further and more crucial distinction that matters to my overall argument, namely, the idea that the solution to the control paradox might be to distinguish between local control and global control and claim that all those instances that might on the surface appear paradoxical are actually cases in which we have a trade-off between local control and global control, either because we enhance local control at the expense of global control (which might turn out to be the more frequent case) or because we enhance global control at the expense of local control. I need to understand how this further distinction between local control and global control could work and, specifically, how it can be squared with my general distinction—based on delegation—between overall control and direct control.

Let me start with some examples. Here it helps that, as I have explained, this chapter is not just about smartphone hardware or the gadget but about all the functions that are accessible to us through that gadget—so apps, software, and so on. And that inevitably still includes—I write in the year 2020—social media, for example. I say that not because I want to get myself worked up about social media—which is another one of my abstinences, having renounced long ago the likes of Facebook, Twitter, and . . . well, that was about it, actually. Rather, social media offers a good example of what I mean by the difference between local control and global control and how trade-offs between local control and global control might actually turn out to be a solution or at least illustration of the control paradox. Warning: I am not going to offer a very original argument here; it has been made before—for example, by Cass Sunstein in *#Republic* (2018) after Trump's 2016 election.

Here it goes: Social media had the potential, among other things, to optimize our interactions, including political interactions and news consumption. It had (notice again the past tense here) the potential, namely, of avoiding the randomness of analog life when it comes to social encounters, whether private (think of dating apps) or public (think of political activism online, otherwise called Twitter). Basically, why leave it to the randomness of analog life to decide who we spend the rest of our lives with (or just have sex with) when some fancy bit of software or algorithm can find the perfect match, whether romantically or politically?

Another way of putting it—but I am still talking about the same kind of potential—is that social media could have been originally thought of as your personal editor, very knowledgeable both about you and your taste (again, romantic, sexual, political, or, indeed, commercial—let's not forget Amazon) and also about what's out there, whether people, news, or shoes.

Here again I don't want to talk about how that has turned out—see part IV on the political paradox for that. I just want to point out how these dynamics can be interpreted in terms of control, and specifically in terms of the distinction between local control and global control—and further, how that relates back to the thin red line between emancipation and alienation.

The idea is the following: You could argue that your own personal "editor"—the algorithm that selects just the people you like, the news you are interested in, and the shoes that you were looking for—enhances your control over your life, because less of your life is left to random chance. If you are not convinced by this intuitive idea, think of it in terms of access: the algorithm is then not your editor but more like your bodyguard. Only the people you are going to like will have access to you; only the news you are going to be interested in is going to be allowed to make its way to you—the rest will be filtered out. And, most important of all (I am Italian, didn't you notice?), only the right shoes will be displayed for your eyes and credit card to indulge in.

And if access isn't control, then I don't know what is. After all—and this is again not my own thought, but I don't remember whom I heard it from—what is the scariest thing about being locked up? (This has actually happened to me, so I am speaking from experience—Santa Cruz PD, I am looking at you.) Those who have not been to prison might plausibly imagine that the scariest element of being locked up is what the term says, namely, the fact that you can't get out. But actually the scariest part isn't that you can't get out, it's that you don't get to decide who gets in—you completely lose control of who has access to your own person—sometimes in brutal ways, in fact. So yes, you lose your freedom, but in a particular sense that might not be obvious at first sight; you lose not only your freedom to wander, you lose your freedom to control who has access to you. And that is—I submit—the worst part.

You might disagree with my brief account of what makes prison the particularly brutal punishment that it is, but that does not matter; my aim is just to illustrate the way access is control and the way the most precious form of control we have is being able to regulate access to our own person or, in fact, property. That's the substance of rights, autonomy, and ultimately liberty—so again, it should not be surprising that this is exactly what we lose in prison.

Whether, then, I am using the editor analogy or the bodyguard analogy, the point is that social media and online shopping algorithms could give us more control because those are effective ways of regulating access, more effective than, say, the randomness of analog life: Will nearby newsagents sell your favorite paper or just tabloids? Or maybe they do sell it but they have run out before you have managed to make your way there this morning. Mutatis mutandis for possible partners or shoes.

Those are forms of local control, I would argue. And if you accept that such technologies have the potential to enhance local control, then my argument is pretty much complete already, because I only have to refer to the political and social mess described in chapter 2 of this book—and further analyzed in part IV—to illustrate the other side of this equation, namely, loss of global control. In a nutshell and simplifying, Facebook promised to give us better control of our relationships and our news consumption—which is (at least a promised of) enhanced local control—and we ended up with Brexit and Trump, which is—the reality of—loss of global control.

Again, the above is not an argument for Facebook having the potential to give us more local control, nor is it an argument for Facebook delivering chaos. Both arguments can be made and have been made at length over the last few years. What I am doing here is just putting those arguments in the context of the distinction between local control and global control.

Now four further questions need to be addressed, two small and the other two more substantial, especially the last one:

1. Does the distinction between local control and global control also have the opposite directionality, in which I have losses of local control together with gains of global control? That would be interesting and important, especially on the assumption that global control deserves some sort of ethical priority over local control (an assumption that is plausible, but I have not defended it here).
2. What consequences does this have for my analysis of smartphones, especially in terms of the thin red line between emancipation and alienation?
3. How does the distinction between local control and global control square with my other control distinction, between overall control and direct control?
4. And finally, what are the consequences for the control paradox of the distinction between local control and global control? Basically—and if you accept the distinction between local control and global control— have I just solved the paradox?

The rest of this chapter is dedicated to answering these four questions. And then you are finished already—with this chapter anyway.

Questions 1 and 3

The importance of Question 1 goes well beyond this smartphone chapter, and it does not depend on the plausible assumption that global control ought to have moral priority over local control. Can you imagine cases in which the supposed trade-off between local control and global control is not one in which you gain local control at the cost of global control—such as, I have hypothesized, with mobile technologies—but rather one in which you gain global control at the cost of local control?

You can, and in fact I have already discussed in some detail one such case: transportation. Intelligent vehicles such as the self-driving cars of chapter 8 are supposed to be beneficial not just to the individual driver—whose cognitive resources are spared and can be reinvested in watching Netflix or playing with her kids—but also to the whole transportation system, because of increased coordination and consequent reduction of traffic, travel times, and accidents—which results in further reduction of traffic and in turn further reduction of travel times. If this is true, then does it not constitute an enhancement at the global control level rather than the local control level?

In fact, here one could argue that in the particular case of self-driving cars you have potential for enhancement at both the local and global control levels, assuming also that software can "drive" the car in more precise and efficient ways than human drivers can (enhanced local control) and that the consequences for coordination and traffic are positive (enhanced global control). So it is that ugly expression again, a win-win.

Given my delegation framework and the distinction between overall control and direct control, it is also difficult in this case to resist local control enhancement on the grounds that, actually, at the local level you have control losses, because if software really is superior to human drivers, then all you have at the local level is loss of direct control at the most. But that won't do, given that it might result in enhanced overall control at the local level. This point might seem redundant, but it is made firstly in the interest of clarity and secondly to specify that overall control and global control are two independent concepts in my framework, such that I can have overall control at the local level too—and maybe there is also just enough space for direct control at the global level.

Self-driving cars, then, don't necessarily qualify as a trade-off of loss of local control for the benefit of enhanced global control, but they have nonetheless helped me clarify both the concepts of local control and global control and also how these concepts relate to the other crucial concepts in my delegation framework, overall control as opposed to direct control.

Given that I have already achieved my narrow aims of conceptual clarification in this section, I am ready to move on; still, I don't want to leave you without a more plausible example of the trade-off between local control and global control, because such examples are not that difficult to find, especially as I move toward the political paradox of the next part of this book. Think, for example, of centralization as opposed to federalism in political institutions. Assuming some benefit from centralization, then the argument for centralization in those cases will in fact be a case of trading off local control for some beneficial outcomes at the level of global control.

European common currency—the euro—could be taken to be a basic example of this, in which countries were sold on a promise of commercial and fiscal benefits by having a shared monetary policy and currency; no longer being able to set one's own interest rates was, in that scheme, the price in terms of local control that had to be traded off against the promised benefits at the shared global level.

What is important to understand is that a trade-off between local control and global control is not the same thing as the control paradox—the euro might, for example, qualify as an example of a trade-off of local control losses for global control gains without thereby qualifying as an example of the control paradox.

Before moving on to the next question, let me just stress that I have hereby provided an answer not just to Question 1 but also to Question 3 about the relation between the local/global control distinction and the direct/overall control distinction, so that after having dealt with Question 2 in the next section, I can move directly to Question 4.

Questions 2 and 4

Where does the local/global control distinction leave me with the issue of smartphones and whether these technologies are emancipatory or alienating? First of all, what the local/global control distinction allows me to say is the following: that smartphones might not give rise to the control paradox—because maybe all they give rise to are local/global control trade-offs—does not mean that these mobile technologies are not disruptive and do not give rise to interesting ethical issues. Again, the control paradox is itself not an ethical assessment of some technology or practice; it is just an action-theoretical framework that can be used in providing such ethical assessment. So no control paradox does not mean that all is good.

Also, it might be that other features of smartphones and apps really are paradoxical: think of the so-called quantified-self movement and all the self-monitoring and self-tracking that comes with it. If you think of that as a way of giving you more control over your body and self but it ultimately results in compulsive exercising or an eating disorder (I am not saying that it does; just a hypothesis), then it will be difficult to argue yourself out of that appearance of paradox with a local/global distinction. You could try to say that in order to enhance your control over your six-pack (local control) you ended up losing control over your life because of too much exercise or even steroids (global control). But that would be pushing it and does not sound very plausible. The control paradox, in these particular sets of circumstances, sounds much more plausible.

You have learned, then, to distinguish between the control paradox and local/global control trade-offs and also to accept that different tasks or different functions of technological devices can give rise to different analyses—that's not even very surprising when you think about it.

Still, you might demand an answer to the main question of this chapter: are smartphones or mobile technologies in general more emancipatory or more alienating? Have I made any progress toward answering this question by introducing the distinction between local control and global control?

In just the same way I have distinguished between empowerment and emancipation, I believe here I need to distinguish alienation from surveillance and the related privacy and liberty/autonomy risks of these data-driven technologies. The reason I introduced the concept of alienation in this chapter was, if you remember, not actually to argue that smartphones can end up alienating you (in fact, it might very well be that it is the nonusers like myself who are alienating themselves from the modern world). The reason I introduced the concept of alienation was to draw an analogy between smartphones and jobs that was supposed to show the risks of emancipatory potential.

Basically the argument was the following: even something with the great and documented emancipatory potential of joining the workforce could be alienating because of the economic structure of waged labor. So it should not surprise us then if a lesser candidate for emancipatory potential such as smartphones also turned out to be dangerous for us. But in this particular case, the danger is not alienation as such but, rather, commodification through surveillance—or what has been recently called "surveillance capitalism" (see the volume *The Age of Surveillance Capitalism* by Shoshana Zuboff [2018]; others have talked about "attention economics"; see the volume *Reality Lost* by Vincent Hendricks and Mads Vestergaard [2019]).[3]

The argument has often been made over the last few years, so I won't repeat it here; I will just clarify that the basic idea that we as sources of valuable data have made ourselves into a commodity for the Big Five and beyond is different from the claim that we are also being manipulated. Those are independent arguments, even though the force of both might turn out to depend on the computational capacities of the Big Five's algorithms.

Before you draw the wrong conclusions from my argument in this chapter, let me make some clarifications: Yes, it might turn out that the control paradox does not actually apply to smartphones and other data-hungry tech. And yes, it might turn out that the thin red line between emancipation and alienation does not work for smartphones the same way it works for . . . well, I can't write "work" again, can I? So let's say "employment."

Still, I think there is something important about control that emerges from this chapter: namely, the connection between the potential for empowerment and emancipation of these technologies and the reality of surveillance and commodification is indeed a matter of control; it is the very same source that is supposed to empower us—for example, just to mention two crucial cases, knowing more about one's body and self or filtering out irrelevant possibilities, be they partners, news items, or shoes—that also results in our commodification and, ultimately, oppression.

It is the very data that allow us to know ourselves and our bodies better that then turn us into commodities; it is the same data that allow us to find the right partner, the more interesting commentary, the best shoes, that then end up being the instrument of our oppression. So it might not be paradoxical, but it is, to a certain extent, self-inflicted—and it is very tempting to conclude that we are lured into this trap by the control-based promise of self-empowerment. And what else if not control is it that we lose when that very same information is then used to monitor and manipulate our future behavior?

Two final points for this chapter, one of which is my answer to Question 4. First, let me admit that it is difficult to imagine that the arguments regarding control that I have put forward in this chapter have no bearings on questions of responsibility, but this is not the place to address that; for a discussion of responsibility and the control paradox, you will have to wait until the final chapter of this book.

Second and finally, here is my answer to Question 4: Is the local/global control distinction my solution to the control paradox? Here I need to distinguish between two different kinds of "solutions," one that shows that there is no genuine paradox or that the appearance of the control paradox can be explained by something else, and the other that actually recognizes the control paradox and its risks and offers a way of dealing with it by minimizing risks for control loss (or maximizing the potential for control enhancement). Now, the local/global control distinction is a version of the former kind of "solution," namely, a dissolution of the paradox, according to which cases that look like the control paradox can often be explained by appealing to simple (well, not that simple, but you know what I mean) trade-offs between local control and global control. On the other hand, my account of successful delegation, developed especially in part II (but also throughout), represents the latter kind of solution: through practices of responsible and successful delegation in which you spare resources through lack of direct control while at the same time enhancing overall control, you can ultimately avoid or alleviate the risk of control loss and thereby the control paradox.

Chapter Ten

Health Data and Healthcare Algorithms

Medical AI

Collecting health data on a huge scale is supposed to empower us twice: big data and precision medicine promise treatment tailored all the way down to the individual patient and also more control over our own health-related practices, such as eating, fitness, and sleep. At the same time, through the recording and collecting of our health data, we fear losing control to tech companies such as the Big Five.

In the context of the control paradox, talking about these technological developments within healthcare is, I believe, particularly crucial because there is a fundamental ethical asymmetry between healthcare and other domains in which autonomous and intelligent technologies are increasingly being used, such as, say, the military, the justice system, or finance and commerce. Basically, nobody disputes the value of health and healthcare: more and better healthcare is a basic intuitive good in a way that more and better weapons, prisons, or derivatives will never be, whatever your politics.

In that respect, if the control paradox applies within the healthcare domain too, that would be particularly important for my argument, because it would show the relevance of the paradox in a domain that is, otherwise, *ethically* pretty straightforward: better outcomes in healthcare are a basic social good, and whatever delivers those is prima facie good news. So even though my control paradox is not an ethical argument, it matters a lot whether it finds application within healthcare—because basically if not even healthcare is safe, then nothing is.

There is another reason trying out the control paradox on healthcare is particularly useful, namely, it is not obvious, within healthcare, that control is what we care about; as above, what we care about within healthcare are clinical outcomes, full stop. If we have therapeutic systems that can be shown (through randomized control trials [RCTs], for example) to deliver improved outcomes, then we adopt such systems.

A focus on healthcare, then, allows me to test the paradox from at least two novel points of view: a context that is not ethically controversial, and a context where the focus is on outcomes rather than control. Let me start from the latter, because it matters a good deal to the overall argument of the book.

PERFORMANCE, OUTCOMES, AND CONTROL

One possible general objection to my argument in this book is that I have put too much focus on control and specifically on the value of control. After all, whatever you make of the control paradox, the whole idea originates from control gains and control losses being assumed to be important and ethically relevant.

Even without disputing the value of control gains and control losses, one could argue that the value of control depends on the context or sector I am analyzing. So, for example, if you are driving your kids to school (which I never do, by the way; we always cycle—we don't even have a car, so please don't shoot us first when the revolution comes), control is probably pretty high on your list of priorities, but if, say, you want to cure disease or even mild pain, control might be a lower-ranked priority. In that case it would be outcomes and results that matter more—if that means anything—than control.

Let me look at this comparison in some more (boring) detail to make myself clear, and again suppose *you* are driving your kids to school. Your kids' education will be a very high priority; your kids' regular attendance at school almost as high, supposedly; and further, their getting to school in good time important and a functional priority—as in, functional to their regular attendance and the general success of their education.

So while you drive your kids to school, it matters that you—well, they, but you (or maybe the software, definitely not the kids) are driving—make it to school on time, which where I am from means between 7:50 and 8:00 a.m. (definitely too early if you ask me). Not arriving late matters, and you will take some minimal risks within reason to make sure that you don't arrive late—you might, say, reasonably go through a yellow but not a red. If, on the other hand, you are just—for comparison's sake—picking up your kids from a friend who said come get them between six and seven and it is quarter past six and you are five minutes away, then you might reasonably go through the green but not the yellow, because there is no rush, basically.

I am supposing, then, that given the high priority of school punctuality, going through a yellow light might be reasonable, but a red would not be, simply because not being involved in an accident is an even higher priority, especially with your kids in the back of the car. When it comes to driving your kids to school, then, you have to weigh the importance of punctuality against the risk of speeding or even causing an accident. While a yellow light or even a speeding ticket (maybe they have an important exam or favorite class in the first hour) might sometimes be within reason, a red light or carelessness would never be. This is another way of saying that, while driving, control will hardly ever be outweighed by other performance-related considerations (Formula One drivers might be an exception here, but that shit ought to be abolished anyway, so it don't count).

Other times, outcomes and performance matter more—relative to control and in comparison to the above case, that is. As I mentioned, I have chosen healthcare as one of the chapters for this book not because I work at a medical faculty but because I think it provides a good example of a result-centered and performance-focused sector in which control is important but is not as high a priority as in, say, driving and, therefore, must be weighed constantly against other considerations (still, it admittedly does depend on what kind of healthcare specialty and what kind of conditions and diseases we are talking about, because with public health crises such as the spread of infectious diseases—have you heard of the new coronavirus?—controlling the disease is crucial).

Given what I have said about control and driving above, I can now compare it to control and medicine: while I would happily sacrifice or give up the outcome based on not having enough control in the driving case (you would not drive the kids to school if your brakes were malfunctioning), I would probably be less willing to sacrifice the outcome in the healthcare case, because sacrificing healthcare outcomes will often lead to worsening of the disease, chronic conditions, or even death.

You might worry that—having introduced life and death into the picture—I am cheating by comparing apples to oranges (which is which, though?). But I think this argumentative move is absolutely legitimate: the difference between healthcare and transportation is indeed that, on average, the stakes are higher in healthcare than they are in transport. It is as simple as that, and in fact the whole reason I have introduced healthcare: because the stakes are higher, that makes some ethical issues simpler, others more complicated.

Take one case that people might have already heard of, Watson, which is an IBM computer program that is supposed to support clinicians. I have written at length on IBM Watson for Oncology elsewhere (Di Nucci 2019;

Di Nucci et al. 2020; Grote & Di Nucci 2020; Tupasela & Di Nucci 2020), so here I will only touch on the main points most relevant to the paradox, like I did in previous chapters. I will refer to the system as "Watson" even though I am only speaking about a particular oncology version of it, namely, IBM Watson for Oncology. Also, notice the danger of personifying such systems by giving them names, and of researchers embracing these risks by, for brevity's sake, referring to the system as "Watson." With this caveat in the bag, and given that IBM Watson for Oncology is both a mouthful and a brand, I will use Watson from now on.

Watson is supposed to assist oncologists in making therapeutic decisions. Some people call it artificial intelligence, some other people refer to the machine learning algorithms powering it, but the easiest and most neutral way of thinking of it is as a decision-support system, while at the same time being careful not to beg the question of who is the decision-maker; like with "self-driving" cars or "autonomous weapons," such labels are not neutral, ethically or theoretically speaking.

What the "decision-support" label is supposed to emphasize is both the task that Watson is deployed to fulfill and also that the computer system is not itself making any (relevant) decisions. Decisional authority is still with the doctor, or so the label emphasizes anyway. This emphasis can go both ways though. You might be reassured that the system is neither so advanced as to make its own decisions nor the programmers so irresponsible as to give the system that decisional authority. But there is a dark side to that reassurance. Namely, you might, rather than being reassured that the system does not have decisional authority or capacity, be fooled or deceived into thinking that the system does not have decisional authority and capacity, because, plausibly, whether or not the system will ultimately have decisional authority and capacity partly depends on the behavior of the end users, in this case medical doctors. And you might be worried that medical doctors will ultimately end up relying too much on the system, and in relying too much on the system erode their own decisional authority and make room for more decisional authority for the system.

Additionally, given that these systems learn from new data and therefore increase in functionality the more we use them, excessive reliance on such decision-support systems among medical professionals will both improve the systems' overall performance—that's the idea, at least—but also give them more decisional authority and capacity, and ultimately control.

That is exactly why the dialectic between performance and control that I emphasized at the beginning of this chapter is so crucial, within healthcare and beyond—because performance and control are clearly not independent of each other, and these two criteria might be feeding each other in circles that are potentially virtuous but ultimately vicious. That is what I want to find out in this chapter. It will then ultimately be up to you, reader, to apply my findings from the healthcare sector to other domains, mutatis mutandis.

How does Watson support the medical professional's decision-making? In the particular oncological focus that has been the subject of my previous work on this topic, what decision support basically means is that Watson compares the patient's clinical profile with available evidence (established therapeutic protocols but also new scientific studies) and generates multiple ranked therapeutic recommendations.

You will be shocked to hear that the ranking is even color-coded—amazing how much you can get away with just because doctors are busy. So basically, the system will give you, say, three outcomes in the form of three alternative therapeutic options, one of which will be green and the other two yellow—let's forget about red for now to keep things easy.

Based on these recommendations—and in consultation with the patient, colleagues, and others—the oncologist is supposed to make the therapeutic decision, and that decision is supposed to be somehow preferable to the decision the oncologist would have come to had they not used the system—otherwise IBM's product won't sell.

In comparing the doctor's decision-making with the assistance of the Watson system and the doctor's decision-making without the assistance of the Watson system, I can rely on some of the progress I made in previous chapter. The difference between economic delegation and strategic delegation could, for example, give me multiple ways of comparing assisted decision-making to unassisted decision-making. And for now, let me stick to the simple option of still holding on to the doctor's deciding alone—given some evidence or advice—instead of more theoretically complex options such as the doctor and Watson deciding together.

How does the assisted decision compare to the unassisted decision? First of all, through my framework of economic delegation and strategic delegation, you can see that the assisted decision does not necessarily have to deliver a better outcome for the patient than the unassisted decision (in order for the system to be worthwhile, that is). It could be, for example, that the assisted decision delivers a comparable outcome for patients to the unassisted decision (call this a thought RCT, if you like) but requires less of doctors' resources. For example, doctors do not need to defer decisions to a time after they have consulted with senior colleagues, say, thereby sparing resources and time for all three parties involved: the doctor, the patient, and the senior colleague.

You might object that I am again running the wrong comparison, because consulting with a senior colleague would also constitute an assisted decision. That's true, but quite obviously for the thought RCT above, what I meant by "assisted decision" was assisted by Watson—because that's what I am trying to evaluate. So it is legitimate to compare performance with Watson assistance both to performance with other assistance and without assistance, which might mean the doctor deciding alone given the evidence she currently has or the doctor deferring the decision to a time after she has consulted new evidence or run some additional tests or whatever is relevant in this particular case.

The economic delegation framework basically gives me a way of comparing even performances in terms of outcomes: if the decision-support system leads to resource economizing (and that again does not have to mean money but might often mean money in the end) but no improvement in performance, that's good enough. In fact, given enough resource economizing, even under-par performance might do as long as it is good enough—this might be particularly relevant for healthcare systems, which are often under pressure, say in third-world countries or a rich healthcare system in crisis mode.

Where does control come into this picture? One plausible way of dismissing this as irrelevant for control would be to argue that—as far as decision-making authority remains with the human expert, the physician—there is no reason to worry about loss of control. One peculiar consequence of this strategy is that there would also be no obvious control enhancement as a result of using the system, but at least one could speculate about control enhancement down the line if the healthcare professional has more time or the system more resources or the performance improved in terms of patient outcomes.

The problem with this strategy is the plausibility, in practice if not in theory, that using such decision-support systems, especially given that they are programmed to get better, would make no difference to the physician's decision-making authority. Here are some reasons to think that it might, and that would be directly or ultimately relevant to the doctor's control:

Scenario A: A physician might be initially skeptical of the system's recommendation but, with time, realize that—despite her being on the lookout for bugs or drops in performance—the system does seem to generate recommendations that are effective; this doctor always double-checks those recommendations in the beginning by consulting colleagues, comparing them with her own previous recommendations in similar cases from the files, checking the evidence that the system claims to support these recommendations, and doing all the other things that a responsible clinician and decision-maker is supposed to do in high-stakes contexts such as healthcare, where it is plausible to think that, because the ethical stakes are higher, the epistemic thresholds are accordingly higher as well. Given that the evidence proves strong and that the outcomes are improved, it would not be surprising—indeed, it might even be a welcome development—if this particular physician started checking a bit less—which might even be just a question of consulting fewer items among the literature that Watson points to with every recommendation. Suppose that in the first few months of use, this oncologist was consulting the full list and that, after a few months of good performance backed up by plausible evidence, she starts to consult only the first page of results. It would be difficult to criticize such behavior, especially given that—within the economic delegation framework—part of the point of implementing the system was to spare resources, so if the doctor is reinvesting her time, that should actually be good news, right? And in fact—given good outcomes and plausible evidence—this might turn out to be exactly what we were aiming for all along. So what I should ask in this scenario is not just how to evaluate this change of clinical behavior from the doctor but also what other consequences this change might have, even given a positive evaluation of it. Has—for example—the doctor given away some of her direct control over clinical decision-making by relying more on the system? I am not going to attempt an answer to this question right now, but already posing the question alone at least makes clear that there are control-related issues at stake here too, even though control might play a different role within healthcare than it plays in the contexts and sectors I have analyzed so far.

Scenario B: The scenario above is one that could have been taken from a resourceful (as in, wealthy) healthcare system. I emphasize this because I think we should take a global perspective when thinking of what kind of consequences and ethically relevant issues the growing use of so-called AI and machine learning algorithms might have. In my previous publications on this topic (Di Nucci et al. 2020; Tupasela & Di Nucci 2020), for example, I have emphasized how a lot of the studies that involve Watson have been conducted both with IBM funding and by healthcare systems in second- or third-world countries. The worry is the following: if, as in scenario A above, there is a risk of overreliance on the decision-support system even in resourceful healthcare systems where medical professionals have alternatives, then that risk will likely be even greater in healthcare systems where there might not be as many readily available alternatives, and this could apply both globally and locally, with in the latter a difference between urban and rural healthcare environments. If you are—say—the only oncologist with a certain expertise in your small city, your capacity to consult colleagues might be limited, if not by communication or geographic constraints then by the fact that you are less familiar with other oncologists with similar expertise who work somewhere else and whom you only contact by phone if circumstances require. This is a point about vulnerability: if overreliance on medical AI systems presents risks, then those risks are greater for more vulnerable environments, be they the healthcare system in a third-world country or the primary care unit in a rural area.

I think both scenarios A and B have to be taken seriously when analyzing control-related issues to do with medical AI decision-support systems—and, by the way, there are a lot of systems that are being developed, tested, and already deployed that are not purely decision support but that actually deliver outcomes, for example, computer-based pathology systems for biopsies, which are apparently really good at lowering the human false negative rate but are not very good at improving on the human false positive rate. As in, pathology computer-based systems are better at identifying more cancers and not missing some genuine ones than human pathologists, but the computer systems still deliver too many false positives, which has led people to argue in favor of a human–computer collaboration in which the computer systems are initially deployed to eliminate a lot of "easy" (for the computer) negatives and then humans come in to sort out the false positives from the positives (here see Fry [2018] for a summary of the relevant evidence).

Back to scenarios A and B: the asymmetry between A and B in terms of the vulnerability of different healthcare systems does not necessarily need to be interpreted negatively, as there is also great potential. Just like in the pharmaceutical industry, if expertise from resourceful healthcare systems can be technologically replicated into a pill or computer system and thereby made available to healthcare systems globally that might otherwise have fewer resources to develop and maintain that expertise themselves, isn't that good news? Aren't we just spreading the love (and expertise) through commercialization?

Doesn't the technological and commercial replication of such expertise democratize healthcare? This is a complex issue, and it is, mostly, a political rather than an ethical one. Let me first of all admit that there is definitely potential for making expertise—be that meds or computer-based decision-support systems—widely available. Second, let me make a cheap point, namely, that the love won't be spread for free, given the commercial nature of such enterprises. What that means is, for example, that underfunded healthcare systems might have to make difficult choices between paying for expensive treatment from abroad and—say—funding their own medical schools or research environments. What you get, then, is a sort of *healthcare neocolonialism* (Di Nucci et al. 2020; Tupasela & Di Nucci 2020).

This healthcare neocolonialism worry is further entrenched by the nature of the systems we are talking about—this is true of the pharma industry but probably even more so of the "medical AI" industry—if we can call it that (and we must; it might not be true AI, but it certainly is true industry). Two points here:

- Given the initial asymmetry, it is almost inevitable that, at least to begin with, the health data powering those algorithms will be overwhelmingly skewed toward patients in resourceful healthcare systems, so that the kind of advice and recommendations that these systems—informed by biased data—will deliver might not be targeted and tailored to the healthcare systems that the products are being marketed to. Watson is, for example, developed by IBM together with oncologists from Memorial Sloan Kettering Cancer Center in New York. That does not prevent them from using global data, but even if they were using global data (and there might be ways health data from poorer countries would be even more accessible than healthcare data from richer countries, for example, because they have fewer restrictions on accessibility or consent requirements), it is not implausible to worry that not only the data (and therefore the algorithm's fuel) will be biased but that also the developer's advice from U.S. oncologists will not be easily translatable to, say, a rural Indian healthcare environment.

- There is a second data-driven neocolonialist worry, namely, that the big corporate players, like the Big Five, who have the most data—and therefore the most algorithmic power—are not healthcare-only businesses like big pharma but are rather mostly involved in other sectors. Different corporate practices could boost innovation but also generate ambiguities about what are health data as opposed to other kinds of data—as lots of data that are not directly health data are still relevant, even more so if you endorse some version of the social determinants of health approach. Also, currently, healthcare appears to be a side project for a lot of these big companies, and that might itself influence their strategy.

Whole books have been written about these issues (Topol [2019] being one of the most influential and talked about recent examples, but again see also Fry [2019], who does not focus only on healthcare but has a very useful chapter on it), so I have to be careful not to lose my focus on control and the control paradox, because not all of the above considerations are directly relevant to control.

Here again one of the distinctions from previous chapters comes in handy, this time my distinction between local control and global control—which, let me remind you, is not about geography but rather about particular tasks (local control) as opposed to more general practices (global control).

This distinction can now be tried out on medical AI systems such as Watson: the idea would be that while delegating literature searches and staying up to date with new studies to Watson might be a good way of optimizing resources—depending on Watson's price tag, admittedly—if what begins at the local level as delegating only literature searches turns into overreliance and healthcare neocolonialism, then you might be trading off some economic delegation gains at the local level for global control losses.

I know what you are thinking. The above argument is, even in its best-case scenario in which there are genuine global control losses, a so-called slippery slope argument; namely, overreliance does not follow from local task delegation, nor does an increased risk of overreliance follow from local task delegation. What I need is an argument supporting the claim that local task delegation might lead to overreliance and thereby further to global control losses. The possibility that local task delegation might result in overreliance and that overreliance will then lead to global control losses isn't just not good enough; it is no argument at all.

This is true, and I must be careful not to rely on slippery slope arguments. On the other hand, what I have done so far in this chapter has actually been to provide arguments that there are risks related to local task delegation to medical AI systems such as Watson leading to overreliance, such as the fact that it is in the design of these systems that they improve performance the more data they can be fed, which does suggest that it is part of these systems' design to generate more reliance through—at the same time—more data and improved performance.

My argument in this chapter can therefore be criticized like any other argument as being either unsound or invalid, but it is not a slippery slope argument, having provided reasons for increased overreliance risks. Still, even if you grant both local task delegation and the overreliance risk, I must still address the question of control loss, whether at the global level or in some other way. If these systems improve performance and deliver better outcomes for patients,

- Who cares about control?
- Even if you did care about control, what's the reason for thinking that increased use of such systems will lead to control losses, for example, at the global control level?

I believe I have already addressed the former question by arguing that even though admittedly in healthcare—at least in some sectors and specialties of healthcare, anyway—control does not have as high a priority as in other domains (say, transport), this does not mean that control is not important in healthcare. My argument has been, basically, that control plays a different role in healthcare, and you might be willing to take more control-related risks in healthcare than in other domains because the stakes are higher.

The second question is more complex: if medical AI systems improve clinical performance—for example, diagnostic performance—and ultimately therefore deliver better outcomes for patients, why worry about control? I have already made some progress toward answering this question, but let me now look at two specific hypothetical cases.

Watson for Oncology

Imagine that, through Watson, an oncologist is presented with a therapeutic possibility that she would herself not have thought of, maybe because the relevant RCTs have been recently concluded or the relevant medication has just been approved; basically, the idea would be that Watson is, in this particular circumstance, more up to speed or up to date than this particular oncologist or the oncology unit where she works. Still, the new therapeutic strategy suggested by the medical AI system is not so radical that our imaginary oncologist cannot evaluate it or try it out. After due diligence, evaluation of the evidence, and consultation with relevant oncologist colleagues, our imaginary oncologist decides to proceed with this new therapeutic strategy suggested by Watson, and, indeed, patients outcomes are significantly improved. Without going into too much detail, what is crucial for this thought experiment is the following counterfactual: *had Watson not suggest this new therapeutic option, patient outcomes would not have improved.*

My focus in this chapter is on Watson as a decision-support system, but I want to also introduce a second hypothetical case that presents some relevant differences both in the interaction between human and computer system and also in the task itself:

Pathology Lab

In this second thought experiment, imagine the kind of human–computer interaction that I have earlier suggested would combine both strengths and thereby reduce both false negatives (medical AI system better than human pathologist) and false positives (human pathologist better than medical AI system). Again, please refer to my previous discussion about the current feasibility of this scenario, which is for my purposes again no more than a thought experiment (don't shoot me, I'm just a poor philosopher; I know nothing—I grew up thinking Socrates was brave, but was he actually a coward?). In this second scenario, then, the local pathology lab has implemented a protocol where all slides are first checked by a new computer system that rules out a lot of the obvious negatives while at the same time catching positives that the local human pathologists alone would have missed; still, in a second stage a team of human pathologists goes through the slides selected by the computer system in the first round and eliminates the false positives—the computer had been very generous, its data gluttony being notorious. As a result of the implementation of this system, the following counterfactual will be assumed to be true: *had the local pathology lab not implemented the new systems, there would have been both more false negatives and also more false positives.*

What these two thought experiments illustrate is, first of all, that I will not make much progress by insisting that decision-making authority remains with humans, because the whole issue is what that means in theory and how that is implemented in practice. And you have seen this problem in previous chapters already, such as with AWSs, VAR, and also self-driving cars and MHC (okay, three acronyms in one sentence is too much; let me at least remind you of the last one: MHC stands for meaningful human control).

One could attempt a clear distinction between, for example, delegating advice and decision support to the computer systems while retaining decision-making for oneself on the one hand, and on the other hand delegating not only advice and decision support but also decision-making to the computer system. How would this supposedly clear distinction apply to the two cases above?

One possible analysis is the following: while there is no decision-making by the computer system in the Watson for Oncology scenario, there is genuine decision-making by the system in the Pathology Lab scenario, because in the latter scenario there are slides that the human pathologists don't even get to analyze because in the first stage only the computer system is involved. So even though the pathology AI system is, we are supposing, supposed to be particularly good at avoiding false negatives and anyway better than humans at avoiding false negatives, if in our scenario the system rules out a genuine positive (thereby making one of these false negative mistakes that they were supposed to be so good at avoiding), then it is too late for the human pathologist to correct that mistake. And the human pathologist might have anyway not even been capable of correcting that mistake, given that we are assuming (based on the evidence from earlier in the chapter) that the computer system is better at avoiding false negatives than the human pathologist.

Still, the protocol is such that human pathologists can only correct false positive mistakes by the computer and not false negative mistakes. And there is a reason that's the protocol, because if the human pathologists were to reassess all cases looked at by the computer, then there would be no point in making the investment to buy the software, as the humans would have to redo the work anyway. So here the question is not whether the protocol makes sense (it does, given the evidence, and some risk assessment and judgment about acceptable risk thresholds is inevitable for any protocol). The question is whether given such protocol we can say that decision-making and not just decision support or advice has been delegated to the computer system or pathology AI system. (I know it's annoying that I keep referring to these supposedly AI systems as "just" computer systems; it makes the whole thing so old-fashioned sounding, but it is just my small reminder not to overestimate the machine and not to overlabel it with the magical term *AI*.)

To answer this question, it makes sense to compare Pathology Lab with Watson for Oncology, because it is not clear that in the latter case there is anything comparable in terms of delegating actual decision-making and not just decision support to the AI system, basically because the system is not ruling out any therapeutic options available to the human oncologist; at best (or worst), what the system is doing is not prioritizing or recommending therapeutic options that the human oncologist might have expected.

While in Pathology Lab the false negative mistake is gone and outside the reach of the human expert—so that effective intervention will inevitably be delayed by this mistake—in Watson for Oncology a comparable mistake (say, the system does not recommend a good or even the best therapeutic option or does not rank it accordingly at number one or near the top) can still be corrected by the human expert, or to be more precise, the comparable mistake will not necessarily compromise the human expert's decision-making, as the human expert can ignore the system's recommendations or override them based on her own experience and clinical judgment.

This kind of fallback—to import useful terminology from a previous chapter—is available to the human expert in the Watson for Oncology scenario but is crucially not available to the human expert in the Pathology Lab scenario. Accordingly, one could claim that the human expert in the oncology scenario has meaningful human control while the human expert in the pathology scenario does not have meaningful human control.

I wonder, though, whether this conclusion is too quick. The idea of clearly distinguishing in terms of control between our two scenarios underestimates, I would argue, a statistical perspective on the different practices described in the Watson for Oncology scenario and in the Pathology Lab scenario. Namely, while it is—empirically speaking—true that human oncologists in the former scenario have a kind of access and intervention capacity that human pathologists lack in the latter scenario, over the course of tens of thousands of cases, we cannot expect that the human oncologists will always check on all the steps taken by Watson, simply because in that case there would be no point in using Watson in the first place.

In fact it is likely that, over many cases, error rates between the two kinds of scenarios would end up converging, especially over time—this does not assume overreliance; it just makes a basic psychological assumption about the likelihood of cognitive systems such as ours (human medics) checking less and trusting the system's judgment more as time goes on—that is, after all, what experience is (also see chapter 3 on control, automaticity, and habits).

The reason error rates can be expected to converge is that, over many cases and over time, both error rates in pathology cases and error rates in oncology cases would end up resembling the computer system's error rates. The only scenario in which there is no long-term convergence is one in which either one of the two systems performs so poorly that it has to be shelved or, alternatively, a scenario in which human oncologists are required to do so much extra work in order to mitigate the system's problems that, again, the system is no longer worth it (especially this latter case will sound familiar to a lot of healthcare staff confronted with the rollout of the latest digital platform; see Di Nucci et al. [2020], specifically chapter 7 but also chapter 8 from the same volume).

I now have a dialectically interesting problem: there seems to be a clear ground to make a theoretical distinction about the kind of control that the human pathologist has in the Pathology Lab case and the control that the human oncologist has in the Watson for Oncology case, because the human pathologist doesn't even get to see the slides that—in the first stage—the medical AI system has ruled out as obvious negatives and can therefore not correct for the (admittedly few, we are supposing) false negative mistakes by the AI system. Under certain assumptions we have made about the Watson for Oncology thought experiment, the human oncologist in this latter case does not have the same particular control problem that her pathology colleague has.

But the question is whether this clear control difference in theory justifies the claim that only one of the humans—the oncologist—has MHC while the other human lacks MHC. (Have you already forgotten? MHC is meaningful human control.) This question is also important from a purely ethical point of view: suppose that one of the many AI ethics guidelines now proliferating stipulated that some practice or technological system was only morally acceptable or ethically justified—or call it responsible innovation—on the (necessary) condition that some person could be attributed MHC. On that simple ethical principle—which I will not defend here—Pathology Lab would be ethically impermissible while Watson for Oncology would be, or at least not ethically impermissible on the grounds of lack of MHC (there could be other reasons the Watson for Oncology scenario is ethically impermissible that have nothing to do with MHC).

Now I have a genuine question about the conditions for control attributions: should these conditions be based on what is possible for human agents (for example, in terms of intervention or, as in my original "street definition" of control, influence), or should they be based on how much intervention or influence human agents can be reasonably expected to exercise?

In order to answer this question, I can again rely on what's probably this book's most important distinction, between direct control and overall control, for the following reason: one could argue that, in order for the pathology scenario also to meet meaningful human control conditions and thereby a necessary condition on ethical permissibility, I should revise the established practices and organization within Pathology Lab in order to give human pathologists access to the first stage so that they can correct the AI system's false negatives.

In this revised scenario, Pathology Lab II, I still have the involvement of both the AI system and the human pathologist and also still have two stages in which the work is organized, but human pathologists can if necessary go back to stage one to make corrections.[1] As discussed above, I could then argue that, given this revision, Pathology Lab II would meet the conditions for meaningful human control and thereby would also meet the MHC condition for ethical permissibility.

The only problem is that, unfortunately, Pathology Lab II does not make sense. Here is why (and you should have already guessed, actually): the whole point of organizing the clinical work as described in the original Pathology Lab was the evidence pointing to software being more vulnerable than human medics to false positives while human medics are more vulnerable than software to false negatives. Obviously one could dispute that evidence, but that's beyond the philosopher's pay grade, so it won't do in a philosophy argument. Assuming then that the relevant evidence is strong, asking human medics to go back to stage one to correct false negative mistakes made by software would be like asking a medical student to correct a consultant's mistakes. A consultant makes mistakes too, and there will even be—across many cases—consultants' mistakes that not even a medical student would have made, and some of those could be such that indeed a medical student could correct the consultant.

At the systemic level, though, we ought to assume that the average consultant will make fewer mistakes than the average medical student and that, therefore, implementing a system in which medical students are asked to check on—and if relevant correct—the mistakes of consultants would be not only inefficient but counterproductive. It would, namely, lead to even more mistakes over many cases. The same goes for Pathology Lab II: given the existing evidence that we are assuming here, Pathology Lab II would lead to more false negatives than the original Pathology Lab rather than fewer.

So here I have *a* control paradox: a system with more control—Pathology Lab II—leads to more mistakes (in this case false negatives) than a system with less control, the original Pathology Lab scenario.[2] Whatever you make of my original control paradox, I think this particular control paradox can be solved by pointing out that Pathology Lab II does not constitute a system with more control than the original Pathology Lab. Rather, given my distinction between direct control and overall control, I can say that Pathology Lab II merely constitutes an organizational system with more direct control but not more overall control than the original Pathology Lab, and that indeed given the distribution of tasks in the original Pathology Lab, the latter is a system in which there is more overall control than in Pathology Lab II, because there is a better task distribution in terms of the skills of the different parties.

Here I then have a very good case of how the distinction between direct control both generates an apparent paradox and also offers a way of resolving that apparent paradox: it only looks as though Pathology Lab II has more control than the original Pathology Lab because we are biased toward human intervention and access. But—as I have argued at length in other chapters—given a particular context and skill set, more human intervention and access is counterproductive and leads to less control rather than more. And the different Pathology Lab scenarios here constitute another such context in which it is important to distribute tasks without being biased by the idea that more human intervention and access is always better.

What is the consequence of my argument for the concept of meaningful human control? MHC should not be spelled out in terms of direct control and more human intervention and access but rather in terms of unbiased task distribution based on relative skill sets, like in the original Pathology Lab. Interestingly, then, you see that within the MHC concept, there might in the end be a tension between its "meaningful" element and its "human" element, because sometimes more "human" is less "meaningful" and less "human" is more "meaningful."

Part Four

The Political Paradox

Chapter Eleven

Taking Back Control

From Brexit to Trump and the Control Paradox of Representative Democracy

The control paradox is to blame for Brexit and Trump—but my delegation-based solution to the paradox might also work as an antidote to populism. Those are the courageous and controversial claims that this chapter will try to defend.

This being chapter 11—and actually the twelfth chapter in this book since I, like Danish schools, started from 0 with an introduction rather than 1—you should have a good idea by now of how the control paradox is supposed to work. I am sure I could have applied it to more technological phenomena than what I chose in part III, but I think there is something even more worthwhile that I can do with the publisher's space and my—and your—time: namely, show that once the control paradox has been introduced and properly understood, it can be used to analyze phenomena that go beyond technological practices.

That is why in this chapter I want to get political, if I may. There are multiple ways to apply the control paradox to the political domain: when I first presented my idea to my colleagues here in Copenhagen, for example, Allan Krasnik, who specializes in migrant health, they pointed out that the way the European Union tried to stop migrants from Africa and the Middle East in the now infamous 2015–2016 period resembled a control paradox. Basically, in order to get what people were referring to as a migration and refugee crisis back under control,[1] the EU outsourced the control of its outer borders to Turkey. Erdogan was generously compensated in order for Turkey to deal with the problem instead of the EU itself.

Here the point is not whether this is a genuine case of the control paradox or whether what happened back then between the EU and Turkey should be thought of as a form of control delegation, but it is at least plausible to think that there was both control enhancement (the number of migrants and refugees dropped dramatically once Turkey took over) and control loss, because it was a nonmember state who was put in control of access to member states.

The control paradox, then, is not just about technology. Here I want to focus on a different political application of the control paradox, one that I have already introduced in chapter 2: the distinction between *representative* democracy and *direct* democracy and how these different political forms can be used to understand recent populist and anti-expertise developments (again, see chapter 2 for some concrete examples, such as recent vaccine skepticism).

It is in fact dialectically difficult for me to apply the control paradox to democratic theory for the simple reason that I am no longer sure whether it is in fact the distinction between direct democracy and representative democracy that was the original model for my distinction between direct control and overall control.

Direct democracy : representative democracy
Direct control : overall control

I have argued so far that the practice of delegation should be understood in terms of giving up direct control in order to enhance overall control, so if direct control and overall control are closely related to the concepts of direct democracy and representative democracy, it should be no surprise that the practice of delegation is central to the functioning of democratic political systems—and in fact in many jurisdictions political "representatives" are called "delegates," for example, at the state level in many U.S. states, there are "state senators" and "delegates" (while at the federal level they are indeed just called "representatives").

Some of this stuff is so conceptually obvious that I hardly need to write it down, but I don't think that weakens my argument. What happens in representative democracies is that some crucial political tasks are delegated by the people (or better, voters—as in many political systems lots of people are disenfranchised from voting, so that "the people" and "voters" are not coextensive in terms of voting rights, let alone actual turnout) to their representatives in a parliament or congress.

It is interesting to reflect on what it is that is delegated in representative democracies—but first of all, let me once again state the obvious by saying that within a direct democracy there is no delegation, and the absence of delegation is indeed the definition of a direct democracy.

Here there is the fascinating question of whether total absence of delegation is even possible on scale, but that's beyond my scope here; let me just say that, if you think in terms of individual decisions rather than over time, no delegation might be at least possible (advisable is a completely different matter that this chapter will have to address in some detail later), referenda being the prototypical example of exceptions to the "norm" of delegation for decisions that are deemed particularly crucial, such as constitutional ones. Here again, see obviously Brexit but also at the end of that same year—2016—the constitutional referendum that brought down the Renzi government in Italy (needless to say, Trump was also elected in that now notorious year 2016, but U.S. presidential elections are not referenda, and in fact, in a way, the opposite is true: namely, the count that was closer to a referendum—the popular vote—was won by Hillary Clinton, and Trump only won the Electoral College).

Back to delegation. What gets delegated in a functioning representative democracy? It would be very tempting to answer that what is delegated is *power*. Power is, after all, the normatively important concept—the equivalent of control, once you make this chapter's transition from technology to politics.

Two questions come up when I hypothesize that representative democracies are founded on the delegation of power:

- Does power function similarly to control so that when power is delegated it is not necessarily lost but in fact potentially enhanced? The analogy between control and power is then crucial for the evaluation of the whole system of representative democracy, it would seem.
- The second question has to do with whether power is the correct candidate for delegation, given that the whole idea of democracy is that *power lies with the people*. But here again, the analogy between power and control is crucial, because if power works like I have argued that control works, delegating power does not mean losing power. So the answer to this second question might depend on the answer I provide to the first question.

Let me take stock of the different steps in my argument so far:

1. The difference between direct democracy and representative democracy consists in which tasks are delegated in the latter system and not delegated in the former system.
2. One obvious candidate for delegation could be power, so that power would not be delegated in direct democracy, but it would be delegated, according to this interpretation, in representative democracies.
3. If power is what is delegated in representative democracy as opposed to direct democracy, that would not necessarily imply that power is given up by the people within representative democracy, at least on

the assumption that power works like control and is therefore not lost through delegation.

This is a philosophy book, and it isn't even a book of political philosophy, so there is a limit to the amount of basic political science that I can go into, but at least the further distinction between executive power and legislative power is in order here if I am to find out what it is that gets delegated in representative democracies as opposed to direct democracies. The distinction between executive power and legislative power (to which traditionally one must also add judicial power) is, for example, relevant if one considers that within representative democracies both executive power and legislative power are delegated, while within direct democracies only executive power is delegated while legislative power is not delegated.

Two points from the argument summarized above I will assume (and therefore not argue for): the crucial role of delegation in distinguishing between direct democracy and representative democracy, and also the claim that control is not lost through delegation—see the relevant previous chapters for an extended argument about delegated control, especially part II.

What I must answer, on the other hand, is both the question of whether power is the right candidate and the question of whether there indeed is an analogy between power and control; as I said, if there is an analogy, that might help make the case that power is the right candidate. So I will start with this latter issue.

POWER AND CONTROL

Does power in politics and society function like I have argued control functions within technological practices? And, more in general, what is the conceptual relationship between power and control? This latter question is important beyond the scope of the control paradox, in fact.

I can start with a bit of conceptual mapping: if power is supposed to function similarly to control, then there ought to be some kind of distinction similar to the one between direct control and overall control, and there ought to be some form of power delegation such that power is not lost. So are there such concepts as *direct power*, *delegated power*, and *overall power*? All I have so far is the basic pretheoretical distinction between legislative power and executive power. Does that help with the control analogy?

I need to distinguish multiple questions within this supposed analogy between control and power:

• Is power what is delegated within representative democracies?

- What happens to power when it is delegated? As in, is delegated power still "real" power the way delegated control is still "real" control? Another way of addressing this is by comparing the idea that control is not lost when we delegate it (and indeed can be enhanced through delegation) with the hypothesis that power is similarly not lost when we delegate it. But how could power be enhanced through delegation?
- What does control have to do with power and power delegation within representative democracies? Could it be, for example, that power is the way we exercise control within politics? This is different from the idea that power is politics' version of control; here the idea would rather be that control is still what matters also in politics, and through the exercise and delegation of power in politics we gain or keep control. This latter question has the added benefit that through an analysis of political power I might actually learn even more about control.

LOTTOCRACY?

Before I address the questions above, let me be clear that even though I am assuming that the difference between direct democracy and representative democracy is a question of delegation, delegation is not necessarily the only game in town. Alex Guerrero (2014) and Hélène Landemore (2017) have, for example, recently argued for a so-called *lottocratic* system or *lottocracy*. No, folks, philosophers aren't very good at coming up with new terminology (and in fact, Landemore just calls it "open democracy," which doesn't say what it is but at least isn't ugly), but here's the idea and, please, don't prejudge it by its name: a lottocratic system is supposed to be a deliberative democratic system that represents an alternative to both representative democracy and direct democracy.

What this already tells the uninitiated is that you should distinguish between deliberative democracy and representative democracy, so that you can do deliberation without representation—and you can do so, the lottocrats argue, without having to rely on the dangers of direct democracy (these "dangers" Guerrero summarizes as "direct democracy—we are told—would lead to bad policy" [2014, 135]).

This is not the place to properly engage with this proposal (for a critical perspective, see, for example, Umbers [2018]). I only want to "use" it to illustrate some elements relevant to my discussion about power delegation and control. The first thing I learn is that there are at least theoretical alternatives to representative systems that are not necessarily "direct." Does this also mean that there are alternatives to delegation?

It is not obviously clear how delegation fits the lottocratic alternative to representative democracy. On the one hand, you could say that, given that there is no representation and no representatives, there is also no delegation in lottocracy. But on the other hand, those individuals who will be chosen through lottery to deliberate on our behalf for their allotted time could also be argued to be our delegates and, in fact, our representatives. After all, the fact that their time as delegates or representatives is limited doesn't matter, because time limits are also a feature of "classic" representative systems.

What this suggests is that lottocracy is not an alternative political system to either representative democracy or direct democracy, but rather that the lottocratic system is just a different electoral system (and this isn't necessarily a surprise, given the title of Guerrero's original article putting this forward, "Against Elections").

There are different ways to choose our delegates or representatives; some of them are forms of delegation while others are not forms of delegation. Birthright, for example, is a way of choosing one's rulers that does not constitute delegation, I would argue. So the question really is just whether lottocracy is a way of choosing one's rulers that involves delegation or whether, like birthright, it does not constitute delegation. But isn't there a difference between representatives and rulers? This is where I go back to the difference between legislative power and executive power and, in fact, also to the difference between democratic rule and nondemocratic rule.

Things get quite complex pretty quickly, and I am not a political theorist, but basically I can simplify by saying that I should first distinguish between democratic and nondemocratic political systems or regimes and that, within democratic systems, I should further distinguish between direct democracy, representative democracy, and—maybe—also lottocratic or open democracy. But the question is whether this simple taxonomy is already buying too much into the lottocratic critique of representative democracy, because an alternative analysis could hold on to the distinction between direct democracy and representative democracy and then, in a further step within different representative systems, distinguish between different ways of organizing representation (or delegation), where elections could be one way and lotteries could be another way.

The reason this matters for my purposes is because I want to understand which forms political delegation can take, where the question is if lottery systems should also count as forms of political delegation—on the assumption that electoral systems do count as delegating systems (what the objection to delegation will turn out to be is—as I already said—a different question, with which I will deal at a later stage in this chapter).

Are there any reasons to believe that lottery systems are not forms of delegation while electoral systems are forms of delegation? Let me start from Guerrero's own use of the concept of delegation, which is mentioned only twice in his original article, one of which is relevant:

In discussions of the use of lottery selection, the most common worry is competence. Wouldn't entrusting political decision-making to a randomly selected body of citizens be a disaster, much worse than delegation to elected representatives? Maybe electoral politics has its problems, but at least those selected have to be at least somewhat intelligent, socially competent, hardworking—or so the thought goes. (Guerrero 2014, 172)[2]

This passage seems to both recognize that representative systems are based on delegation and suggest that lottocratic systems are not based on "delegation to elected representatives." If that is indeed Guerrero's position (this assumption seems plausible, but I will not argue for it here), what grounds are there to think that lottocratic systems are not based on delegation?

In the above-quoted passage, Guerrero is discussing competence. While competence could well be a reason for delegating—in my framework, competence is a strategic reason for delegation—a difference in competence between the decision-makers in a representative system and the decision-makers in a lottocratic system doesn't as such say anything about whether delegation is at play.[3]

A more promising way seems to be the following. Ask yourself, why would we organize such a lottery to choose our decision-makers in the first place? The reason doesn't have to do with the supposed problems with representative democracy but rather with the supposed problems with direct democracy—namely, deliberation is difficult on scale. So we need to cut the numbers down to a size that allows for meaningful deliberation.

And if you don't believe the above, just look at political debate online: people seem now to generally recognize that online political debate lowers, exacerbates, and polarizes deliberation rather than informing it or making it more inclusive or democratizing it. Still, here I don't have the time to engage with the many hopefuls of online or digital direct democracy. The point is just that if you are worried about direct democracy and scale, online developments over the last couple of decades offer you a case study. And I don't have to argue that you should be worried about direct democracy and scale, but the lottocrats seem themselves worried about it, otherwise the lottery wouldn't be necessary and we could just stick to good old-fashioned soviets (the distribution and multilevel character of which [of the soviets, I mean] was also, let me remind you, a way of dealing with the problem of direct democracy and scale).[4]

Lotteries are then supposed to be a way of guaranteeing the quality of deliberation without sacrificing inclusivity and, basically, the democratic principle. But isn't that also what voting is meant to achieve? And if voting is delegating, then why aren't lotteries also delegating?

The answer to this question is not obvious. You could argue that lotteries are not forms of delegating because the lucky ones (or unlucky ones, in the case of jury duty?) are not necessarily deciding on our behalf. Depending on the ethical, legal, and political constraints of different lottery systems, it is at least not obvious that those who are picked shouldn't just be allowed to decide based on their own particular interests, so that when an academic is picked she will decide in the interest of education, research, and the like while when a commercial pilot is picked she will decide in the interest of her own sector.

The problem with disallowing the above self-interested way of coping with the lottery systems is that we risk turning the system into a representative one in which we have part-time politicians instead of full-time politicians. And indeed different representative systems across space and time have had more or less full-time politicking, and in Western democracies the number of so-called career politicians has certainly grown, for example.

There are, then, reasons for thinking that lottery systems would be such that those picked—as opposed to chosen through elections—would not necessarily be deciding on behalf of the rest. That would turn out to be a neat way of also arguing that, because they are not deciding on behalf of the rest, they are not representing the rest. And this consequence would in turn mean that what happens in lottery systems is not a form of delegation. On the other hand, if certain restrictions against self-interested decision-making are put in place within a lottery system, that might make the system more plausible from the point of view of democracy, but it might turn it back into a representative system based on delegation.

Assuming no such constraints, would those not picked have any power in lottery systems? The answer to this question might further illuminate the nature of the practice of delegating power and control within politics. Basically, it seems to me that—unsurprisingly, perhaps, given the title of this book—the main difference between representative systems and lottocratic systems is in terms of control, namely, the control that voters are supposed to have over those elected as opposed to the lack of control that those not randomly picked have over those randomly picked.

Now, political theorists, in contrasting representative systems with lottocratic systems, might be most worried about the quality of deliberation on the one hand and fairness and basic democratic principles on the other hand. For these reasons, one would want to be very careful in organizing such lotteries so that everybody has the same chances of being picked, for example. And this would admittedly be an improvement—from at least the point of view of inclusion—over the voter disenfranchising and low turnout of many representative democracies.

While this might deal with worries about fairness and equality, it says very little about the relationship between those picked and those not picked after the lottery. And the possible constraints discussed above about not abusing one's luck will not do either, because even the most stringent constraints would—at least in principle—fail to distinguish lottocratic systems from the legal and ethical constraints on politicians within representative democracy.

What's missing, it seems to me, is very simple: those not picked do not control those picked once they are picked, nor do they control them before the lottery. This is the crucial missing element of representation in lottocratic systems, and it is, importantly, neither about quality of outcome nor about equality—which are supposed to be the two standard measures by which we evaluate representative democracy against direct democracy.

DEMOCRATIC CONTROL

The third measure is control. Now you might well think I am being very naïve in relying on the claim that voters control politicians after they have elected them. If they have any leverage at all, then surely it comes before and not after electing them. But it is not too ambitious, I believe, to think of a functioning representative democracy in terms of power being delegated by voters to politicians through election without control being relinquished.

And—surprise, surprise—you can guess what I am going to claim is the kind of control that voters do relinquish within representative democracy: yes, it is in fact direct control, just like you have seen throughout this book. And, as in previous chapters, direct control being relinquished does have a price. And that price might very well include—as I claimed at the outset of this chapter—recurring cycles of populist uprisings like the ones we have seen across Western democracies over the last few years.

The loss of direct control is the price of representative democracy. But— and that's the crucial difference—within the lottocratic alternative there is no control at all, and no amount of fairness or quality of outcome can compensate for that lack of control. Remember, though, my argument contrasting representative systems with lottocratic systems has been very quick because that's not what I am interested in here. I make the contrast only to emphasize this additional feature of representative systems, namely, that they are organized like many of the other practices I have discussed in this book: direct control is sacrificed on the altar of some (supposed) enhancement. But giving up direct control does not mean giving up control altogether—and that applies to representative democracies just like it applies to technological systems.

I now have the analogy I was looking for: power is delegated through the voluntary loss of direct control within representative democracies. Overall control is not thereby lost (whether it is enhanced as in previous chapters is another matter). But the price for voluntarily abdicating direct control can be steep, especially over time, and result in the kinds of populist backlashes that we have seen over the last few years (Brexit and Trump above all else). The populist slogan should really be "Taking Back Direct Control."

This is not a joke. If the populist slogan had been "Taking Back Direct Control," I believe that slogan would have been accurate. And the fact that the slogan for Brexit was instead "Taking Back Control" tells me a few interesting things: First of all, as political slogans go, it was quite brilliant, being almost accurate in a business in which accuracy is rare and beside the point. Second, there was some truth in that slogan, namely, there is genuine political cost to the loss of direct control, and representative democracies ought not to forget or underestimate what it costs voters to lose direct control (the same way computer system designers ought not to forget it, for example). Third, as this book should have made clear by now, there is a big difference between "control" and "direct control," so that in fact in the end the slogan was inaccurate: there was no need to take back control because control had not been lost or given away, since when we delegate successfully we do not lose control altogether but only direct control. And in fact the disagreement between the populists and the establishment might have in the end been over the success of power delegation within recent representative democracies.

As I emphasized in chapter 2, whether power delegation has been successful might very well depend on which group or minority you belong to. Some groups' material conditions have notoriously deteriorated over the last few decades (for example, what Europeans refer to as the "working class" and Americans rather tend to call the "middle class")—see wage stagnation, but also drops in life expectancy for some groups (again, I refer you back to chapter 2 for the relevant evidence on this).

I can now identify at least three kinds of political systems based on my control framework:

Direct Democracy: These are political systems in which the people (as John Steinbeck used to call them—ironically, I always believed, or hoped?) are supposed to keep direct control—direct-democratic systems; they present, on scale, massive problems of organization and also of quality of outcome—but that's not my concern here.

Nondemocratic Regimes: These are political systems in which the people lose, whether voluntarily or involuntarily, or never had overall control. You might think of traditional oligarchic systems or historically the institution of the monarchy as such systems (involuntary loss of overall control for both). But there is maybe a more interesting instantiation of this category for our purposes, namely, populist backlashes where the people voluntarily give up overall control (to a strongman?) on the grounds that they want to reclaim direct control.

Representative Democracy: Finally, there are systems in which the people voluntarily give up direct control for the purpose of—supposedly—improving governance and ultimately outcomes. Lottocratic systems might still count as a subgroup of this category, in which the people (those not picked this time by the lottery) have no control over the decision-makers but still retain overall control over the lottery and its rules—but how, given that they have not been picked and there is nothing they can do apart from wait for the next lottery and hope to be lucky? Anyway, the lottocractic alternative is not my concern here, but it served well to tease out some features of other democratic systems.

This is where the control paradox comes in, for the following reason: the difference between giving up just enough direct control in order to enhance outcomes and giving up too much direct control so that there is overall loss of control (say, populism, but I can think of other possibly worse outcomes such as some voluntary totalitarian outcomes in Europe in the twentieth century) is ultimately the difference between a democratic regime and a nondemocratic regime—therefore, we must get this distinction precisely right.

What constitutes, for example, giving up just enough direct control without giving up too much control within representative democracies? Power delegation must be reversible, for example—through individual accountability. In this respect, one might believe that a representative system such as the British first-past-the-post where MPs are accountable not just to their party but also to their individual constituency retains more overall control than a representative system that is more proportional but has less accountability—for example, because smaller parties are more equally represented in Parliament, but their elected members are chosen top-down rather than bottom-up.

I realize this is newspaper-like simplification of political realities (maybe worse, actually). But, first of all, that's philosophy for you. And, second, the point here is not the details of the different systems and how to better implement representative systems. My point is that evaluation of democratic systems should be based (also) on the kinds of control criteria analyzed in this book. And above, I gave you just one example of how purely from a control point of view a system that is less representative (the UK first-past-the-post) might be more democratic than a system that is more representative (the German 5 percent threshold).

You are welcome to disagree on the merits of this particular case, but—you know what—I don't care, nor do I need to care. My point is just that control should be one criterion of evaluation among others. And if a less representative system generates more accountability, then that's a consideration worth including in the evaluation.

One caveat here is that I have used "representative" in a less than perfectly accurate way. Accountability between individual elected politicians and voters can itself be argued to be "representative" because it is through the sum of having been elected by those voters plus being accountable to those voters that we get "representation"—again, see the contrast with the lotto-cratic alternative. So if my use of "representative" above was less than clear, then you can make the following distinction between "representative" and "proportional (representation)": political systems can be more representative in virtue of being less proportional (or proportionally representative). That would be the difference that I have just emphasized between the current UK electoral system and the current German electoral system.

To be sure, electoral systems are just one element of a political system, and I certainly do not want to argue that the only way control is exercised is through elections and electoral systems. A free press, for example, is a clas-sic further element of control and accountability. And there are forms of control that go possibly too far. I am thinking of referenda, which are meant to be direct-democratic exceptions to power delegation in which the people reclaim direct control over individual decisions. The worry is that if direct control is reclaimed for the wrong question—for example, because the gener-al public does not have the relevant expertise to answer that question—this form of reclaiming direct control might result in a loss of overall control. Maybe Brexit was such a case, with Parliament arguably in the end empow-ered by the fine complexities generated by the outcome of the initial referen-dum. The world is, as usual, much more complicated than philosophy.

POLITICAL CONTROL PARADOX

This chapter has, I believe, achieved its goals: an analysis of the ways control is relevant to political power, which at the same time further illustrates my crucial concepts of delegation and direct control. There is only one thing left to do, and that's asking whether the control paradox itself applies to the political realities I have been discussing in this chapter.

The basic idea of the political control paradox—as I already introduced it in chapter 2—is that we delegate power in representative democracies for both economic and strategic reasons (remember, those are technical terms as defined in this book and do not mean exactly what they normally mean—just in case you picked up this book for chapter 11 to read about Trump or Brexit). Economic delegation of power is so that we don't have to invest too much of our resources for the purposes of political decision-making—after all, we are busy making a living, changing nappies, and so much more. In this respect, direct democracies could be construed as systems in which there is no need for economic delegation—if they work well and the resource distribution is worthwhile, as with rich Athenian men who had plenty of slaves and women home to do the Ancient Greek equivalent of changing nappies.

Strategic delegation might turn out to be more controversial, because the idea would be that within representative democracies it is in our not only economic but also strategic interest to delegate power to our representatives, supposedly because they are better than we would be at political decision-making. This is the kind of delegation to the experts that otherwise happens in domains such as healthcare. But while people normally don't find it too difficult to recognize that medical doctors, given their experience, training, and particular skill set, are better placed than themselves when it comes to, say, clinical decision-making (with exceptions, see vaccination skepticism in chapter 2), it is common to deny politicians the relevant expertise that makes them, supposedly, better decision-makers. And in fact it is common even among politicians to deny such a particular skill set and instead to portray themselves as men (mostly) of the people.

Assuming nonetheless that the average politician in a representative democracy is a better decision-maker than the average voter, we get strategic delegation—warning: you might not be able to assume as much; lottocrats might, for example, deny a skill gap between politicians and voters, Guerrero's idea being that as long as the average voter has good quality expert advice—namely, the kind of advice that politicians should listen to—there is no reason the average voter should be thought a better decision-maker than the average politician. So I suppose, on Guerrero's lottocratic proposal, you cannot assume strategic delegation reasons for delegating power; still, the lottery is there for the kinds of simplification purposes that are behind economic delegation, as you have already seen.

We delegate political power to representatives, then, in order to use our attention resources more efficiently and also in order to improve outcomes—you will recognize this picture from previous chapters. Now, in order to get the control paradox (or the power paradox, for that matter), I need two more conditions to be met: there needs to be control loss or power loss (or anyway increased risk of control loss or power loss or, finally, reasonable fear of control loss or power loss—you know the drill by now). And the second condition is that the very purpose of the delegation is what undermines it—the paradoxical bit, if you like. Namely, as you have seen in previous chapters, if the actual dialectic turned out to be outcome enhancement that results in control loss, then that would not be paradoxical (the same for control enhancement that results in, say, worse outcomes).

It is not clear that the strategic reasons for power delegation in representative democracies have to do with control enhancement or power enhancement: delegation is the way the people exercise their power (also don't forget the genuinely still open question of whether delegation is voluntary within representative democracies) rather than a way of enhancing one's power. So there might be no genuine paradox here after all.

The loss of control or the loss of power are more promising (but remember, the conditions are not alternative—both need meeting in order to get the paradox). As I have said, giving up direct control has its costs, and those costs can have serious political consequences, such as the rise of populist movements that end up endangering the foundations of representative democracies—thereby undermining the very purpose of delegating power.

Populism might in fact represent a case in which you start with strategic and economic power delegation that should result in only giving up direct control and in a more efficient and successful exercise of power by the people, but you end up with genuine loss of power by the people to, say, a perceived strongman such as Trump.

Suppose the above is the case for at least some historical occurrences, whether very recent ones such as Brexit and Trump or older ones. One question is whether this would count as a genuine instantiation of the control paradox, but a possibly more urgent question is why: namely, how do you go from power delegation, which should create efficiencies and enhance outcomes, to populism?

A clarification here will help me answer this question: there are, in the process described above, two different control losses, and distinguishing between those two is important to better understand the phenomenon in question. On the one hand, there is the perceived control loss, which is supposed to rationalize, from a populist point of view, the idea of taking back control. Namely, populists argue that there has been genuine loss of control or power by the people through delegation and representative democracy, and that therefore control (and power) needs to be won back.

This perceived loss of control isn't, though, the loss of control that I have identified previously as possibly resulting in a control paradox. That other loss of control was about the fact that, through populism, the people genuinely lose control over political proceeding by giving power to a perceived strongman. The complexity here depends on the fact that perceived loss of control leads to wanting to take back control, which leads to genuine loss of control—this, I speculate, is what happened with Brexit and Trump.

What's funny is that here, in the end, I might have a control paradox but one that is different from the original control paradox as I defined it early on in this book. This new control paradox has to do with the paradoxical character of genuinely losing control as a result of wanting back a control that one has not actually lost but only perceived to have lost. And the reason for that inaccurate perception is simply having mistaken loss of direct control for loss of overall control. And this—I again speculate, but I have also put forward relevant arguments in chapter 3—has to do with a psychological bias in favor of direct and conscious control over other forms of control. It is ultimately this bias that causes populist backlashes by leading people to believe that power delegation needs to be reined in.

As this book isn't and cannot even aspire to be a critique of populist movements, at least one caveat to the above argument needs to be discussed, namely, the possibility that loss of direct control within contemporary representative democracies doesn't just result in perceived loss of control but in actual loss of control. This is particularly relevant given the different interpretations of the paradox: it could be that, say, loss of direct control does not result in loss of actual control, but it does result in reasonable fear of loss of control. And that would be good enough given my definition of the original paradox.

Additionally, it could be that in many recent instances power delegation has been unsuccessful, resulting again in either loss of overall control instead of just direct control or at least increased risk or reasonable fears. But this is where political science comes in and the philosopher ought to stop. I have already pointed out possible empirical evidence that could be relevant here (both in chapter 2 and earlier in this chapter), about wage stagnation for the middle classes, for example, or drops in life expectancy for some groups. Still, it is important to emphasize that data pointing to genuine worsening of the material conditions of some groups—even if backed up by evidence that those very groups were overwhelmingly supporting, say, Brexit or Trump—does not necessarily mean that there was genuine loss of control for these groups, even just relative to former generations.

In conclusion, in this chapter I have shown how the control concepts developed in this book can be applied also to political processes and systems, such as with the difference between direct democracy and representative democracy. I have argued that there is an analogy between power delegation within political systems and control delegation within technological systems, and that the loss of direct control involved in power delegation might be one of the root causes of recent populist movements. Finally, I have concluded that here there might be a control paradox of sorts at play (even if not my original paradox): perceived loss of control (due to genuine loss of direct control through power delegation) leads to populist movements seeking to "take back control"—but those movements might ultimately end up causing genuine control loss, as with Brexit and Trump.

Chapter Twelve

Delegating Responsibility?

This is the last chapter. You've made it; well done! Which is also to say that there will be no conclusion or appendixes; once this chapter concludes, it's over—so I'd better say everything still left to say within the boundaries of this chapter. In fact, I think in a certain sense the main argument of this book has already been brought to a conclusion: I have said what the control paradox is and how it is supposed to work—through delegation (had you already forgotten?)—and then I applied the paradox to different plausible technological and nontechnological phenomena and practices, which was both a way of better understanding these phenomena and practices but also, hopefully, a way to delineate more precisely the conditions for the application of the paradox—that's why the results of some chapters were negative rather than positive, as in not all cases that I analyzed turned out to be genuine applications of the paradox.

I am not quite finished, though. There is one final important issue that needs dealing with, and it has to do with the normative consequences of the paradox. One crucial element of the paradox is, you will remember, the idea that control can be delegated, and that when we delegate control, we do not necessarily lose it—in fact, when we delegate control successfully, we necessarily do not lose control but only lose—and necessarily lose—direct control, and that is, as I said, the whole point of delegation.

The above is, as I see it, the most important insight resulting from the control paradox, and it therefore constitutes, I believe, this book's most important theoretical contribution. It is for that reason that in this final chapter I want to analyze the practical side of this theoretical insight, namely, the idea of delegating responsibility. My hypothesis here—as I have previously anticipated—will be that responsibility cannot be delegated; only control can be delegated, but crucially, when we delegate control, we do not also thereby delegate responsibility.

When we delegate control, in short, we keep responsibility. We are and remain responsible for what our delegates do, and this should not be a surprise given my overall argument: since when we delegate control we do not lose control, then we do not lose responsibility either. Still, there is a difference between the claim that we remain responsible after delegating control and the claim that we do not delegate responsibility along with control. And that difference is, basically, that there is something important that is lost when we delegate control—namely, direct control. But there is no equivalent to the loss or abdication of direct control when I move to the practical and normative realm of responsibility. Normatively speaking, there is no such thing as *direct* responsibility.

Nothing changes to our responsibility when we delegate control—that is the main claim that I defend in this chapter. Still, this hypothesis must be unpacked in two different ways:

1. There is no such thing as "delegating responsibility," so talk of "delegating responsibility" is a category mistake because, conceptually, responsibility cannot be delegated.
2. When we delegate control, we do not also delegate responsibility (because of the point above); also, when we delegate control, we remain responsible even though control has been delegated.

These two claims are quite obviously related, but you must not mix them up, for the following reason: it could be that the first conceptual claim about "delegating responsibility" is true while the second claim is not, because there might still be a change to our responsibility when we delegate control even if that change is not that responsibility itself has also been delegated.

There are also two further claims that are not implied by the above hypotheses: namely, it does not necessarily follow from either the claim that "delegating responsibility" is a category mistake or from the claim that we keep responsibility when we delegate control that (1) nothing changes to our responsibility when we delegate control, nor does it follow that (2) nothing changes to the responsibility of the delegate when we delegate control.

These two claims would make the main hypothesis of this chapter even stronger, but also less plausible. So in going through my analysis, I must be careful to keep separate the idea of "delegating responsibility" as a category mistake (and the related idea that we keep responsibility when we delegate control) and the idea that nothing changes in our responsibility when we delegate control, and also the further (and even stronger) idea that nothing changes in the delegate's responsibility. You can think of these claims as decreasing in theoretical magnitude, starting from

1. When we delegate control, nothing changes ino the responsibility of either the delegating party or the delegate.
2. When we delegate control, nothing changes in the responsibility of the delegating party.
3. When we delegate control, the delegating party keeps responsibility.

I will go through all the three different possibilities in this chapter, but let me already say that it is only the last and weakest possibility that I want to defend; the first and strongest claim is, I believe, pretty obviously false, and the truth of the second claim will ultimately depend on one's account of responsibility.

CONTROL AND RESPONSIBILITY

As you have seen in earlier chapters, a lot of the philosophical literature only uses the concept of control to talk about responsibility (Fischer and Ravizza [1998] being a classic example), so the idea of distinguishing between control and responsibility is already, of itself, controversial, but clearly that is what is at stake in a chapter dedicated to the conceptual impossibility of delegating responsibility that comes at the end of a whole book dedicated to delegating control.

Here I must begin by asking what the difference and relationship between the concepts of control and responsibility are. I will not get into the whole free will and determinism debate, but starting from the notorious PAP—the principle of alternate possibilities—will help me frame the conceptual relationship between responsibility and control.

According to PAP, you can only be responsible for some action A if you had an alternative to doing A. And that is why PAP is an incompatibilist argument, because in a universe where causal determinism applies, then if you did A, you could not have done otherwise than A, and then, if PAP is true, you could not be held responsible for A. Now you might think that PAP is an intuitive way of cashing out control: you only have control over your action A if you could have done otherwise than A—say not A or B or whatever. After all—going back to my street definition of control—if you did A and you could only have done A, how did you have any influence on your own A-ing?

Then along comes Harry Frankfurt (in 1969) with his cases supposed to show that responsibility does not require PAP—and you have already encountered such a case in this book, as the dual-control car case by Fischer and Ravizza (1998) is a Frankfurt-type case. Sally turns left without any intervention or coercion by the driving instructor—but given dual controls, the driving instructor could have and would have intervened to make Sally turn left if Sally hadn't done it on her own. Sally, according to Fischer and Ravizza, has guidance control even though she lacks regulative control—and as long as guidance control is enough for responsibility, Sally is responsible even though she lacks alternate possibilities, which in turns shows that PAP fails.

This helps me in the following way: in Frankfurt's original argument, you don't need any talk of "control," as the case goes straight from alternate possibilities to responsibility. But Fischer and Ravizza insert two control concepts in the argument to show that, basically, compatibilists and incompatibilists are talking past each other by using different notions of control. I am not interested in whether this constitutes any progress in the free will debate but only in the idea that we do not have some logical space between responsibility and control. On the assumption that Sally is responsible for turning left, then you can have responsibility without control—regulative control anyway, while guidance control would still be necessary for responsibility.

This is enough for now: minimally, the above shows that control and responsibility are not coextensive concepts, so analyzing the concept of "delegating responsibility" in light of my analysis of "delegating control" is at least not meaningless, conceptually speaking. Having established that much, here are six exemplary cases that I will use to argue against the delegation of responsibility. To be sure, by an argument against "delegating responsibility" I clearly—given what I have said so far—do not mean that delegating responsibility is wrong, impermissible, irresponsible, or anything normative like that. I simply mean that it is impossible to delegate responsibility. And ought implies can, so no need to argue for its wrongness apart from the interesting further claim that trying to delegate responsibility would be wrong (here see a recent paper about agency laundering [Rubel et al. 2019]—thanks to Sven Nyholm for pointing this out to me):[1]

1. Mary is John's boss and gives—in her capacity as his boss—John the following task: finding out and reporting back to her last year's net profits of company C, a competitor to the company where Mary and John work. John finds out and reports back to Mary.
2. This scenario is exactly like (1) but with a twist: while in (1) the financial data John found out about and reported to Mary were accurate, in this new scenario John reports back a mistaken number or set of data to Mary.
3. Hospital H implements a new computer system in which biopsy slides are evaluated by software based on machine learning algorithms. Only cases where the software reports inconclusive outcomes (under a certain confidence threshold) are further evaluated by a human pathologists. Above that confidence threshold of 96 percent, outcomes are

automatically passed on to the treating clinician, who will inform the patient. The clinician on duty receives a positive outcome with a 98 percent confidence value and reports it to the patient, recommending the relevant treatment plan.

4. This scenario is exactly like (3) but with a twist: while in (3) the positive outcome was accurate, in this new scenario the outcome is a false positive. Still, given the confidence value of 98 percent, it is reported to the clinician, who informs the patient, recommending the (same) relevant treatment plan.

5. A rural Scottish constituency elects M as their new MP on the promise that once in Parliament she will vote to stop construction of a new motorway that cuts through this rural constituency. Once elected, M votes to stop the new motorway.

6. This scenario is exactly like (5) but with a twist: in this new scenario, M once elected votes in support of the new motorway.

Why have I chosen the six scenarios above? Pretty clearly, these are all scenarios of delegation as defined in this book: respectively, delegation to other human agents (scenarios 1 and 2), delegation to technological systems (3 and 4), and delegation of power (5 and 6). For each pair, the difference between the former member of the pair and the latter member is that in the former delegation goes as planned while in the latter delegation does not go as planned; whether this is the same as to say that delegation was not successful is a further important question that I will address in this chapter.

Who are the bearers of responsibility in each case? Remember that, given my claim that there is no such thing as "delegating responsibility," each scenario ought to be such that—if my claim is right—the delegating party offloads none of the responsibility by delegating control to the delegate—that is, there is no change in the responsibility of the delegating party. Namely, I don't have with responsibility what happens with control, in which at least its "direct" element (of control) is lost by the delegating party in delegation.

Before I look at each case, let me emphasize a similarity between what I have said in this book about control and what I am saying in this chapter about responsibility. While the analogy breaks down because of the "direct control" component, which has no equivalent when it comes to responsibility, there is still an important analogous element, namely, that just like when we delegate control we do no lose control—because we keep or enhance overall control—when we delegate we also keep responsibility; it's just that what we delegate in this case isn't responsibility to begin with, but the relevant task (which might be control or something else—choice, for example).

SIX CASES STUDIES IN THE IMPOSSIBILITY
OF DELEGATING RESPONSIBILITY

Having made this further small conceptual clarification, let me now analyze the six cases. I actually do not need to analyze each separately, as I really have three pairs—and the easiest assessment of responsibility, at least intuitively, can be delivered for cases (2), (4), and (6) where things go wrong—it is, after all, particularly in such cases that we are, as individuals but also as a society, interested in attributing responsibility and blame.

How does my general claim that there is no loss of responsibility through delegation work in these three particular instances? There are, basically, two different controversial aspects of my claim:

• The first is that there is no loss of responsibility through delegation, where an opponent might want to argue that if the mistake is the delegate's alone, then the delegating party cannot be blamed or, at least, cannot bear *all* the blame—this use of "all," as I have already anticipated, is one of the aspects I find problematic with this alternative approach. More on this to come.

• Second, even someone sympathetic to my general claim that there is no loss of responsibility through delegation might be less sympathetic to my application of this general claim across domains as diverse as human organizations, technological systems, and political power—so this particular opponent might want to accept my claim that responsibility is not lost through delegation for technological systems but not for, say, human organizations or political power.

As these two ways of resisting my argument are independent of each other, I will have to deal with them in turn. But let me start with the cases, focusing on the latter variant in each pair.

INACCURATE INFORMATION

In case (2), Mary delegates a task to John: finding out a set of financial data. John finds out and reports back to Mary, as requested. The only problem is that the data set John reports to Mary turns out to be inaccurate. Who is to blame? Who is the bearer of responsibility? The case as I have presented it so far is way too underdescribed for an attribution of responsibility. But before I fill in the details, let me make clear whose responsibility I am interested in, because I am interested in a specific question—namely, whether Mary has lost or given up or ceded (or abdicated) responsibility by delegating the task to John. My normative claim, let me remind you one last time, is that no responsibility is lost through delegation.

Now suppose Mary herself needed those numbers for the next board meeting, at which she presents the inaccurate data set, costing her company a significant amount of money—imagine they are supposed to decide whether to take over the competitor in question, whose profitability data Mary is presenting to the board. Mary's company decides in favor of a takeover, but their old competitor turns out to be much less profitable than the data presented by Mary to the board suggested—the result is a share price drop for the newly merged company; job losses follow.

Who is responsible for the above? We have three obvious candidates: the board, Mary's office, John (I haven't quite decided whether John is high enough in the company to have his own office or whether he is just Mary's subordinate; let's see if that makes a difference to responsibility attributions). Also remember a couple of obvious caveats: responsibility can be shared so that more than a single party is responsible; also, it could be that nobody is responsible; finally, a less obvious candidate could be responsible—maybe the competitor has hacked Mary's company's IT system and inserted the inaccurate data without anybody realizing.

Let's imagine the following happened: Trying to establish the profitability of C involved some complex modeling by John—who is the specialist for that kind of thing within Mary's team. In modeling C's profitability, John made a small mistake that turned out to increase the expected profitability of C by a significant margin. John did not notice his mistake and passed on the inflated numbers to Mary, who presented them to the board.

Imagine further that John's mistake was not careless and that John was properly trained for the task Mary delegated to him, as his role in the team suggests. Why are these further elements important? Go back to our three pairs of cases: the difference between (1) and (2), for example, turns out not to be that in (1) Mary delegates successfully and in (2) Mary's delegation is unsuccessful. Mary delegates successfully in both cases, but the results are different because of John's small mistake. Delegating's success, it turns out—but you already knew given the conditions I established in part II of this book—does not entirely depend on the results of the delegation. Mary's delegation was both economic and strategic, intentionally speaking: John was the specialist on the team, so by delegating to him Mary followed her organization's structures and practices, creating efficiency and also—in theory—enhancing the outcome, as neither she nor anybody else on her team would have had the skill set and training to carry out the necessary financial modeling that John specializes in. Things just went wrong in a nonculpable way, as sometimes is the case.

Is Mary responsible for the data she presents to the board? Probably. Is she responsible for John's mistake? Again, probably. Bosses are responsible for their subordinates. Is that it? Is my story of delegation and responsibility as simple as that? Actually, I don't even have to argue that Mary is responsible for the data she presents to the board or for John's mistake, even though she probably is. Given that my claim is simply that by delegating one gives up direct control but does not give up responsibility—basically because direct control is not a necessary condition on responsibility, which ought not to surprise many—what I really need to compare is Mary's responsibility in the case in which she delegates with Mary's responsibility in the case in which she does not delegate—assuming the same outcome, clearly.

Imagine, then, a twin scenario in which Mary presents to the board inaccurate data that are the results of her own modeling—John was on holiday, or busy, or Mary had always wanted to try her own hand at modeling. It follows from my account that Mary cannot justify, excuse, or even mitigate (Hart 1968) her responsibility by appealing to John's role in the original case.

In fact—and this might seem paradoxical, but that's the whole point of the book—it seems to me that it would be easier for Mary to try to excuse herself or mitigate her mistake if she did the modeling herself: "My data scientist was on holiday," "It was my first time doing this kind of modeling myself," "The data scientist on my team was busy on another project so I did it myself." Those are probably not very good excuses and won't save her job after the merger fails, but still these attempts sound more plausible than saying, "My best data scientist did it" or "I didn't come up with the number myself; my specialist did it."

What this shows—and I happily admit that I am also appealing to intuition here as philosophers often do—is that Mary isn't any less responsible for the data she presents to the board in virtue of having delegated the task; indeed, if at all, she is all the more responsible in virtue of having done the proper thing of delegating—and in fact, if you are not sure yourself, just compare case (2) with case (1), in which the data is accurate and the merger a success. You wouldn't want to take any praise away from Mary just because she didn't do the modeling herself: she delegated to the expert, to the right person for the job, and that's exactly the role of a good manager—who should then share the praise with her team, obviously.

I am aware that this sounds a lot like the captain going down with her ship or being the last one to leave her ship, but I don't mind. The only thing I would add to that kind of rhetoric, in fact, is that often we talk of such cases as *taking* responsibility, as in praising especially virtuous individuals for taking their duties and responsibilities seriously. But there is no such thing, conceptually, as taking responsibilities for your team, your subordinates, or your delegates: you just *are* responsible. And the fact that some less virtuous individuals often try to deny that responsibility when things go wrong doesn't show anything or, if at all, shows that there is something there to deny in the first place.

Remember: do not confuse what I say above about Mary's responsibility in the different cases with John's responsibility. John is also responsible as the one carrying out the task; it's just that John's responsibility does not exonerate Mary. And John's responsibility for his mistake in the original scenario is a complex matter, but again, here I am only interested in Mary, so I don't need to get into it.

Small caveat: you might worry that I am being too friendly to the bosses, with all this talk of one's responsibility for one's subordinates and of not caring to spell out an account of why John is responsible. But while it is true that in this particular case there is a hierarchical structure such that the delegating party is above the delegated-to party, I have already anticipated in previous chapters that it is not always that way around, and indeed in the next two cases—healthcare and politics—it *is* the other way around, and the less powerful party—patients or voters—delegates to the more powerful party— medics or politicians.

Before moving on to the next case, I want to offer a further argument for the claim that no responsibility is lost through delegation. Given my account of delegation as giving up direct control, showing that no responsibility is attached to direct control is another way of demonstrating that, when by delegating we give up direct control, we do not thereby also give up responsibility.

Direct control does not, alone, make you responsible—which is another way of saying that direct control is not sufficient for responsibility (and I have already claimed earlier that direct control is not necessary for responsibility). So I can now say that direct control is neither necessary nor sufficient for responsibility.

Imagine Mary, instead of delegating to John, delegates the task of finding out the profitability of C to Jeremy, who has never done that kind of work before and normally does marketing. If Jeremy makes a mess of assessing the profitability of C, it will be difficult to blame him, given that he was not qualified or trained for that particular task and Mary knew it. The blame will naturally reside alone with Mary in that particular scenario. So the direct control that Jeremy has over the task in virtue of Mary's delegation doesn't warrant any attribution of responsibility. And my account has an explanation for this: given that Jeremy lacks the relevant skills and training, he has no overall control over the task—his mere direct control doesn't amount to much (for example, it won't get the job done), and it certainly doesn't count toward responsibility. It is like ceding the steering wheel to someone who can't drive: an irresponsible act.

Final caveat: an interesting feature of this further variant of case (2) is that Mary, by delegating to the wrong employee, has herself lost overall control over the completion of the task. That's a case of unsuccessful delegation, independent of the outcome (Jeremy might by a stroke of luck get the profitability of C just right, but that still would not amount to control because it was just a random occurrence). While on the other hand, delegating to the specialist John amounts to successful delegation even if the outcome is not the one aimed at; again, delegation is an intentional concept and not an extensional one, and that allows also for negative outcomes.

FALSE POSITIVE

One of the most controversial arguments in this book is probably offering the same account of delegation between different human agents for the interaction between human agents and technological systems. That analogy becomes even more controversial when it comes to responsibility, given the assumption that most technological systems (and very likely all technological systems that will be available this century anyway) are not capable of moral responsibility, not being the right kinds of agents to bear responsibility.

This is an important difference, when it comes to responsibility, between what in part II of this book I referred to as social control and delegation as opposed to technological control and delegation. Still, given that my interest has been primarily in the analysis of human agents delegating tasks to other human agents as opposed to human agents delegating tasks to technological systems (instead of technological systems delegating tasks to human agents, that is)—and that in this final chapter I am focusing on the responsibility of the delegating party instead of the responsibility of the delegate—the mere fact that with technological control and delegation the delegate is not the right kind of agent to bear responsibility is not necessarily an obstacle to a comparative analysis of the responsibility of the delegating party in the human–human case and the responsibility of the delegating party in the human–tech case—that is what case (4) is meant to achieve.

Cases (3) and (4)—which are obviously based on the Pathology Lab scenario in chapter 10—are such that a false positive generated by the algorithm results in the wrong treatment (case 4), while case (3) is the same but the result of the biopsy is accurate and the relevant treatment is given to the patient. One further feature of cases (3) and (4) that is particularly interesting for my purposes is that I don't just have humans delegating to machines (hospital management decides to delegate the task of evaluating pathology slides to software, and human pathologists implement a system that depends on the machine's outcome without relevant human fallback); I also have machine outcomes that automatically result in further human agency down the line, so that human clinicians take the outcome—which in case (4) is inaccurate—and run with it. While this cannot be considered a case of the software delegating a further task to the human clinician, it is a further machine–human interaction that generates extra complexity—is the clinician, for example, in a position to question the medical AI's results? This will likely make a difference to attributions of responsibility. Two further clarifications are in order here:

1. The idea that we as human agents take some outcome generated by a computer and work with it without knowing how the machine generated that outcome or how to evaluate or question the veracity of that machine outcome is neither very new nor very fancy, so I don't really need to bother with the AI label for it. But on the other hand, this is a reminder that in a high-stakes domain like healthcare, practices that have elsewhere become commonplace or innocuous might still need careful ethical analysis.

2. The second point has again to do with a special feature of these cases involving so-called intelligent systems, namely, the idea of possible "responsibility gaps," where the complexity of the systems involved—and the fact that the humans involved do not necessarily understand or have access to that complexity—might generate outcomes for which nobody can be plausibly held responsible (see Matthias [2004] and Sparrow [2007] for the classic formulations of this particular worry—I have also discussed it in Di Nucci [2017] and Di Nucci and Santoni [2016].)

Back to case (4): who is responsible for the clinical mistake that occurs when a patient receives the wrong treatment? Remember, as usual, that what I am interested in here is not responsibility all around but specifically the responsibility of the delegating party, which in this case is either hospital management or the unit that decided to implement that pathology AI system that resulted in the false positive. Further reminder: as I explained at length in chapter 10, so far the evidence points to medical AI systems being better than human pathologists at avoiding false negatives but worse than human pathologists at avoiding false positives, so our case (4) here, albeit fictional, is in line with available evidence.

Again, as with case (2), for case (4) I am particularly interested in the comparative analysis of the responsibility of the delegating parties, who in this thought experiment happens to delegate to a machine, as opposed to their responsibility in alternative scenarios in which they carried out the task themselves (or, specifically for this case, in which they delegated to human pathologists instead of medical AI systems). The question is the same: has delegation "cost" any responsibility loss to the delegating party? As I previously emphasized, this talk of "cost" is ironic, as people are often tempted to and guilty of trying to off-load or outsource responsibility. That's a helpful way of describing this argument that I have not used so far: attempts to off-load or outsource responsibility necessarily fail because responsibility delegation is not possible. So again, off-loading or outsourcing responsibility is not just wrong, it is impossible—but trying might be wrong. Here I might have to look at the possibility that there is a difference between off-loading and outsourcing on the one hand and delegating on the other—maybe the latter is impossible but the former just wrong.

In order to carry out the comparative analysis necessary for case (4), think of the following scenario: The clinic's management has the same evidence that I presented in chapter 10 about the comparative abilities of the medical AI and the human pathologists; the former are good—or anyway better than the latter—at avoiding false negatives, while the latter are good—or anyway better than the former—at avoiding false positives. Further, imagine that the financial commitment required by the medical AI system is lower than what human pathologists would cost.

Based on the evidence, imagine that in this new version of the scenario clinic management decides that patients would not understand the switch from human medics to medical AI and keeps in place its less precise and more expensive practice of having a human pathologist look at each slide.

Before proceeding, a caveat: you might object that, in comparison with case (2), I am mixing up two different possibilities here: the possibility of not delegating and the possibility of delegating to humans rather than machines. I disagree: given the complex structures of a hospital, it makes little sense to imagine a system in which reviewing pathology slides would not be delegated. Who would be supposed to do it in that scenario, the hospital's CEO? So the only practical alternative is not between delegating and not delegating, but which tasks to delegate to which party. So here it is really the alternative between delegating to human pathologists and delegating to medical AI that is the only dilemma I need to analyze.

I have, then, scenario 4A and scenario 4B. In each of these two scenarios, a false positive results in the wrong treatment. In scenario 4A the false positive is generated by a medical AI system, in 4B by a human pathologist. Suppose clinic management is sued by the patient, or even just accused of malpractice in the newspaper (which I am using as a placeholder for moral responsibility as opposed to the civil or penal legal accountability of a suit, which might lead me into complex questions of strict liability and the like that I want to avoid). Could the clinic point to its delegating practices in order to try to off-load, outsource, or avoid responsibility?

Given the inevitability of delegation from the point of view of an organization's management, here it is probably more fruitful to think in terms of the medic responsible for the pathology unit: could she try to off-load responsibility by pointing out that the mistake was actually the medical AI system's? Things do not get simpler but actually more complex by distinguishing between clinic management and the human medic responsible for the pathology unit, because the implementation of the medical AI system was likely decided above the pay grade of the human medic who runs the pathology unit—after all, investments of that magnitude (such as buying a Watson license from IBM) can only be approved by the board.

Still, would the human medic in charge of the pathology unit be "more responsible" for the false positive if she had not delegated the task of analyzing biopsy slides to the medical AI system but rather had done the analysis herself or tasked a human colleague with it? Is any responsibility lost? Again, I don't see why it should be: if a programming error led to this particular false positive, one could look into the code to check whether the bug was the result of any recklessness. That might result in an off-loading of responsibility on the company who sold the clinic this particular AI system—but that would not be a case in which it is delegation itself that results in any loss of responsibility on the part of the delegating party. And indeed something similar could be said of the training of the human pathologist tasked with analyzing the slides.

Imagine that it turns out this person was not properly trained (she got her MD from a university that did not actually have degree-granting authority). Here again, the clinic could off-load responsibility onto the medic in question or her university, but that would not depend on delegation itself. Still, what these different possibilities show is the following: by delegating, further parties are included in the transaction. Namely, delegating is such that it increases the number of possible responsible parties. But this does not mean that responsibility is diluted, though it does mean complexity is increased, possibly making the attribution of responsibility more difficult.

This is a simple distinction, between who the bearer of responsibility is and how difficult the attribution of said responsibility to its appropriate bearer can be. Like in distinguishing between knowledge and truth, you should not assume that the difficulty involved in responsibility attributions—because of increased complexity due to delegation, for example—means that any responsibility is lost. The truth might just be a little bit more difficult to find out, but it's still there (I wasn't quite finished with lame slogans, I know).

I have found out something important about delegation and responsibility: delegation necessarily increases complexity; complexity in turn necessarily increases the number of possible bearers of responsibility. But these two necessities do not have the consequence of diluting responsibility, even though they might have the consequence of making responsibility attributions more difficult in practice, as you have just seen in this medical AI scenario.

In conclusion, who is responsible for the particular false positive I have been analyzing? Probably management, for the following reason: accepting outcomes over a confidence threshold of 96 percent means that, over a few hundred cases, there will inevitably be a few mistakes. Implementing a system with such confidence intervals might still be a good idea for both economic and strategic reasons; it might be the best outcome for the money, for example. Still, the decision-makers implementing such a system and accepting the risk threshold attached to the system are inevitably responsible for the mistakes that the system makes and that are within the risk thresholds that had been accepted to begin with.[2] This seems to be a plausible principle of responsibility, that errors within the accepted risk thresholds should be the responsibility of those who decided to accept the relevant risk thresholds. But even if you want to dispute this principle, it would not have any bearing on my argument against delegating responsibility.

CROOKED POLITICIAN

Case (6) is the last and possibly most complicated of my analysis, so allow me the following premise, which actually applies to the whole chapter: I would be happy for my account of responsibility and delegation to be a progressive or anyway normative one. Namely, I am not just trying to map established attributions of responsibility practices; I would also be happy if the outcome of this chapter was actually to reform established responsibility attribution practices, showing that some stakeholders bear more responsibility than normally assumed.

If the above premise was slightly unclear to you, let me make it explicit using the political scenario: voters are, normally, responsible for their representatives' decisions. Why are voters responsible for the decisions made by their representatives? Because voters voluntarily delegated power to their representatives, and specifically the power to make the very decisions in question. This is the controversial aspect of my account of delegating responsibility that I was referring to above.

Before I start analyzing this final case, let me also make a conceptual clarification. I have argued that delegating control means voluntarily giving up direct control in order to enhance overall control. I have further argued that—when we delegate control—we do not lose responsibility in virtue of such control delegation and that there is no such thing as "delegating responsibility." Through this chapter, though, a possible better way of expressing this argument has now emerged: just like when we delegate direct control we might actually gain better overall control, delegated responsibility does not mean a loss of responsibility. So maybe we can, after all, delegate responsibility—as long as that is not misunderstood as off-loading or outsourcing responsibility.

This new way of expressing my argument has the advantage that it allows room for the fact that, when control is delegated, a new stakeholder is introduced, who might be a bearer of responsibility. Now, even if this new stakeholder turns out to bear responsibility, the delegating party will still be responsible, as I have argued. But further distinguishing between delegating responsibility and off-loading or outsourcing responsibility, as I am doing now, enables me to distinguish between having a further responsible party (delegating responsibility) and scapegoating that further stakeholder.

How does all this come to bear on my political example? In representative democracies, voters ought to carry the burden (responsibility) of the decisions made by their politicians, as long as delegation of power to their representatives was successful. As in other cases, power delegation's success will not be measured through outcomes alone, so voters might end up being responsible for the decisions of their politicians even if those politicians do not make the decisions voters expected them to.

Take case (6) and suppose that, despite promising to vote against the new motorway, M had a track record of being close to the car industry. Say it was a matter of public record that some of her advisers were previously employed by car manufacturers (and the papers reported this fact—that's an important additional condition, I believe). This kind of evidence ought to have been enough to be skeptical of M's promise during the campaign. So if M does in the end break her promise and support the motorway, given the evidence, voters cannot excuse themselves by pointing out that M had promised to vote against the motorway.

Make no mistake: M is still guilty of breaking her electoral promise and is responsible for her corrupt behavior. But here, as usual, I am not interested in the responsibility of the delegate; I am only interested in the responsibility of the delegating party, namely, the voters. But how can I make voters responsible for a decision that they not only did not make themselves but would not have made had they had the chance (see lottocratic systems in the previous chapter)—a decision, additionally, those voters disagree with? Obviously, I am talking of the responsibility of those voters who elected M while not wanting the motorway—the others are uninteresting for my purposes.

In order to answer this question, I must first remember that I am assuming the system is a representative democracy in which there are economic and strategic reasons for delegating power. Further, I am assuming that delegation was successful: this is important, because it rules out things like voter fraud, for example. The system functioned as it was supposed to in electing M. It is just that voters who did not want the motorway and still voted for M made a mistake, and, given the available evidence, that's a mistake that they cannot blame on anyone but themselves.

As with previous cases, let me compare case (6) with a version of it in which there is no delegation. Say in the constituency in question there was a referendum on whether to build the motorway or anyway allow its route to go through that particular constituency. Here the right comparison is not between a voter who votes against the motorway in the referendum and a voter who voted for M but is disappointed when M supports the motorway. The correct comparison to determine responsibility (for the motorway being built) is a voter who voted for the motorway in the referendum and a voter who voted for M but did not want the motorway.

It seems to be that, given the available evidence—and the fact that the voter is epistemically to blame for having disregarded such evidence—M's voter is as much to blame for the motorway's ultimate construction as the yes supporter in the referendum. After all, both voters in these parallel scenarios had available to them an effective way of stopping the motorway and neither pursued it: the referendum voter could have voted no, while M's voter could have supported a different candidate who was genuinely against the motorway. Further, both voters' votes contributed to the building of the motorway and did so in an effective and organic way—again, there was no deception (because M's true feelings were actually public knowledge) or voter fraud.

When we delegate power to our representatives, we entrust them with great responsibility—but that does not make us any less responsible for their decision-making; after all, it is we who put them there in the first place. This, as I emphasized in the last chapter, is only true on condition that power delegation was successful, namely, that there was no abuse, so that I can still truly claim that the people have not lost power through delegation—and this in turn might depend on which systems are in place to, for example, recall politicians who break their promises. The paradox, as I argued in the previous chapter, is that attempts—such as referenda—to keep power in our own hands often ultimately result in loss of power (see Brexit). And this consideration is relevant to my discussion of responsibility in this chapter, because the sooner we realize that we are responsible and have no excuses for the political decisions that our representatives make on our behalf, the more readily will we live up to our epistemic duties of due diligence as voters.

Notes

INTRODUCTION. THE CONTROL PARADOX FOR DUMMIES

1. See, for example, Lin 2015; Nyholm & Smids 2016; Santoni de Sio 2017; and Liu 2017.

2. For recent data, please see Zenko and Mae Wolf (2018). The literature on the ethics of drones and autonomous weapons is already too large to be referenced in any complete way, so here are just some examples that I hope are somewhat representative: Beauchamp & Savulescu 2013; Brunstetter & Braun 2011; Byman 2013; Coeckelbergh 2013; Cronin 2013; Di Nucci 2014b; Di Nucci & Santoni de Sio 2014, 2016; Enemark 2011, 2013; Franke 2014; Gregory 2011; Kirkpatrick 2016; Paust 2010; Santoni de Sio & Di Nucci 2016; Singer 2009; Strawser 2010, 2013; Wall & Monahan 2011; Williams 2013.

3. Unfortunately philosophers from my neck of the woods don't have much time for the practice of delegation, but it is very well researched and discussed elsewhere; see, for example, Bruno Latour's work (as Jim Johnson, 1988).

4. See both the relevant psychological literature (e.g., Bargh & Chartrand 1999; Bargh et al. 1996; Beilock et al. 2002; Beilock et al. 2004; Gigerenzer 2007) and the philosophical literature (Di Nucci 2008, 2013; Dreyfus & Dreyfus 1984; Gendler 2008; Levy & Bayne 2004; Montero 2016; Pollard 2006; Rietveld 2008).

5. Let me be clear about why this would be a waste of time: my point is not that resisting the power of habit to avoid those trade-offs would be impossible and therefore trying would be a waste of time; habits are powerful, but whether they are irresistible is empirical and beyond the scope here; what I mean by waste of time is rather a normative claim: that we cultivate our habits and automatic actions likely means we endorse those trade-offs, supposedly because the few mistakes are worth the amount of spared resources. So we are making—even if only implicitly—a normative call about sparing cognitive resources being more advantageous than avoiding the resulting few *familiar* mistakes.

6. Refer to "Implicit Bias" (2015) for an excellent overview on the literature on implicit bias.

7. For example, Matthias 2004 and Sparrow 2007.

8. See, for example, Miller & Wertheimer 2009.

9. This is a good place to mention that, when it comes to particular cases, there may be fine lines between delegating, delegating too much, and ceding or abdicating control, so in some specific case there may be not only the general distinction between successful delegation and abdication of control but also a murkier distinction among delegating, delegating too much, and finally abdicating—where even though agents have delegated too much, they have not completely abdicated control. A relevant case here could be patients—or even friends—who trust

you a little too much for their own good; that may be more than successful delegation and still fall short of actual abdication. The rest of this book will hopefully give you the tools to navigate all kinds of tricky cases.

1. THE PARADOX

1. Eyre 2019; Kim & Maglio 2018; Mauss et al. 2011; Schooler et al. 2003.
2. Mudde & Kaltwasser 2017. Before you ask me for a definition of populism, here we go: "agreement is general that all forms of populism include some kind of appeal to 'the people' and a denunciation of 'the elite'. Accordingly, it is not overly contentious to state that populism always involves a critique of the establishment and an adulation of the common people. More concretely, we define populism as *a thin-centered ideology that considers society to be ultimately separated into two homogeneous and antagonistic camps, 'the pure people' versus 'the corrupt elite,' and which argues that politics should be the expression of the* volonté générale *(general will) of the people*" (Mudde & Kaltwasser 2017, 5–6; emphasis in the original). I will have more to say about this, but this should do for now as a working definition.
3. The philosophy book I am currently reading—Ryan Patrick Hanley's *Our Great Purpose* (2019)—is a particularly good example of how philosophers are terrified of being confused with self-help authors, as it not only claims not to be a self-help book but also extends the claim to the books of the philosopher discussed in the book, Adam Smith. All of it is very plausible, but still I am left wondering why philosophers of all people—and moral and political philosophers especially—are so scared of the self-help tag. Btw, if you think that Adam Smith has nothing to do with my book, think again: you will see when I come to delegation that it has a lot to do with division of labor and Smith's superior productivity of specialized labor.
4. That's very much "your" pockets because my phone is not smart; I thought you should know that before reading on.

2. CONTROL AND THE EMPOWERMENT ILLUSION

1. There are also clear political advantages in not having to send troops into foreign territory. One example? Obama's drones were very active in western Pakistan at precisely the time when Obama was being awarded the Nobel Peace Prize. And indeed President Obama was explicit in arguing for the advantages of deploying drones. See my own article "Drones and the Threshold for Waging War," freely available at this address: https://static-curis.ku.dk/portal/files/188457338/27642_63603_1_SM.pdf.
2. Would I be begging the question to just call them *technocrats*?
3. Then again, you wanted speed? You certainly got speed: things have gone to shit, but at least it happened fast.
4. Boseley 2018.
5. I have removed the name of the author from the tweet, but you will be all too familiar with it anyway. If you must, see here: https://twitter.com/realdonaldtrump/status/449525268529815552?lang=en.
6. See WHO (2019) for more information on this and also the other nine threats to global health.
7. Here thanks are due to my colleague Klaus Hoyer for pointing out to me that there is a socioeconomic difference between the two audiences, where vaccination skeptics tend to be—on average—wealthier and better educated than supporters of right-wing populist movements such as Trump and Brexit. Also allow me to use this footnote to thank my colleague Iben Mundbjerg Gjødsbøl for helpful comments on an earlier draft of this chapter.
8. Just a little anecdote to stress the first-world obsession with technological threats: *The Age of Surveillance Capitalism* by Shoshana Zuboff (2018) is easily one of the most talked

about recent books about the risks of information technologies. Well, on page 2 of this very long book the author falsely claims that more people have access to the internet than to electricity—an easily falsifiable claim. It's a small blunder, but it is symptomatic of a certain loss of perspective when discussing the benefits and risks of technological innovation, or if I were in a less generous mood, just a techno-apocalyptic slip.

9. For example, the WHO (n.d.) estimates that, globally, between 2010 and 2015 at least ten million deaths were prevented through vaccination.

10. Maybe you have heard this one already. How long has it taken the following three innovations to get one hundred million users? The old-fashioned landline telephone took one hundred years; the iPhone, two years, and *Pokemon Go*, only four weeks (Feldenkirchen 2018). I have not been able to verify this one apart from this Spiegel article, but never spoil a good story with the truth, right?

11. Here again it is easy to see the link to technological innovation; just think of the basic income narrative, which is very much based on technophile undertones: Once production and services will be taken care of by robots and algorithms, we will have lots of time on our hands for direct democracy. Basic income would then be the solution to technological unemployment.

12. On the same topic of so-called *epistocracy*, see also the new volume *10% Less Democracy: Why You Should Trust Elites a Little More and the Masses a Little Less* by Garett Jones (2020).

3. THE CONCEPT OF CONTROL
AND DIRECT CONTROL

1. I will have the chance to properly talk about this later on in the book, but it is important to stress from the outset that when thinking about control and the relations between human agents and technological systems, we should neither assume it is always a one-way relationship in which humans either control or fail to control machines—because the other way is crucial too; nor should we make the mistake of taking the direction in which humans either control or do not control machines as paradigmatic. For now we need to stay genuinely open-minded about the directionality and also whether there is any power asymmetry.

2. Wendy Wood was kind enough to read this book of mine, as well as comment on and endorse it—thanks!

3. Here there could admittedly be an issue in terms of separating the topic of habits and habitual action from the topic of expertise and expert action; after all, it's true that experts have been getting bad press of late—well, bad Twitter press anyway. But expertise is supposed to be a plus, while habits have often also been understood as something from which we want to free ourselves, such as breaking the smoking habit. So we should be careful in not mixing up habits and expertise as if they were the same; for the purposes of my argument, though, all I am saying here is that we can interpret the Beilock experiments—whether we apply them to habits or expertise—in terms of less attention resulting in more control, or at least more control resulting in less attention. And this point could be something that habits and expertise have in common. More generally, these similarities between habits and expertise are probably important in themselves and should be made more of, just not quite here. For now it's enough that you do not make the following confusion: I am not saying that experts are always acting habitually when acting within their expertise; nor am I saying that we are the experts of our habits—even though at least the latter claim is a plausible and easily defensible one.

4. Again, this might sound as though we do the turning off actively and consciously, but it is more plausible to think that the turning off itself happens automatically.

5. For a more precise definition, see Bill Pollard's: "What I propose is that a habitual action is a behaviour which has three features. It is (i) repeated, that is, the agent has a history of similar behaviours in similar contexts; (ii) automatic, that is, it does not involve the agent in deliberation about whether to act; and (iii) responsible, that is, something the agent does, rather than something that merely happens to her" (Pollard 2003, 415). See also William James on

habits: "habit diminishes the conscious attention with which our acts are performed" (James 1890, 114). And Gilbert Ryle: "When we describe someone as doing something by pure or blind habit, we mean that he does it automatically and without having to mind what he is doing" (Ryle 1949, 42).

6. For a good introduction to these topics, two in fact, see the *Stanford Encyclopedia of Philosophy* (*SEP*), which is a free online resource; for many philosophical topics, the *SEP* should really be the first port of call for both the uninitiated and the initiated. In this particular case, the two most relevant entries are "Free Will" (https://plato.stanford.edu/entries/freewill) and "Compatibilism" (https://plato.stanford.edu/entries/compatibilism). If you prefer a good introductory book instead, see, for example, Kane (2005).

7. This is not my claim but the authors' own. Fischer and Ravizza define guidance control as when the following two conditions are met: "the decisional mechanism leading up to X should be (1) 'moderately reason-responsive' and (2) the decisional mechanism should be 'the agent's own'" (Santoni de Sio & van den Hoven 2018, 5).

4. SOCIAL CONTROL AND TECHNOLOGICAL CONTROL

1. This point raises an interesting further dialectical possibility for my argument in this book: namely, even if it turns out in the end there is no *control* paradox, we might still be right about the paradoxical nature of these innovations; it's just that the paradox would not necessarily be a *control* paradox, like in the remark above.

2. If you don't know the story of how Stanislav Petrov "saved the world" on September 26, 1983, by narrowly avoiding nuclear catastrophe, you can start by reading these two articles: Matthews (2019) and Chan (2017); and then if you want more, check out the following two books: Downing (2018) and Ambinder (2018).

3. Do you want another sign of the times? The *New York Times* article reporting the Democratic congressman's death refers to him as "uncontestably the most conservative member of Congress" (Krebs 1983).

4. "A 1979 report by Congress's Office of Technology Assessment estimated that a full-scale Soviet assault on the US would kill 35 to 77 percent of the US population—or between 82 million and 180 million people in 1983. The inevitable US counterstrike would kill 20 to 40 percent of the Soviet population, or between 54 million and 108 million people." (Matthews 2019). The full 1979 report by the Congress's Office of Technology Assessment can be found online here: https://ota.fas.org/reports/7906.pdf.

5. I don't have the time or the expertise to get into this, but you should not assume an oversimplified version of chains of command in which those above can without reason overrule those below, not even in the military. There are bureaucracies and processes in place—there were even in the Soviet Union, supposedly—that make these issues more complex than a merely philosophical account can do justice to. My point here is just that, if you are going to claim that Petrov was in charge of the overall process even though he had no direct control over the machine and that, in virtue of Petrov's overall control, you can also claim that Petrov was in control of the machine (because he could influence its role in the overall process) even though Petrov did not control the machine itself as such, then this claim would also depend on Petrov's position in the overall chain of command, because his position would be crucial to how much influence he had over the whole process. It is then beyond my scope here to make an assessment of general chain-of-command principles in the Soviet Union in the 1980s or of the specific chain of command that September morning in 1983. As an aside: while I write this, I cannot help but think about both the differences and the similarities between the story of Stanislav Petrov and what happened in Chernobyl, but I can't pursue this here either, I'm afraid (and if you haven't seen the HBO miniseries *Chernobyl*, then please stop reading this book now, go binge on it, and only come back to my book once you are finished with it).

5. DELEGATING CONTROL AND THE
PRACTICE OF DELEGATION

1. See Merriam-Webster on *delegate*: https://www.merriam-webster.com/words-at-play/delegate-meaning-origin.

2. There might be some justified skepticism about the idea that the patient–doctor relationship is one of delegation. But here I am not arguing for this idea; I am just using this example among many others for the purposes of illustration, to emphasize differences and similarities between disparate practices. Later in the book, I will talk more about healthcare, and that will be the right place to evaluate whether patient–doctor relationships fit the delegation framework or whether that's a stretch.

3. I remember that former British prime minister Tony Blair, after leaving office in 2007, said he had never had a mobile phone, because supposedly before entering office in 1997 mobile phones weren't yet very common, and in his ten years as PM he had one or multiple "phone" persons, so that he didn't have a "personal" mobile phone and only government phones managed by other people. It goes to show how things have changed, especially when you think how over the last decade the phones of prominent foreign leaders have been spied on and surely still are being spied on, by both allies and enemies, such as the United States hacking into Angela Merkel's phone. So maybe the old-fashioned solution of not having a personal phone for politicians of that caliber and having all government devices managed by other human agents isn't that silly after all.

4. See Nicas 2018.

5. Elliot & Long 2016; see also Gaskell 2016.

6. I would be genuinely interested in any explanations or even just hypotheses about why acronyms are so widespread within sociology of science as opposed to philosophy—again, feel free to email me if you have any suggestions: ezio@sund.ku.dk.

7. For the record, despite being Italian, I am not picky about my coffee (and find coffee snobs quite annoying too). I will drink anything—the thing I am currently drinking as I type this at the office I refer to as "cola" because it doesn't deserve the label "coffee"—but I wish it were cola! Still, I happily drink many coups of this cola every day, and it goes without saying that without it this book could never have been written.

8. Having put all these different elements of delegation in place, I should also not lose sight of what the practice of delegation as such says about the tasks that we delegate instead of perform ourselves. Namely, I'm sure most of us have some idea of the tasks we would rather accomplish ourselves as opposed to delegate to others—and there are probably tasks and actions that we would never delegate, maybe even some that are impossible to delegate. Would you delegate lovemaking, for example? And what would it even mean, actually, to delegate something as intimate and personal as lovemaking? So maybe it is not just that we would rather do it ourselves, but that there are tasks and actions that are only conceivable in terms of doing it ourselves as opposed to having someone do it on our behalf. And clearly, with social and technological progress, what is possible or acceptable to delegate both in terms of tasks and in terms of delegates changes continuously—don't just think of technologies but also of slavery, or even just what a particular social class in a particular culture deems acceptable. Should you clean your own apartment, for example? And what about cooking?

6. CONTROL, DRONES, AND
AUTONOMOUS WEAPONS

1. Some representative discussions: Beauchamp & Savulescu 2013; Brunstetter & Braun 2011; Byman 2013; Coeckelbergh 2013; Cronin 2013; Di Nucci 2014b; Di Nucci & Santoni de Sio 2014; Enemark 2011, 2013; Franke 2014; Gregory 2011; Kirkpatrick 2016; Paust 2010;

Santoni de Sio & Di Nucci 2016; Singer 2009; Strawser 2010, 2013; Wall & Monahan 2011; Williams 2013.

2. I have already made the argument that using the term *AI* might bias my discussion. The same worry applies here: it seems as though calling these systems "robots" is trying to sound at the same time both familiar and scary for the purposes of public opinion. The philosophical and more generally academic debate has made this mistake too, with an early paper that is now widely cited also using the "killer robots" language (Sparrow 2007), but now academics seem to have settled on the use of the AWS terminology, autonomous weapon systems. This avoids talking of "robots," but on the other hand it might be presupposing what needs demonstrating, namely, that these systems are in fact in any sense "autonomous." Here are some representative sources on the way the debate has developed over the last decade and has settled on AWSs and not robots: Kastan 2013; Bhuta 2016; Noone & Noone 2015; Liu 2012; Krishnan 2016; Bieri & Dickow 2014; Toscano 2015; Meier 2016; Klincewicz 2015; Sauer 2016; Etzioni & Etzioni 2017; Foy 2014; Sparrow 2009; Jain 2016.

3. But trust philosophers to always find some further clarification to make. For example, given the evolution of war, it is not necessarily the case that a drone pilot in Florida would be safer than a fighter jet pilot hovering above Pakistan. Think of the following case: international terrorism could be justified exactly with the consideration that—since there are no longer boots on the ground—the enemy has to be targeted where it is, and given that it is pretty difficult to spot a drone pilot in Florida, this might justify indiscriminate practices. Whether or not that would be ethical, it must be admitted that the same ethical criteria that apply to the targeting of boots on the ground would have to apply to remote enemies. And that might end up justifying or at least excusing some acts of what we would otherwise normally refer to as terrorism.

4. Btw, I am only using the example of Pakistan because of the documented targeting through drones that happened in Pakistan during the Obama administration. I am not making any specific claims about the security situation in Pakistan—take it as a thought experiment, if you like.

5. I am not going to say anything about whether any of the three groups deserves priority, for example, whether the safety of our own military personnel should take ethical priority over the safety of "enemy" civilians. Those are difficult questions that are, luckily, not directly relevant to my discussion of AWSs for the simple reason that, if AWSs can deliver better outcomes for each of the three groups, then I don't need to think in terms of which groups deserve priority. In fact, you could argue that this is in itself an argument in favor of developing and deploying AWSs, that these systems allow us to skip complex decision-making around prioritizing between our own military personnel and enemy civilians, for example, by reducing risks for both. But that would still be just a pragmatic solution, which would not actually answer the normative question of who deserved priority.

7. VAR, AUTHORITY, AND LOSS OF CONTROL

1. The VAR rules go on for a bit, but I did not want to get bogged down in too many details. See the source (IFAB 2018) if you want the rest.

2. What this means is that a lot of difficult and close calls will remain difficult and close no matter how many times you watch the episode or from how many perspectives or how good the resolution is or how much you can slow down the footage and so on; in fact, maybe the opposite is the case, that some episodes are simply best judged live by the referee on the pitch, end of story. This is a bold claim and one that I do not need to make; less bold is the claim that there is intrinsic discretion in a lot of referee decision-making, in football and beyond.

3. If you are interested in more VAR statistics, you might also want to look at evidence that VAR results in more penalties, but I don't think that's relevant for my discussion here, so I will just drop it in this footnote: Ward (2018).

4. I leave you with a good write up of that day (in Italian though): D'Ottavi (2019).

8. SELF-DRIVING CARS AND
MEANINGFUL HUMAN CONTROL

1. Some people call them "self-driving cars," some people call them "autonomous vehicles," others call them "driverless cars." I choose the first label for the following two reasons: the "autonomous" label, like I said in, for example, chapter 6, is question begging, so it's out. (Is there anything worse than being question begging in philosophy, by the way? I still remember when I was told the meaning of the term in graduate school [by Mike Ridge] . . . felt very small that day about having made it to philosophy graduate school without having encountered "question begging.") Enough autobiography—that's why "autonomous vehicles" is out. "Driverless" is a less obviously problematic label, but I prefer not to use it because, in the first place, it is not true that there is necessarily no driver in a self-driving car; self-driving cars are typically not unmanned. And also "driverless" points to something missing in a way that I don't think is obvious. There is a driver; it's just that the driver is software. Finally, some people object to the idea that such cars drive themselves because they are driven by software. But I think that's lame, because it assumes a traditional understanding of cars as separate from their software. It is true that the very early self-driving cars were traditional cars plus software, but I don't think that's true anymore. This should be enough to explain my choice of "self-driving cars" over other terms.

2. See, for example, Lin 2015; Nyholm & Smids 2016; Santoni de Sio 2017; and Liu 2017.

3. Conceptually, it might be worth pausing for a second to think about the following: do I really need to specify at the same time both "human driver" and "manually driven," or is that repetitive and superfluous? Obviously I don't mean the difference between manual and automatic gears; rather, the question is whether it makes any sense to think of something other than a human driver "manually" driving the car. This is exactly where having already analyzed similar technologies comes in to help: when it comes to self-driving cars, it seems as though the literature focuses on whether the vehicle is being maneuvered by a human sitting inside the car or by software installed in or connected to the vehicle. But obviously there is no theoretical or technological reason for that divide, which excludes one obvious solution that I have already encountered, namely, the idea that something is remotely controlled by someone—human or otherwise—who is outside the vehicle or independent of the vehicle, like with drones or AWSs. And obviously both who is in control and where the agent (human or otherwise) in control is located are ethically relevant. What this side note really shows is that when thinking of the differences between, say, drones and self-driving cars, I must also be aware of both the social and historical context in which these technologies have evolved, so that we already have remotely controlled drones but with cars we seem to have skipped that step. Equally, those remotely controlled drones currently in operation do not have people in them, while cars are primarily still thought of as a vehicle for private transportation. This further distinction I will take up again later on in the chapter.

4. Btw, don't worry, I am not that much of an asshole; this book is safe and you will not find out the ending of *Game of Thrones* or any other spoilers—one less excuse to stop reading, I'm afraid.

5. Or as John Danaher calls it in his recent book *Automation and Utopia* (2019), "human obsolescence." He takes an interesting, less apocalyptic view of automation there.

6. This argument is obviously too quick, but given the role it plays in the overall argumentation, I think that should be okay. There is obviously a difference between the attention resource efficiency provided by public transport and the attention resource efficiency provided by your private car or taxi/Uber/car share. For one thing, only in the latter scenarios do you get to decide who is sitting in the vehicle with you, and that might make a difference to your attention resources, if you are trying to write philosophy, say, on a busy and loud train journey. So there are obvious differences. Also, in terms of the flexibility of the journey, your car or taxi can take you exactly where you need to go, but trains, buses, metros, and other public transport do not serve individual needs. But the basic point of my short argument—and the reason I think it is good enough—is just that delegating transportation to others, whether humans or techno-

logical systems, in order to free up time and other resources does not necessarily require cars or even private transportation.

7. See these reports on the five autopilot fatalities: Felton 2018; Yadron & Tynan 2016; Vlasic & Boudette 2016; Green 2018; NTSB 2019.

8. See Eliot (2019) for some more precise numbers on U.S. car fatalities.

9. Some useful resources on the different automation levels: Taeihagh & Lim 2019; Joerger & Spenko.

10. If I really needed to distinguish between level 4 and level 5, I could appeal to differences in other domains and apply them to driving, for example, with drones and AWSs, the difference between a fully automated mission in which the commanding officer only inputs a target and a time frame and a fully automated mission in which the system identifies the target by itself without manual input or authorization. Once I apply this kind of distinction to driving and the difference between level 4 and level 5, I might have the difference between a car that needs to be switched on by someone sitting inside it and then does everything by itself and a car that can be remotely activated from a distance so that it comes to pick me up, or something like the difference I previously identified between a competent person inside the car and no person inside the car or an incompetent person inside it. These differences could be captured by the distinction between level 4 and level 5.

11. See also Horowitz & Scharre 2015; Heikoop et al. 2019; Wagner 2019; Cummings 2019; Bojarski et al. 2016; Calvert et al. 2019; Surden & Williams 2016; and Mecacci & de Sio 2019.

12. Here I want to make clear that increased surveillance or manipulation might even be paternalistic. Maybe it's to reduce speed and accidents, for example. But even if such forms of surveillance and manipulation through software ended up having benefits that everybody acknowledged, that would not mean that those liberty costs would be thereby erased. So it is legitimate—whatever the actual consequences of these interventions—to think of these in terms of control loss. And if the manipulation or surveillance is not paternalistic, then the argument is even easier to make, obviously.

9. SMARTPHONES, FROM EMPOWERMENT TO SURVEILLANCE

1. Hopefully you don't care enough about my personal life to want to know why I don't have a smartphone, but just in case, let me tell you anyway: it's not because of any surveillance or manipulation worries; it's just because I would end up using it too much and, also, because I want to try to delay as much as possible the time when my kids will want—and then get—one. Whether this latter consideration is itself, in turn, dependent on some kind of manipulation or surveillance worry once-removed on behalf of my kids, that's a good question that I don't really need to go into here, I reckon, because it could just as well be that I want to avoid my kids using it too much as well. No, I am not on social media either, in case you were wondering, which—note to my publisher—probably means this book won't sell. Sorry.

2. Speaking of smartphones and emancipation as nondependency, it seems pretty obvious to me that my family could not function if we had no smartphone—not even multiple iPads, say, could quite cover for that. So I have a clean/dirty hands problems on my hands, where I am relying on my wife's smartphone without "compromising" myself with one—it's like if a vegetarian waits for his kids not to finish their meat in order to then eat it as leftovers. In fact, on a recent trip, my wife lost her smartphone on our way to visiting some friends; getting there turned out to be a nice challenge (we did make it, in the end).

3. I am providing a link for this book because the whole volume is open access: https://www.springer.com/gp/book/9783030008123.

10. HEALTH DATA AND
HEALTHCARE ALGORITHMS

1. And, yes, it is easy enough to imagine a further scenario in which the AI system has access to stage two in order to correct the human pathologist's false positives, but what I will say in a second about Pathology Lab II will also apply to this further alternative scenario.

2. This would apply, as I anticipated in the previous footnote, also to the possible Pathology Lab III, in which the computer system reviewed stage two; it would lead to more false positives, supposedly, even though in this case it is not clear that giving software access to stage two would result in more control, because the MHC condition would not necessarily be met just in virtue of giving software access to stage two. Which leads me to a fourth possible scenario, call it Pathology Lab IV, in which both the AI system and the human pathologists have access to both stages.

11. TAKING BACK CONTROL

1. Here "control" admittedly refers, from the EU point of view, to a reduction in the number of human beings allowed the chance for a better life—so it is not obvious that this is a form of control, but it is at least fair to say that, from the point of view of the EU, better controlling access to its borders was what they were trying to achieve by delegating to the Turks.

2. See also Lupia & McCubbins 1998 and Kuklinski & Quirk 2000.

3. If you are interested in this question of competence, another source is Jason Brennan's book *Against Democracy* (2016), where he argues for epistemic constraints on who should be allowed to vote.

4. In fairness, it might very well be that what Guerrero has in mind are classic soviets. This would make his proposal less original but not necessarily thereby less interesting or promising, but again here I am not interested in the merits of the lottocratic alternative as such, so the interpretative details are not important. Still, take a look at the three elements of lottocratic systems that Guerrero emphasizes and judge for yourself if what we are actually talking about isn't just classic old-fashioned soviets (see also Pettit 2010): "The three distinctive features of the full lottocratic system as I envision it are: (1) that the legislative function is fulfilled by many different *single issue* legislatures (each one focusing just on, for example, Agriculture or Health Care), rather than by a single, generalist legislature; (2) that the members of these single-issue legislatures are chosen by *lottery* from the relevant political jurisdiction; and (3) that the members of the single-issue legislatures hear from a variety of *experts* on the relevant topic at the beginning of each legislative session" (Guerrero 2014, 155–156).

12. DELEGATING RESPONSIBILITY?

1. Full disclosure: I am one of the editors of the journal where this particular paper was published, *Ethical Theory and Moral Practice*, which makes it particularly embarrassing that Sven had to point out this paper to me, given how relevant it is to my own book and that it was published in *my* journal. Btw, another recent publication that is also relevant to this book is Sven's own *Humans and Robots* (Nyholm 2020).

2. Here there might be a relevant difference between whether these risk thresholds had been just foreseen/accepted and whether they had been intended—but I have written a whole book on that further distinction, which is the basis for the so-called Doctrine of Double Effect, so I will not comment on it here (see Di Nucci 2014a).

References

Adams, E. (2019, October 31). Cirrus' private jet can now land itself, no pilot needed. *Wired*. https://www.wired.com/story/cirrus-garmin-vision-jet-autoland-safe-return/

Ambinder, M. (2018). *The brink*. Simon & Schuster.

Anderson, E. (2017). *Private government*. Princeton University Press.

Anscombe, G. E. M. (1957). *Intention*. Basil Blackwell.

Aristotle. (1998). *Nicomachean ethics*. Oxford University Press.

Bargh, J. A., & Chartrand, T. L. (1999). The unbearable automaticity of being. *American Psychologist, 54*, 462–479.

Bargh, J. A., Chen, M., & Burrows, L. (1996). Automaticity of social behavior. *Journal of Personality and Social Psychology, 71*(2), 230–244.

Beauchamp, Z., & Savulescu, J. (2013). Robot guardians: Teleoperated combat vehicles in humanitarian military intervention. In B. J. Strawser (Ed.), *Killing by remote control: The ethics of an unmanned military*. Oxford University Press.

Beilock, S. L., Bertenthal, A. M., McCoy, A. M., & Carr, T. H. (2004). Haste does not always make waste. *Psychonomic Bulletin and Review, 11*, 373–379.

Beilock, S. L., & Carr, T. H. (2001). On the fragility of skilled performance: What governs choking under pressure? *Journal of Experimental Psychology: General, 130*(4), 701–725.

Beilock, S. L., Carr, T. H., MacMahon, C., & Starkes, J. L. (2002). When paying attention becomes counterproductive. *Journal of Experimental Psychology: Applied, 8*, 6–16.

Beilock, S. L., & Gonso, S. (2008). Putting in the mind versus putting on the green: Expertise, performance time, and the linking of imagery and action. *Quarterly Journal of Experimental Psychology, 61*(6), 920–932.

Bhuta, N. (Ed.). (2016). *Autonomous weapons systems: Law, ethics, policy*. Cambridge University Press.

Bieri, M., & Dickow, M. (2014). Lethal autonomous weapons systems: Future challenges. *CSS Analysis in Security Policy, 164*, 1–4.

Bohlin, I. (2000). A social understanding of delegation. *Studies in History and Philosophy of Science, 31*(4), 731–750.

Bojarski, M., Del Testa, D., Dworakowski, D., Firner, B., Flepp, B., Goyal, P., Jackel, L. D., Monfort, M., Muller, U., Zhang, J., Zhang, X., Zhao, J., & Zieba, K. (2016). End-to-end learning for self-driving cars. *arXiv*, 1604.07316.

Boseley, S. (2018, December 21). Measles cases at highest for 20 years in Europe, as anti-vaccine movement grows. *Guardian*. https://www.theguardian.com/world/2018/dec/21/measles-cases-at-highest-for-20-years-in-europe-as-anti-vaccine-movement-grows

Bostrom, N. (2014). *Superintelligence*. Oxford University Press.

Bratman, M. (1984). Two faces of intention. *Philosophical Review, 93*, 375–405.

Bratman, M. (1987). *Intention, plans, and practical reason*. Harvard University Press.

Brennan, J. (2016). *Against democracy*. Princeton University Press.

Brockman, J. (2019). *Possible minds: 25 ways of looking at AI*. Penguin.

Brunstetter, D., & Braun, M. (2011). The implications of drones on the just war tradition. *Ethics & International Affairs, 25*(03), 337–358.

Byman, D. (2013). Why drones work. *Foreign Affairs, 92*(4), 32–43.

Calvert, S. C., Heikoop, D. D., Mecacci, G., & van Arem, B. (2019). A human-centric framework for the analysis of automated driving systems based on meaningful human control. *Theoretical Issues in Ergonomics Science, 21*(4), 478–506.

Chan, S. (2017, September 18). Stanislav Petrov, Soviet officer who helped avert nuclear war, is dead at 77. *New York Times*. https://www.nytimes.com/2017/09/18/world/europe/stanislav-petrov-nuclear-war-dead.html

Clark, A., & Chalmers, D. (1998). The extended mind. *Analysis, 58*(1), 7–19.

Clarke, R. (2014). *Omissions*. Oxford University Press.

Coeckelbergh, M. (2013). Drones, information technology, and distance: Mapping the moral epistemology of remote fighting. *Ethics and information technology, 15*(2), 87–98.

Collins, H., & Kusch, M. (1998). *The shape of actions: What humans and machines can do*. MIT Press.

Cronin, A. K. (2013). Why drones fail. *Foreign Affairs, 92*(4), 44–54.

Cummings, M. L. (2019). Lethal autonomous weapons: Meaningful human control or meaningful human certification? *IEEE Technology and Society, 38*(4), 20–26.

Danaher, J. (2019). *Automation and utopia*. Harvard University Press.

Davidson, D. (1980). *Essays on actions and events*. Oxford University Press.

Desilver, D. (2018, August 7). For most U.S. workers, real wages have barely budged in decades. Pew Research Center. https://www.pewresearch.org/fact-tank/2018/08/07/for-most-us-workers-real-wages-have-barely-budged-for-decades

Di Nucci, E. (2008). *Mind out of action*. VDM Verlag.

Di Nucci, E. (2011). Automatic actions: Challenging causalism. *Rationality Markets and Morals, 2*(1), 179–200.

Di Nucci, E. (2012). Priming effects and free will. *International Journal of Philosophical Studies, 20*(5), 725–734.

Di Nucci, E. (2013). *Mindlessness*. Cambridge Scholars.

Di Nucci, E. (2014a). *Ethics without intention*. Bloomsbury.

Di Nucci, E. (2014b). I droni tra progresso ed etica. *AREL La Rivista, 1*, 108–115.

Di Nucci, E. (2017). Sex Robots and the Rights of the Disabled. In J. Danaher & N. McArthur (Eds.), *Robot Sex: Social and Ethical Implications* (pp. 73–88). Cambridge, MA: MIT Press.

Di Nucci, E. (2018). *Ethics in healthcare*. Rowman & Littlefield.

Di Nucci, E. (2019). Should we be afraid of medical AI? *Journal of Medical Ethics, 45*, 556–558.

Di Nucci, E., Jensen, R. T., & Tupasela, A. M. (2020). Kunstig intelligens og medicinsk etik: Tilfældet Watson for Oncology. In *8 cases i medicinsk etik* (pp. 169–192). Munksgaard.

Di Nucci, E., & Santoni, F. (2016). *Drones and responsibility*. Routledge.

Di Nucci, E., & Santoni de Sio, F. (2014). Who's afraid of robots? Fear of automation and the ideal of direct control. In Fiorella Battaglia & Natalie Weidenfeld (Eds.), *Roboethics in film* (pp. 127–144). Pisa University Press.

Di Nucci, E., & Santoni de Sio, F. (2016). *Drones and responsibility*. Routledge.

Domingos, P. (2015). *The master algorithm*. Basic Books.

D'Ottavi, M. (2019, October 4). Storia orale del contratto tra Ronaldo e Iuliano. *l'Ultimo Uomo*. https://www.ultimouomo.com/ronaldo-e-iuliano-fallo-contatto-storia/

Downing, T. (2018). *1983*. Da Capo Press.

Dreyfus, H., & Dreyfus, S. (1984). Skilled behavior: The limits of intentional analysis. In E. Lester (Ed.), *Phenomenological essays in memory of Aron Gurwitsch*. University Press of America.

Economist. (2018, June 25). VAR increases refereeing accuracy, but not the total penalty count. https://www.economist.com/graphic-detail/2018/06/25/var-increases-refereeing-accuracy-but-not-the-total-penalty-count

Eliot, L. (2019, May 30). Essential stats for justifying and comparing self-driving cars to humans at the wheel. *Forbes*. https://www.forbes.com/sites/lanceeliot/2019/05/30/essential-stats-for-justifying-and-comparing-self-driving-cars-to-humans-at-the-wheel/#73973b5146 ed

Elliot, C. S., & Long, G. (2016). Manufacturing rate busters: Computer control and social relations in the labour process. *Work, Employment and Society, 30*(1), 135–151.

Elmore, J. G., Longton, G. M., Carney, P. A., Geller, B. M., Onega, T., Tosteson, A. N., Nelson, H. D., Pepe, M. S., Allison, K. H., Schnitt, S. J., O'Malley, F. P., & Weaver, D. L. (2015). Diagnostic concordance among pathologists interpreting breast biopsy specimens. *JAMA, 313*(11), 1122–1132.

Enemark, C. (2011). Drones over Pakistan: Secrecy, ethics, and counterinsurgency. *Asian Security, 7*(3), 218–237.

Enemark, C. (2013). *Armed drones and the ethics of war: Military virtue in a post-heroic age.* Routledge.

Esteva, A., Kuprel, B., Novoa, R. A., Ko, J., Swetter, S. M., Blau, H. M., & Thrun, S. (2017). Dermatologist-level classification of skin cancer with deep neural networks. *Nature, 542*(7639), 115.

Etzioni, A., & Etzioni, O. (2017, May–June). Pros and cons of autonomous weapons systems. *Military Review.*

Eyre R. (2019). *The happiness paradox.* Familius.

Fabre, C. (2009). Guns, food, and liability to attack in war. *Ethics, 120*(1), 36–63.

Feldenkirchen, Markus. (2018, November 30). Friedrich Merz: Der fluch des gestern. *Der Spiegel.* http://www.spiegel.de/plus/friedrich-merz-der-fluch-des-gestern-a-00000000-0002-0001-0000-000161087451

Felton, R. (2018, February 27). Two years on, a father is still fighting Tesla over autopilot and his son's fatal crash. *Jalopnik.* https://jalopnik.com/two-years-on-a-father-is-still-fighting-tesla-over-aut-1823189786

Fischer, J. M. (2004). Responsibility and manipulation. *Journal of Ethics, 8*, 145–177.

Fischer, J. M., & Ravizza, M. (1998). *Responsibility and control.* Cambridge University Press.

Foy, J. (2014). Autonomous weapons systems: Taking the human out of international humanitarian law. *Dalhousie Journal of Legal Studies, 23*, 47.

Franke, U. E. (2014). Drones, drone strikes, and US policy: The politics of unmanned aerial vehicles. *Parameters, 44*(1), 121–131.

Fry, H. (2018). *Hello world.* Penguin.

Gaskell, A. (2016, April 29). What it's like to work with a computer for a boss. *Forbes.* https://www.forbes.com/sites/adigaskell/2016/04/29/what-its-like-to-work-with-a-computer-for-a-boss/

Gendler, T. S. (2008). Alief and belief. *Journal of Philosophy, 105*, 634–663.

Gendler, T. S. (2011). On the epistemic costs of implicit bias. *Philosophical Studies, 156*(1), 33.

Gigerenzer, G. (2007). *Gut feelings.* Penguin.

Gilbert, M. (1990). Walking together: A paradigmatic social phenomenon. *Midwest Studies in Philosophy, 15*(1), 1–14.

Green, J. (2018, March 30). Tesla: Autopilot was on during deadly Mountain View crash. *San Jose Mercury News.* https://www.mercurynews.com/2018/03/30/tesla-autopilot-was-on-during-deadly-mountain-view-crash/

Gregory, D. (2011). From a view to a kill: Drones and late modern war. *Theory, Culture & Society, 28*(7–8), 188–215.

Grice, H. P. (1971). "Intention and Uncertainty." *Proceedings of the British Academy 57*, 263–79.

Grote, T., & Di Nucci, E. (2020). Algorithmic decision-making and the problem of control. In B. Beck & M. Kühler (Eds.), *Technology, anthropology, and dimensions of responsibility* (pp. 97–113). Verlag J. B. Metzler.

Guerrero, A. (2014). Against elections: The lottocratic alternative. *Philosophy and Public Affairs, 42*(2), 135–178.

Gulshan, V., Peng, L., Coram, M., Stumpe, M. C., Wu, D., Narayanaswamy, A., Venugopalan, S., Widner, K., Madams, T., Cuadros, J., Kim, R., Raman, R., Nelson, P. C., Mega, J. L., & Webster, D. R. (2016). Development and validation of a deep learning algorithm for detection of diabetic retinopathy in retinal fundus photographs. *JAMA , 316*(22), 2402–2410.

Hart, H. L. A. (1968). *Punishment and responsibility*. Oxford University Press.

Heikoop, D. D., Hagenzieker, M., Mecacci, G., Calvert, S., Santoni de Sio, F., & van Arem, B. (2019). Human behaviour with automated driving systems: A quantitative framework for meaningful human control. *Theoretical Issues in Ergonomics Science , 20*(6), 711–730.

Hendricks, V., & Vestergaard, M. (2019). *Reality lost: Markets of attention, misinformation and manipulation.* Springer.

Hern, A. (2017, September 4). Elon Musk says AI could lead to third world war. *Guardian.* https://www.theguardian.com/technology/2017/sep/04/elon-musk-ai-third-world-war-vladimir-putin

Ho, J. Y., & Hendi, A. S. (2018, August 15). Recent trends in life expectancy across high-income countries: Retrospective observational study. *BMJ, 362*, k2562. https://www.bmj.com/content/362/bmj.k2562

Hofstadter, D. (1980). *Gödel, Escher, Bach*. Basic Books.

Holroyd, J., Scaife, R., & Stafford, T. (2017). Responsibility for implicit bias. *Philosophy Compass , 12*(3), e12410.

Horowitz, M. C., & Scharre, P. (2015, March 16). Meaningful human control in weapon systems: A primer. Center for a New American Security. https://www.cnas.org/publications/reports/meaningful-human-control-in-weapon-systems-a-primer

Human Rights Watch. (2020). Killer robots. https://www.hrw.org/topic/arms/killer-robots

IFAB. (2018). Laws of the game. https://img.fifa.com/image/upload/khhloe2xoigyna8juxw3.pdf

Implicit bias. (2015, February 26). *Stanford Encylopedia of Philosophy.* https://plato.stanford.edu/entries/implicit-bias

Jain, N. (2016). Autonomous weapons systems: New frameworks for individual responsibility. In *Autonomous weapons systems: Law, ethics, policy* (pp. 303–324). Cambridge University Press.

James, W. (1890). *The principles of psychology*. Macmillan.

Joerger, M., & Spenko, M. (2017, December). Towards navigation safety for autonomous cars. *Inside GNSS*, 40–49. https://par.nsf.gov/servlets/purl/10070277

Kahneman, D. (2011). *Thinking, fast and slow*. Farrar, Straus and Giroux.

Kane, R. (2005). *A contemporary introduction to free will*. Oxford University Press.

Kastan, B. (2013). Autonomous weapons systems: A coming legal singularity. *Journal of Law, Technology and Policy , 45*, 45–82.

Kim, A., & Maglio, S. J. (2018). Vanishing time in pursuit of happiness. *Psychonomic Bulletin & Review, 25*, 1337–1342. https://doi.org/10.3758/s13423-018-1436-7

Kirkpatrick, J. (2016). State responsibility and drone operators. In Ezio Di Nucci & Filippo Santoni de Sio (Eds.), *Drones and responsibility* (pp. 101–116). Routledge.

Klincewicz, M. (2015). Autonomous weapons systems, the frame problem and computer security. *Journal of Military Ethics, 14*(2), 162–176.

Krebs, A. (1983, September 2). Rep. L.P. McDonald of Georgia among the Americans lost on jet. *New York Times.* https://www.nytimes.com/1983/09/02/obituaries/rep-lp-mcdonald-of-georgia-among-the-americans-lost-on-jet.html?module=inline

Krishnan, A. (2016). *Killer robots: Legality and ethicality of autonomous weapons*. Routledge.

Kuklinski, J., & Quirk, P. (2000). Reconsidering the rational public: Cognition, heuristics, and mass opinion. In A. Lupia, M. McCubbins, & S. Popkin (Eds.), *Elements of reason: Cognition, choice, and the bounds of rationality* (pp. 153–182). Cambridge University Press.

Landemore, H. (2017). Deliberative democracy as open, not (just) representative democracy. *Daedalus: Journal of the American Academy of Arts & Sciences, 146*(3), 1–13.

Latour, B. (as Jim Johnson). (1988). Mixing humans and nonhumans together: The sociology of a door-closer. *Social Problems, 35*(3), 298–310.

Latour, B. (1996). On actor-network theory: A few clarifications. *Soziale Welt, 47*(4), 369–381.

Levy, N., & Bayne, T. (2004). Doing without deliberation: Automatism, automaticity, and moral accountability. *International Review of Psychiatry, 16*(3), 209–215.

Lin, P. (2015). Why ethics matters for autonomous cars. In M. Maurer, J. C. Gerdes, B. Lenz, & H. Winner (Eds.), *Autonomes Fahren* (pp. 69–85). Springer.

Liu, H.-Y. (2012). Categorization and legality of autonomous and remote weapons systems. *International Review of the Red Cross, 94*(886), 627–652.

Liu, H.-Y. (2017). Irresponsibilities, inequalities and injustice for autonomous vehicles. *Ethics and Information Technology, 19*(3), 193–207.

Lubben, A. (2018, March 19). Self-driving Uber killed a pedestrian as human safety driver watched. *Vice*. https://www.vice.com/en_us/article/kzxq3y/self-driving-uber-killed-a-pedestrian-as-human-safety-driver-watched

Lupia, A., & McCubbins, M. (1998). *The democratic dilemma: Can citizens learn what they need to know?* Cambridge University Press.

Marx, K. (1891). *Jeder nach seinen Fähigkeiten, jedem nach seinen Bedürfnissen*. Kritik des Gothaer Programms.

Matthews, D. (2019, September 26). 36 years ago today, one man saved us from world-ending nuclear war. *Vox*. https://www.vox.com/2018/9/26/17905796/nuclear-war-1983-stanislav-petrov-soviet-union

Matthias, A. (2004). The responsibility gap: Ascribing responsibility for the actions of learning automata. *Ethics and Information Technology, 6*(3), 175–183.

Mauss, I. B., Tamir, M., Anderson, C. L., & Savino, N. S. (2011). Can seeking happiness make people unhappy? Paradoxical effects of valuing happiness. *Emotion, 11*(4), 807–815.

McDougall, R. J. (2019a). Computer knows best? The need for value-flexibility in medical AI. *Journal of Medical Ethics, 45*(3), 156–160.

McDougall, R. J. (2019b). No we shouldn't be afraid of medical AI; it involves risks and opportunities. *Journal of Medical Ethics, 45*, 559.

Mecacci, G., & de Sio, F. S. (2019). Meaningful human control as reason-responsiveness: The case of dual-mode vehicles. *Ethics and Information Technology, 22*, 103–115.

Meier, M. W. (2016). Lethal autonomous weapons systems (laws): Conducting a comprehensive weapons review. *Temple International and Comparative Law Journal, 30*, 119–132.

Miller, F., & Wertheimer, A. (2009). *The ethics of consent*. Oxford University Press.

Mittelstadt, B. D., & Floridi, L. (Eds.). (2016). *The ethics of biomedical big data* (Vol. 29). Springer.

Montero, B. G. (2016). *Thought in action*. Oxford University Press.

Mudde, C., & Kaltwasser, C. R. (2017). *Populism: A very short introduction*. Oxford University Press.

Murphy, S. L., Xu, J., Kochanek, K. D., & Arias, E. (2018, November). Mortality in the United States, 2017. CDC National Center for Health Statistics. https://www.cdc.gov/nchs/products/databriefs/db328.htm

Neal, D. T., Wood, W., & Drolet, A. (2013). How do people adhere to goals when willpower is low? The profits (and pitfalls) of strong habits. *Journal of Personality and Social Psychology, 104*(6), 959–975.

Nicas, J. (2018, October 25). Apple News's radical approach: Humans over machines. *New York Times*. https://www.nytimes.com/2018/10/25/technology/apple-news-humans-algorithms.html

Noone, G. P., & Noone, D. C. (2015). The debate over autonomous weapons systems. *Case Western Reserve Journal of International Law, 47*, 25–35.

NTSB. (2019, May 16). Highway preliminary report HWY19FH008. National Transportation Safety Board Highway Accident Report. https://www.ntsb.gov/investigations/AccidentReports/Reports/HWY19FH008-preliminary.pdf

Nyholm, S. (2020). *Humans and robots*. Rowman & Littlefield.

Nyholm, S., & Smids, J. (2016). The ethics of accident-algorithms for self-driving cars: An applied trolley problem? *Ethical Theory Moral Practice, 19*(5), 1275–1289.

Obermeyer, Z., & Emanuel, E. J. (2016). Predicting the future—big data, machine learning, and clinical medicine. *New England Journal of Medicine, 375*(13), 1216–1219.

Pasquale, F. (2015). *The black box society*. Harvard University Press.

Paust, J. J. (2010). Self-defense targetings of non-state actors and permissibility of US use of drones in Pakistan. *Journal of Transnational Law & Policy, 19*(2), 237–280.

Pettit, P. (2010). Representation, responsive and indicative. *Constellations, 17*(3), 426–434.

Pollard, B. (2003). Can virtuous actions be both habitual and rational? *Ethical Theory and Moral Practice, 6*, 411–425.

Pollard, B. (2006). Explaining actions with habits. *American Philosophical Quarterly, 43*, 57–68.

Reason, J. (1990). *Human error*. Cambridge University Press.

Reason, J. (2000). Human error: Models and management. *British Medical Journal (Clinical Research Edition), 320*(7237), 768–770. doi:10.1136/bmj.320.7237.768

Rietveld, E. (2008). Situated normativity: The normative aspect of embodied cognition in unreflective action. *Mind, 117*, 973–1001.

Robillard, M. (2018). No such thing as killer robots. *Journal of Applied Philosophy, 35*(4), 705–717.

Rubel, A., Castro, C., & Pham, A. (2019). Agency laundering and information technologies. *Ethical Theory and Moral Practice, 22*, 1017–1041.

Russo, N. (2016, April 21). A 2,000-year history of alarm clocks. *Atlas Obscura.* https://www.atlasobscura.com/articles/a-2000year-history-of-alarm-clocks

Ryle, G. (1949). *The concept of mind*. Penguin.

Santoni de Sio, F. (2017). Killing by autonomous vehicles and the legal doctrine of necessity. *Ethical Theory and Moral Practice, 20*(2), 411–429.

Santoni de Sio, F., & Di Nucci, E. (2016). Drones and responsibility: Mapping the field. In Ezio Di Nucci & Filippo Santoni de Sio (Eds.), *Drones and responsibility* (pp. 1–13). Routledge.

Santoni de Sio, F., & van den Hoven, J. (2018). Meaningful human control over autonomous systems: A philosophical account. *Frontiers in Robotics and AI, 5*, article 15.

Sartario, C. (2005). A new asymmetry between actions and omissions. *Nous, 39*(3), 460–482.

Sartorio, C. (2009). Omissions and causalism. *Nous, 43*(3), 513–530.

Sauer, F. (2016). Stopping "killer robots": Why now is the time to ban autonomous weapons systems. *Arms Control Today, 46*(8), 8–13.

Saul, J. (2012). Ranking exercises in philosophy and implicit bias. *Journal of Social Philosophy, 43*(3), 256–273.

Saul, J. (2013a). Implicit bias, stereotype threat, and women in philosophy. In F. Jenkins & K. Hutchison (Eds.), *Women in philosophy: What needs to change* (pp. 39–60). Oxford University Press.

Saul, J. (2013b). Scepticism and implicit bias. *Disputatio, 5*(37), 243–263.

Schooler, J. W., Ariely, D., & Loewenstein, G. (2003). The pursuit and assessment of happiness can be self-defeating. In J. Carrillo & I. Brocas (Eds.), *Psychology and economics* (pp. 41–70). Oxford University Press.

Sie, M. (2009). Moral agency, conscious control and deliberative awareness. *Inquiry, 52*(5), 516–531.

Singer, P. W. (2009). *Wired for war*. Penguin.

Sparrow, R. (2007). Killer robots. *Journal of Applied Philosophy, 24*(1), 62–77.

Sparrow, R. (2009). Predators or plowshares? Arms control of robotic weapons. *IEEE Technology and Society Magazine, 28*(1), 25–29.

Strawser, B. J. (2010). Moral predators: The duty to employ uninhabited aerial vehicles. *Journal of Military Ethics, 9*(4), 342–368.

Strawser, B. J. (Ed.). (2013). *Killing by remote control: The ethics of an unmanned military*. Oxford University Press.

Sunstein, C. R. (2015). *Choosing not to choose*. Oxford University Press.

Sunstein, C. R. (2018). *#Republic: Divided democracy in the age of social media*. Princeton University Press.

Surden, H., & Williams, M. A. (2016). Technological opacity, predictability, and self-driving cars. *Cardozo Law Review, 38*, 121–181.

Susskind, R., & Susskind, D. (2015). *The future of the professions*. Oxford University Press.

Taeihagh, A., & Lim, H. S. M. (2019). Governing autonomous vehicles: Emerging responses for safety, liability, privacy, cybersecurity, and industry risks. *Transport Reviews, 39*(1), 103–128.

Todd, P., & Tognazzini, N. A. (2008, October). A problem for guidance control. *Philosophical Quarterly, 58*(233), 685–669.

Topol, E. (2019). *Deep medicine: How artificial intelligence can make healthcare human again.* Basic Books.

Toscano, C. P. (2015). Friend of humans: An argument for developing autonomous weapons systems. *Journal of National Security Law & Policy, 8*, 189–246.

Tupasela, A. M., & Di Nucci, E. (2020). Concordance as evidence in the Watson for Oncology decision-support system. *AI & Society.* doi:10.1007/s00146-020-00945-9

Umbers, L. M. (2018). Against lottocracy. *European Journal of Political Theory.* Online only. doi:10.1177/1474885118783602

Vlasic, B., & Boudette, N. (2016, July 1). Self-driving Tesla was involved in fatal crash, U.S. says. *New York Times.* https://www.nytimes.com/2016/07/01/business/self-driving-tesla-fatal-crash-investigation.html

Wagner, B. (2019). Liable, but not in control? Ensuring meaningful human agency in automated decision-making systems. *Policy & Internet, 11*(1), 104–122.

Wajcman, J. (2017). Automation: Is it really different this time? *British Journal of Sociology, 68*(1), 119–127.

Wall, T., & Monahan, T. (2011). Surveillance and violence from afar: The politics of drones and liminal security-scapes. *Theoretical Criminology, 15*(3), 239–254.

Ward, J. (2018, June 22). Video review at the World Cup is resulting in more goals from penalty kicks. *New York Times.* https://www.nytimes.com/interactive/2018/06/22/sports/world-cup/video-review-var-penalty-kicks-goals.html

Williams, B. G. (2013). *Predators: The CIA's drone war on al Qaeda.* Potomac Books.

Wood, W. (2019). *Good habits, bad habits.* Farrar, Straus and Giroux.

World Health Organization (WHO). (n.d.). The power of vaccines: Still not fully utilized. https://www.who.int/publications/10-year-review/vaccines/en/

World Health Organization (WHO). (2019, March 21). Ten threats to global health in 2019. https://www.who.int/vietnam/news/feature-stories/detail/ten-threats-to-global-health-in-2019.

Yadron, D., & Tynan, D. (2016, July 1). Tesla driver dies in first fatal crash while using autopilot mode. *Guardian.* https://www.theguardian.com/technology/2016/jun/30/tesla-autopilot-death-self-driving-car-elon-musk

Zenko, M., & Mae Wolf, A. (2018, April 25). Drones kill more civilians than pilots do. *Foreign Policy.* http://foreignpolicy.com/2016/04/25/drones-kill-more-civilians-than-pilots-do

Zuboff, Shoshana. (2018). *The age of surveillance capitalism.* PublicAffairs.

Index

habit, 39. *See also* automaticity
healthcare, 68, 149–150, 156–163
health data, 149

intentionality, 5

labor division, 15–16, 133. *See also*
    delegation
liberty, 61
lottocrazy, 171–175

machine learning. *See* AI
Marx, 19, 133

neocolonialism, 156
normative, xvi, 62, 102, 103, 183

organizations, xxi

PAP, 184
passive human supervision, 103
populism, 13, 14, 20–21, 176–181
power, 12, 16, 23, 68, 169

responsibility, xxi, 9, 46, 184; delegate,
    196
robots, xv, 92

self-driving cars, 117–127
slippery slope arguments, 158
smartphones, 132–147
social media, 12
software, xv–xvi, 68
surveillance, 96

technological apocalypticism, xv, 7
technological innovations, xiii
technophiles, 22
technophobia, 13, 22, 102
tracing condition, 44
tracking condition, 44
trade off, 24, 101, 115, 144

video assistant referee, 105–115

Watson, 152–155, 160–161. *See also* AI

www.ingramcontent.com/pod-product-compliance
Lightning Source LLC
Chambersburg PA
CBHW022309280326
41932CB00010B/1034